Lluís Payrató, Ignasi Clemente
Gestures We Live By

Mouton Series in Pragmatics

Editor
Istvan Kecskes

Editorial Board
Reinhard Blutner (Universiteit van Amsterdam)
N.J. Enfield (Max-Planck-Institute for Psycholinguistics)
Raymond W. Gibbs (University of California, Santa Cruz)
Laurence R. Horn (Yale University)
Boaz Keysar (University of Chicago)
Ferenc Kiefer (Hungarian Academy of Sciences)
Lluís Payrató (University of Barcelona)
François Recanati (Institut Jean-Nicod)
John Searle (University of California, Berkeley)
Deirdre Wilson (University College London)

Volume 22

Lluís Payrató, Ignasi Clemente
Gestures We Live By

―

The Pragmatics of Emblematic Gestures

DE GRUYTER
MOUTON

ISBN 978-1-5015-2674-9
e-ISBN (PDF) 978-1-5015-0995-7
e-ISBN (ePub) 978-1-5015-0987-2
ISSN 1864-6409

Library of Congress Control Number: 2018009948

Bibliographic information published by the Deutsche Nationalbibliothek
The Deutsche Nationalbibliothek lists this publication in the Deutsche Nationalbibliografie;
detailed bibliographic data are available in the Internet at http://dnb.dnb.de.

© 2021 Walter de Gruyter GmbH, Berlin/Boston
This volume is text- and page-identical with the hardback published in 2020.
Typesetting: Integra Software Services Pvt. Ltd.
Printing and binding: CPI books GmbH, Leck

www.degruyter.com

Foreword and acknowledgements

This book is the result of many efforts that have been supported by many people. We want to acknowledge the grant support provided by the Fundació Jaume Bofill, the Ministerio de Ciencia y Tecnología (FFI2014-56258-P), and the Generalitat de Catalunya (2017SGR-942).

Personally, we are in debt especially to Istvan Kecskes and to many colleagues in our departments and at our schools. We would also like to express our gratitude to the informants that contributed their data and to all the people who have contributed their different expertise to the process of writing the book. Precisely, as a book that is in many senses a collective work, we hope that all of them will consider this one as something of their own.

We are especially grateful to our families, without whom we would have probably written the book anyhow; moreover, we would have finished it much sooner! But all in all, it would not have been so much fun, and we would not have felt so accompanied in this book-writing journey.

Contents

Foreword and acknowledgements —— V

Introduction —— 1

1 The historical perspective: A synthesis —— 5
1.1 Forerunners: From classical rhetoric to the 19th century —— 7
1.1.1 Classical rhetoric —— 8
1.1.2 Medieval and later treatises —— 10
1.1.3 The 19th century —— 13
1.2 The 20th century —— 16
1.2.1 Initial period (1900–1941) —— 16
1.2.2 Intervening period (1942–1969) —— 21
1.2.3 Final period (1970–2000) —— 26
1.3 The 21st century —— 28

2 Emblems and other gestures —— 30
2.1 Gestures and emblems —— 30
2.1.1 Pathways towards a definition of gesture —— 30
2.1.2 Pathways to a definition of emblematic gesture —— 39
2.2 Emblem as a category —— 42
2.2.1 Emblem as a semiotic category —— 42
2.2.2 Gestural continua —— 44
2.2.3 Emblematicity criteria: Emblem as a prototypical pragmatic category —— 48
2.3 Types and functions of emblems —— 50
2.3.1 Current speech and current emblems —— 51
2.3.2 Greeting emblems —— 54
2.3.3 Deictic emblems —— 59
2.3.4 Insult emblems —— 62
2.3.5 Technical emblems or emblems for special purposes —— 64
2.4 Other gestures and non-verbal acts —— 65
2.4.1 Co-speech gestures —— 66
2.4.2 Pragmatic gestures —— 67
2.4.3 Vocal items: From sounds to interjections —— 70
2.4.4 Sign language items —— 72

3	**The taxonomical task: Methodology and repertoires —— 77**
3.1	Notation and transcription: Visual representations —— 77
3.2	The compilation of an emblem repertoire: Conception, types and methodology —— 78
3.2.1	Traditional repertoires and methods —— 79
3.2.2	Contemporary repertoires and methods: A sample —— 81
3.2.3	Past and future: Comparisons between repertoires —— 84
3.3	Elaborated repertoires —— 85
3.3.1	Current repertoires —— 85
3.3.2	Other repertoires —— 87
3.4	Gestural lexicography —— 87
3.5	A detailed example: A basic repertoire of Catalan emblems —— 91
3.5.1	Exclusions, order, and repertoire entries —— 92
3.5.2	Compilations established —— 93
3.5.3	Codification test —— 94
3.5.4	Informants —— 95
3.5.5	Questionnaires, interviews, and items —— 96
3.5.6	Precedent repertoires and future projects —— 98
3.5.7	Selection of emblems according to pragmatic and semantic features —— 99
4	**An ecological view on emblems —— 103**
4.1	Origins and historical evolution —— 103
4.1.1	Illustrators or co-speech gestures and image schemas —— 104
4.1.2	Affect displays, adaptors and regulators —— 106
4.1.3	Other sources. Gestural neologisms. Language origins —— 107
4.2	Variation and cultural distribution of emblems —— 108
4.2.1	Emblems, culture, and linguistic variety —— 109
4.2.2	Multilingualism and emblem borrowings —— 110
4.3	Geographic distribution of emblems —— 113
4.3.1	Precedents. Emblems and classical dialectology —— 113
4.3.2	Gestural geography in Europe —— 117
4.4	Social distribution of emblems —— 123
4.4.1	Ethnographic analysis of emblems: A sample —— 126
4.4.2	A background for the ethnographic research on emblems —— 129
4.4.3	Everyday emblems in Catalonia: An example —— 130

5	**The cognitive and interactive dimensions of emblems —— 135**
5.1	Variants and repertoires: What does "the same emblem" (exactly) mean? —— 135
5.1.1	Introduction: Assumptions and basic questions for the research —— 136
5.1.2	Filtering samples: Interpreting items to elaborate repertoires —— 137
5.2	The emblematic web: Organization of emblems within a repertoire —— 141
5.2.1	The prototypical model: Emblems as symbolic associations —— 142
5.2.2	The family resemblance model —— 143
5.3	The interpretation of emblems: From context through relevance —— 147
5.4	Relevance: Common principles and processes in verbal / non-verbal communication —— 151
5.5	Multimodal tropes in emblematization processes —— 157
5.5.1	Around metonymy —— 158
5.5.2	Around metaphors —— 160
5.5.3	Complex combined processes: Metonymy, metaphor and verbal tropes —— 164
5.5.4	Ironic constructions —— 170
5.5.5	Emblems and phraseology —— 172
5.6	Emblems and interaction: Meaning and functional distribution —— 174
5.6.1	Messages conveyed —— 175
5.6.2	Illocutionary force —— 176
5.6.3	Illocutionary types and values —— 178
5.6.4	Illocution and functions: An example —— 181

6	**Conclusions and final remarks —— 185**
6.1	The research on emblems: Present and future: Pragmatic theory and multimodality —— 186
6.1.1	A note on applications —— 188
6.2	Emblems as cognitive constructions —— 189
6.3	Emblems as sociocultural displays —— 191
6.4	Emblems as pragmatic tools —— 193

Appendices

Appendix I	Basic repertory of Catalan emblems —— **197**	
Appendix II	Catalan emblems. Sample of Amades (1957) —— **202**	
Appendix III	Catalan emblems. Sample of Mascaró (1981) —— **204**	
Appendix IV	American Spanish gestures (Venezuela). Cardona (1953–1954) —— **205**	
Appendix V	American Spanish gestures. Kany (1960) —— **207**	
Appendix VI	American Spanish emblems (Colombian). Sample of Saitz and Cervenka (1972) —— **214**	
Appendix VII	Spanish emblems. Sample of Meo-Zilio and Mejía (1980–1983) —— **216**	
Appendix VIII	Other samples of emblems (links to illustrations and videos) —— **219**	

References —— 222

Index —— 243

Introduction

This book presents an analysis of emblematic gestures from a pragmatic view in which emblems are regarded as autonomous gestures that fulfill clear communicative functions, embody illocutionary values, and act as multimodal tools and signals of cognitive relevance.

Emblematic gestures (or emblems) have been given a range of denominations in the literature (*autonomous, quotable, semiotic, folkloric* or *symbolic* gestures, to name a few). Many of these denominations reflect the fact that emblems are easily isolated and recognized, for instance gestures that are used to greet, insult, assess positively or negatively others' conduct, and refer to specific actions (e.g. steal or eat). Emblems are culturally bound gestures. They differ interculturally and intraculturally, i.e. both among different cultural and linguistic areas, and among individuals and social groups inside the same culture. These gestures are easily translated into verbal language, they are equivalent to utterances, and in many cases even have individual names (e.g. Cat. *pam i pipa*, also known as the Shanghai gesture or the nose thumb gesture; Cat. *botifarra* and Sp. *corte de mangas*, the forearm jerk gesture, and Cat. *banyes* and Sp. *cuernos*, the cuckold gesture, see section 3.5.7).

From a pragmatic and ethnographic view, emblems can be conceived as multimodal tools at the frontier between verbal and nonverbal modes, and are part of the communicative repertoire of individuals and sociocultural groups. Emblems illustrate clearly the concept of embodiment in at least two basic ways: meaning is created in and with the body (of the speaker), and interpretation (by the recipient) can only be carried out when taking into account the body. Furthermore, emblematic gestures are susceptible to different processes of metaphorization (contrasting or not with verbal metaphors), metonymy, and interference, or combination between modalities. The applications of the study of emblems are numerous, from lexicography to language acquisition and applied linguistics.

The book is divided in six chapters, followed by several appendices, which include information about repertoires of emblems with photographs and verbal descriptions.

Chapter 1 presents a historical overview that introduces the definition of gesture and its current and technical meanings. The chapter begins with the forerunners, including classical rhetoric, as well as the treatises from Medieval and later periods. Whereas Engel's opus (1785–6) constitutes the most outstanding work during the 18th century, many contributions appear in the 19th century: among others, Bell (1806), Austin (1806), Tylor (1865),

Kleinpaul (1888), Sittl (1890), Hacks (1892), and Ott (1902). From this period, we will give special attention to the work of De Jorio (1832), Darwin (1872), Mallery (1881a, 1881b) and Wundt (1900). The majority of studies of what today are known as emblematic gestures emerge during the 20th century and the beginning of the 21st century. This state of the art follows the different traditions, such as the French, Italian, British and Hispanic, with special reference to scholars such as Efron (1941), Meo-Zilio (1961a, 1961b), Ekman and Friesen (1969) and the more recent contributions of Kendon, McNeill, Poggi, Calbris, Hanna, and Brookes, inter alia.

Chapter 2 examines emblematic gestures and other gestures or non-verbal acts. First, we describe the pathways that have led to contemporary definitions of gesture and emblems, and we propose a description of the notion of gesture understood as a prototype category. Are emblems (and other gestures) really non-verbal items? Emblems have similarities with vocal gestures and also with other co-speech, or coverbal, and pragmatic gestures. However, we analyze the criteria used to establish emblematicity and the gestural continua proposed by different scholars, and we propose that emblems are a distinguishable category (as a prototype) because it constitutes a pragmatic resource with specific illocutionary power and autonomy. We also describe the functions and types of emblems (current emblems, deictic/greeting/insult/technical emblems), which are then followed by an examination between emblems and co-speech and pragmatic gestures, vocal items (interjections, onomatopoeic words, ideophones, sounds) and sign language items.

Chapter 3 concludes the first part of the book and offers information and guidelines regarding the methodology. The taxonomical study requires a system of notation and compilation of emblems (in repertoires). This chapter presents several techniques for the production of basic and complementary repertoires by means of encoding and decoding tests, which are illustrated with several examples from emblem repertoire of Catalan speakers in Barcelona. A section is devoted to the analysis and comparison of the current repertoires related to different languages and cultures, with another section devoted to gesture lexicography, that is, to the lexicographical and technical procedures used to present emblems in dictionaries. Above all, gestural lexicography is currently the broad domain in which research on emblems has been applied all over the world, and the impact of the new technologies in this case is also self-evident.

The second part of the book begins with Chapter 4, an ecological view of emblems in which the origins and the historical, anthropological, and sociocultural aspects of these gestures are analyzed. The sources of emblematic gestures are very often illustrator gestures (i.e. coverbal gestures which reproduce iconically some features of a mental referent) – or affect displays, adaptors (of objects or the body), and regulators (of interaction). In many cases, emblems are based on image schemas or mimetic schemas, for instance RECIPIENT (the head), PAIRING (two fingers), or PATH, CYCLE; CONTACT, WALK, EAT, etc. Some gestural neologisms are related to verbal expressions, i.e. phraseology, lexical items or even orthographical aspects, like the initial letter of a word, as in the highly conventionalized instances of the hand depicting a V for 'victory' or a T for 'time" (or less conventionalized uses such as T or C for "tea" and "coffee" in airplanes by flight attendants who are far from each other). The present cultural and geographical distribution of emblems depends to a large extent on these origins and on the historical evolution of gestures and the ways in which they have spread. Two sections are devoted to aspects of the social distribution of emblems and their ethnographic analysis.

Chapter 5 explores the cognitive and interactive dimensions of emblems. We suggest that as cognitive constructions, emblems can be described in terms of prototypes and family resemblance (within gestural families). The chapter compiles what we know at the moment about the processes of their production and interpretation, their processes of acquisition or development, and gestural and communicative pathologies that may affect them. We propose relevance as a key feature in the processes of production and reception of emblems. Moreover, several types of processes of metaphorization are exemplified and analyzed; metaphor and metonymy underlie many emblems (often together) and may have parallels in the verbal channel, and in the case of ironic expressions. The interrelation between emblems and phraseology is frequently complex and has great interest pragmatically from the point of view of multimodal research. Regarding conversational and communicative interaction, emblems display specific meanings and functions, associated to their illocutionary value and their special effectiveness in manifesting relevance. Emblems provoke a strong impact on recipients' cognitive context while making low processing demands; in less technical terms, they provide a lot of information in a very clear and costless way.

The book closes with a brief chapter on present and future research on emblems and the role of multimodality in a general theory of pragmatics. The chapter begins with a consideration of applications, stressing the need to take into account emblematic repertoires in language learning (especially between distant cultures), in the area of literature and translation, and in the automatic production and recognition of multimodal systems, which have been elaborated as avatars, talking faces, or any form of interactive machine. The last part of the book ends with three concluding and interrelated remarks. First, we highlight how emblems can be considered as cognitive constructions that match gestural forms with symbolic meaning and deploy and concentrate relevance in current interaction. Second, we consider them as sociocultural displays— culturally bound gestures at the frontier of verbality that belong to the communicative repertoire of individuals and sociocultural groups. Third, we point out that emblems are pragmatic tools that perform communicative (deliberate) acts and carry illocutionary force.

1 The historical perspective: A synthesis

In this chapter, we provide a brief introduction to the notion of gesture and its current and technical meanings, which is followed by a historical overview. The historical overview begins with the forerunners (classical rhetoric, Aristotle, Cicero, Quintilian), the treatises from medieval and later periods, including Engel's (1785–6) outstanding work from the 18th century, and the many contributions that appeared during the 19th century (inter alia Austin 1806, Tylor 1865, Sittl 1890, Hacks 1892). Work by De Jorio (1832), Darwin (1872), Mallery (1881a, 1881b), as well as Wundt's (1900) constitute a link between the 19th and 20th centuries. The last part of the historical overview covers work published during the 20th century and the beginning of the 21st century, including the majority of studies of what is known today as emblematic gesture research. This state of the art follows different traditions and trends (French, Italian, British, Portuguese and Hispanic traditions), with special reference to works by Efron (1941), Meo-Zilio (1961a, 1961b, 1980–1983), Ekman and Friesen (1969) and more recent contributions by Kendon, McNeill, Poggi, Calbris, Hanna, and Brookes.

A highly synthesized selection of these contributions can be found in Table 1.1, in order to provide a first presentation of the most relevant studies, as well as their historical genesis. In the following sections, we discuss and contextualize the studies listed in this table, together with other works that are not included but are worthy of being mentioned.

This is a book about emblems, but emblems understood in what sense? Today, we consider emblems as instances of a gestural category that may seem easy to isolate and define. For instance, there is a general agreement that emblems can be used without accompanying speech – verbal language – and that can be translated into words, can be quoted, and can be reproduced with words. However, emblems or emblematic gestures – two terms that are used as synonymous in this work – have been named with different denominations in the literature across history: for instance, *gestures, symbolic gestures, folk gestures, pantomimic gestures, semiotic gestures, autonomous gestures, quotable gestures*, and *quasi-linguistiques*. This terminological diversity shows that the apparent ease in isolating and defining the category should be envisaged with more prudency. A historical overview is fundamental to understand how this category has been conceptualized in the literature over the years and how we have come to propose in this book what constitutes the category of emblematic gesture that emerges from a pragmatic perspective and it is therefore part of an integrated analysis.

Table 1.1: Synthesis of historical contributions to the conceptualization of gesture, and in particular to the conceptualization of emblematic gesture.

		Classical Rhetoric
55 BC	Cicero	De oratore
95 AD	Quintilian	Institutio Oratoria
		Medieval and Later Treatises
1616	Bonifacio	L'Arte de' Cenni
1620	Cresollius	Vacationes Autumnales sive De Perfecta Oratoris Actione et Pronunciatione
1640	Bacon	Of the Advancement and Proficiency of Learning. Book VI
1644	Bulwer	Chirologia: or the Natural Language of the Hand Chironomia: or the Art of Manual Rhetoric
1746	Condillac	Essay on the Origin of Human Knowledge
1785–6	Engel	Ideen zu einer Mimik
		19th Century
1806	Austin	Chironomia or, a Treatise on Rhetorical Delivery
1832	De Jorio	La mimica degli antichi investigata nel gestire napoletano
1865	Tylor	Early History of Mankind
[1865]	Gratiolet	De la physiognomie et des mouvements d'expression
1872	Darwin	The Expression of the Emotions in Man and Animals
1872	Bacon	A Manual of Gesture
1881b	Mallery	Sign Language among North American Indians [...]
1890	Sittl	Die Gebärden der Griechen und Römer
1891	Adams	Gesture and pantomimic action
1892	Hacks	Le geste
		20th Century
1900	Wundt	Völkerpsychologie.I. Die Sprache
1925	Leite de Vasconcellos	A figa. Estudio de etnografia comparativa [...]
1932	Cocchiara	Il linguaggio del gesto
1939	Critchley	The language of gesture

Table 1.1 (continued)

1941	Efron	*Gesture, Race and Culture*
1968	Green	*A Gesture Inventory for the Teaching of Spanish*
1969	Ekman and Friesen	"The repertoire of non verbal behavior: categories, origins, usage and coding"
1972	Saitz and Cervenka	*Handbook of Gestures: Colombia and the United States*
1979	Morris et al.	*Gestures: their origins . . .*
1980–3	Meo-Zilio	*Diccionario de gestos: España e Hispanoamérica*
1981	Kendon et al. (eds.)	*Nonverbal Communication, Interaction, and Gesture.*
1990	Calbris	*The Semiotics of French Gestures*
1992	McNeill	*Hand and Mind*
1996	Hanna	"Defining the emblem"
1998 [2004]	Posner and Müller (eds.)	*The semantics and pragmatics of everyday gestures*
		21st Century
2000	McNeill (ed.)	*Language and Gesture*
2001	Various	*Gesture. A Journal . . .*
2003	Rector et al. (eds.)	*Gestures. Meaning and Use*
2004	Kendon	*Gesture. Visible Action as Utterance*
2007	Poggi	*Mind, Hands, Face and Body: [. . .]Multimodal Communication*
2013–2014	Müller et al. (eds.)	*Body – Language – Communication*

1.1 Forerunners: From classical rhetoric to the 19th century

The historical journey that allows us to understand what is — or what we can say is — an emblem is inseparable from the historical journey of what is — or what we can say is — a gesture. The review that we take here does not aim to be a history of gesture, since there is an abundance of historical studies (Schmitt 1990, Kendon 2004). We propose here to ask and try to answer a more specific/narrower question: when does it become apparent that gesture *means*, that it conveys and it is taken to convey meaning? More specifically, what allows people to *do* (or *say*) similar or almost identical things to spoken words by using gestures? In sum we are interested in analyzing the historical steps that have led to a pragmatics of gesture.

1.1.1 Classical rhetoric

Classical rhetoric is often presented as the oldest precursor to pragmatics and semiotics. The arguments for this interpretation are strong and well known: the interest in language/linguistic use, and in particular, the interest in verbal language/speech, as well as the interest in argumentative and expressive devices, with an emphasis on persuasion research. In particular, classical rhetoric devoted attention to gesture as a mechanism associated to words in the phase of *actio*, that is to say, *declamation*, in updated terminology. As a complement to speech and also an inherent aspect of orality, classical rhetoric has had a significant interest in gesture, which did not necessarily continue in subsequent studies.

The interest of classical rhetoricians/rhetoric is selective and found among only some authors. Aristotle and more generally stoic philosophers move forward towards creating the foundations of semiotics and the characterization of the sign and its different classes, but they have no interest in gesture at all. In fact, Aristotle seems quite opposed to the study of gesture (Kendon 2004: 17; but cf. Dutsch 2013 for an overview). Aristotle seems to imply that gesture should never limit the clarity of speech. Such negative judgment of gesture indeed seems to have been prevalent in many societies and historical periods. Gesture is regarded not as a positive parallel channel to speech contributing to meaning-making processes, but as a negative instrument that diminishes the precision of verbal expression. Gesture is to be limited and censored.

Conversely, Cicero, in his work *De Oratore*,[1] shows that he has a genuine interest in gesture, and establishes a division between *significatio* (expressive gestures) and *demostratio* (representational gestures), a division[2] that is reproduced

---

[1] Cicero, Marcus Tullius. *On the Ideal Orator [De Oratore, 55 BC]*. 2001. New York: Oxford University Press. To facilitate the presentation of classical work, historical references (up to 1900) are listed in this chapter as well as included in the bibliographic references at the end of the book. For rhetoricians and the concept of *delivery*, see Dutsch (2013).

[2] In Efron's own words (1941: 97): "For Cicero the real gesture is that kind of movement which expresses the internal *workings* of the mind; an external, *natural* sign of "affectionum animi,"

by other authors (Meo-Zilio 1961a: 83). Although more implicit than explicit, Efron (1941) seems to indicate that Cicero's *significatio* coincides with his concept of *ideographic* or *logico-pictorial* gesture, whereas *demostratio* coincides with what he calls *physiographic* (see more details in 1.2.2.).

Quintilian, however, is the one who develops an actual complete thesis about gesture and its importance in the context of the speaker's/orator's conduct. It is not anachronistic to state that Quintilian appreciates clearly the pragmatic value of gesture, as it can be seen in his own words:[3]

> As for the hands, without which all action would be crippled and enfeebled, it is scarcely possible tot describe the variety of their motions, since they are almost as expressive as words. For other portions of the body merely help the speaker, whereas the hands may be almost said to speak. Do we not use them to demand, promise, summon, dismiss, threaten, supplicate, express aversion or fear, question or deny? Do we not employ them to indicate joy, sorrow, hesitation, confession, penitence, measure, quantity, number and time? Have they not power to excite and prohibit, to express approval, wonder or shame? Do they not take the place of adverbs and pronouns when we point at places and things? In fact, though the peoples and nations of the earth speak a multitude of tongues, they share in common the universal language of the hands. (Book XI, III.85–87)

If we take into account that Quintilian lived during the first century of our era, it is not an exaggeration to consider this excerpt as the first explicit reference to the performative and illocutionary aspects of gesture. Indeed, the modernity of Quintilian's thinking and writing are evident in his metaphoric description of the "speaking hands" and in his comparison/equating of the actions of the hands with the speech acts formulated in the 20th century: asking, promising, requesting, rejecting, threatening, begging/imploring, and accepting (see 5.6.3, illocutionary types and values of emblems). Quintilian also describes expressive speech acts such as expressions of admiration, joy, doubt, and shame. Furthermore, when Quintilian argues that gestures can function as adverbs and pronouns, he starts an area of study that connects with very recent studies about the possibility that grammar may include gestural items or that grammars may unify speech and gesture production (Arndt and Janney 1987, Fricke 2013, Alturo, Clemente and Payrató 2016). For instance, Quintilian talks about deictic gesture that Levinson (1983) includes in his classical handbook of pragmatics. Moreover, Quintilian

---

in contrast to the pictorial one which expresses merely the *objects* of thought; the latter he calls "gestus scenicus," proper of an actor but unfitting to an orator."

3 Quintilian, Marcus Fabius. 1969. *The Institutio Oratoria of Quintilian [De Institutione Oratoria, 95 AD]*. New York: Putnam. Kendon (2004) presents an excellent analysis of Quintilian's work and also includes the quote reproduced here; cf. also Dutsch (2013).

opens at the end of this quote another recurrent topic in the history of gesture studies: the multiplicity and diversity of spoken language vis-à-vis the universal language of the hands. Although contemporary gesture studies illustrate how gestures need to be analyzed from a cultural perspective, Quintilian's and others' perspective of a universal hand language maintains a long standing.

Bühler (1933) and Meo-Zilio (1961a, 1961b) have underscored the importance of Quintilian's work and refer to his gesture classification (expressive vs. expositive or representative), heir to Cicero's classification. In the 11th book of *De Institutione Oratoria*, Quintilian distinguishes gestures that naturally accompany words from gestures that allow things to be understood. However, such distinction was not carried on afterwards, at least not exactly, and there is no contemporary parallel beyond Efron's (1941) distinction between ideographic or logico-pictorial gesture and physiographic.

1.1.2 Medieval and later treatises

The differences between classical rhetoric and 18th century studies can easily justify our jump here, but nonetheless a number of studies deserve mentioning because they acted as a bridge between the two:
(a) Giovanni Bonifacio's work, *L'Arte de' Cenni* [...].[4] Bonifacio could be considered the first author to create an emblem repertoire (see Tessendorf 2013: 88), or at least to create a gesture repertoire that includes some emblems. Kendon (2004: 23–24) discusses Bonifacio's work in detail and highlights its more relevant aspects, while Wollock (2013: 369) highlights the fact it is a compendium of gestures associated with ideas and internal states, but with an anatomic basis and not a functional one.
(b) The work by the French Jesuit Ludovico Cresollius entitled *Vacationes Autumnales sive: De Perfecta Oratoris Actione et Pronunciatione*, published in Paris in 1620.[5] It is an example of a rhetoric treatise with frequent references to gestures, some of which is related to aspects that have been

---

[4] Bonifacio, Giovanni. 1616. *L'Arte de' Cenni* [...]. Vicenza: Francesco Grossi. For an overview of these authors and their historical milieu, see Wollock (2013).
[5] Interestingly, 1620 is also the year of the first publications to teach the deaf a gestural language: Bonet, Juan Pablo. 1620. *Reduction de las letras y arte para enseñar a ablar los mudos* [sic]. Madrid: Francisco Abarca de Angulo.

recently questioned, such as the statement that hand gestures start from the left and finish to the right.[6]

(c) Francis Bacon's work (1640), *Of the Advancement and Proficiency of Learning. Book VI* (Oxford: Young and Forrest). As Tessendorf underscores (2013:83), Bacon is the first scholar to use the term emblem to refer to a type of gesture:

> This in the meane is plain, that Hieroglyphiques and Gestures ever have some similitude with the thing signified, and are kind of Emblemes. (Bacon 1640: 258–259)

Efron (1941) picks the term from Bacon and also from the use of the term during the Renaissance, as Tessendorf notes (2013: 83). The term *emblem* was used during the Renaissance mostly to refer to the images that accompanied poetic texts or to a concept (and in fact, this latter interpretation and use continue to this day). *Emblem books* were popular throughout Europe during the 15th and 16th centuries.

(d) John Bulwer's (1644) work, which exerted great influence afterwards, two joint books entitled *Chirologia [...]* and *Chironomia [...]*.[7] Bulwer's work is one of the first monographs on gesture. According to Cleary (1974), who was in charge of its re-edition, Bulwer's work "is a thorough and systematic treatise on the movements of the hands and fingers, first, in relation to natural significations, and then in relation to artistic usage in public address" (ix). In a synthetic manner, Bulwer's treatise examines elocution with a focus on the orator's hand and arm gesticulation (cf. Wollock 2013). It moves away from Aristotelian physiognomy and more towards Ciceronian rhetoric. Despite his interest in the organization of the area of hand gestures, he does not expand the categorization outlined by the classical rhetoricians. However, Bulwer discovers important aspects of the gesture study that are greatly modern, such as the discursive character of gestures (the hand as a fountain of discourse) and the relationship between gesture and cognition. Bulwer's "fountain of discourse" metaphor predates by a few centuries McNeill's (1992) understanding of gesture as "a window to the mind." The two aspects, discursive and cognitive, are observable in the following quote:

---

6 All this information can be easily accessed online in an excellent thematic index at https://books.google.es/books?id=A8bynQEACAAJ&pg=RA1-PP20&hl=ca&source=gbs_selected_pages&cad=3#v=onepage&q&f=false

7 Bulwer, John. 1644. *Chirologia: or the Natvrall Langvage of the Hand* and *Chironomia: or the Art of Manuall Rhethoricke*. London: T. Harper, 1644. Re-edition by James W. Cleary (ed.). 1974: Carbondale and Edwadsville: Southern Illinois University Press.

> In all the declarative conceits of gesture whereby the body, instructed by nature, can emphatically vent and communicate a thought, and in the propriety of its utterance express the silent agitations of the mind, the hand, that busy instrument, is most talkative, whose language is as easily perceived and understood as if man had another mouth of fountain of discourse in his hand.
> (Bulwer 1644 [1974]: 121)

If we move to the 18th Century, two works are particularly worth mentioning. The first is Étienne Bonnot de Condillac's (1746) *Essai [...]*,[8] in which he proposes gesture as a phase in the genesis of human verbal language. The second one is Johann Jakob Engel's (1785–6) book *Ideen zu einer Mimik*,[9] in which he takes up the classical distinction between representation or exposition, and expression. Bühler (1933: 59), who discusses Engel's work within the historical context of physiognomy and pathognomy, describes how Engel sets up "painting" as a synonym of 'depicting' or 'representing.' Pictorial gestures constitute the first fundamental class of mimic gestures and expressive gestures the second one. What the soul thinks about is depicted in the first case, and the state of the mind when the soul thinks about it is expressed in the second case. Engel's classification is completed with the subdivision of expressive gestures into *intentional, analogous,* and *physiological*. Intentional gestures involve the start of an action, for instance when drinking; the second reflect internal movements, such as the evolution of thought; and the third are the gestures that accompany a specific physiological reaction, such as blushing (Bühler 1933: 66).

Meo-Zilio (1961a), rebuilding a historical line, links Engel's categorization with much later studies, including Gratiolet's (1865), Darwin's (1872), Mallery's (1881b) (see 1.1.3), as well as his own, as illustrated in Table 1.2.

Table 1.2: Correspondences between gesture types in several classical studies (according to Meo-Zilio 1961a).

Cicero/Quintilian (55 BC/95AD)	Engel (1785–6)	Gratiolet (1865)	Darwin (1872)	Mallery (1881b)	Meo-Zilio (1961a)
Expressive	Expressive	Symbolic	Inherited	Instinctual	Expressive
Representational	Pictorial	Metaphorical	Conventional	Conventional	Expositive

---

8 Condillac, Étienne Bonnot de. 1746. *Essai sur l'Origine des Connaissances Humaines [...]*. Paris: Pierre Mortier. Re-edited in 1973. Auvers-sur-Oise: Galiléee.
9 Engel, Johann Jakob. 1876. *Ideen zu einer Mimik: Mit erläuternden Kupfertafeln*. Berlin: Mylius.

This distinction is certainly questionable, since not all categorizations are quite comparable. For instance, Gratiolet's criteria are clearly different from the other classifications' criteria (see next section). However, these correspondences highlight some similarities and partial overlaps that, despite the obvious differences, trace a shared pathway by studies that are separated by hundreds of years and show the main recurrent parameters used in the description of a general notion of gesture (see 2.1.1).

1.1.3 The 19th century

In the 19th century, the first important work on gesture is Gilbert Austin's (1806): *Chironomia or, a Treatise on Rhetorical Delivery*[10] (see Kendon 2004). Austin's work continues to be relevant today, for instance in regards to his conceptualization of synchronicity between voice and gesticulation, and to his interest in notation. During the first quarter of the 19th century, we find other minor works that nonetheless deserve mentioning. These works examine the anatomy and physiology of expression, such as Charles Bell's (1806) *Essays on the Anatomy of Expression in Painting*,[11] and Gustav Anton von Seckendorff (1816)'s *Vorlesungen über Deklamation und Mimik*,[12] in which he focuses on declamation and mimicry.

These and other treatises culminate in Andrea de Jorio's (1832) *La mimica degli antichi investigata nel gestire napoletano* (Napoli: Stamperia e Cartiera del Fibreno). De Jorio's work is far more relevant to the study of emblems than any other work published during the 19th century, since many gestures that he compiles and examines are indeed emblems. According to Kendon (see Kendon 2004 and de Jorio 2000 [1832]), de Jorio's piece represents the first scientific study of gesture – although we believe this could well be said about the contemporary significance of Austin's (1806) *Chironomia*. Either way, de Jorio's treatise is indisputably the first cultural study – ethnographic *avant la lettre* – of gesture, and as its title announces, a historical study that is a pioneer in many ways.

During the second part of the 19th century, one finds less significant contributions when compared to the much later groundbreaking work by

---

[10] Gilbert, Austin. 1806. *Chironomia or, a Treatise on Rhetorical Delivery*. London: W. Bulmer, and Co. Re-edited in 1966. Carbondale and Edwardswille: Southern Illinois University Press.
[11] Bell, Charles. 1806. *Essays on the Anatomy of Expression in Painting*. London: Longman, Hurst, Rees, and Orme.
[12] Seckendorff, Gustav Anton von. 1816. *Vorlesungen über Deklamation und Mimik*. Braunschweig.

Efron (1941) during the following century. However, as Bühler (1933) notes, they are nonetheless important to explain the intellectual history that have led to the contemporary study of gestures. Generally, these works are found in the field of physiognomy, often from a medical perspective:
(a) Theodor Piderit's (1867) *Wissenschaftliches System der Mimik und Physiognomik* (Detmold: Klingenberg) focuses on facial mimicry movements and their physiology.
(b) Guillaume B. Duchenne (1862)[13] and Louis Pierre Gratiolet (1865),[14] who are physicians like Bell and Piderit, continue to be interested in physiognomy and physiology aspects. In fact, Gratiolet is the first author to distinguish symbolic and metaphoric gestures, although his use of this terminology is unclear, at least not very advantageous (Meo-Zilio indeed argues that Gratiolet "smashes" the terminology and does nothing to what Engels had already said):
  (i) *"Prosbolics"* movements: adaptations in the sense organs
  (ii) *Sympathetic* or *concomitant* movements: joint movements of bodily organs
  (iii) *Symbolic* or *analogous* movements: linked to fantasy
  (iv) *Metaphoric* movements: associated with thought

Another important contribution is the book by Edward B. Tylor, who is often considered one of the founders of cultural anthropology: *Researches on the Early History of Mankind and the development of civilization* (1865, London: John Murray). Tylor includes numerous references to the sign languages used by the deaf, as well to the relationship between verbal and non-verbal language (see Kendon 2004: 50–54).

In the latter part of the 19th century, Charles Darwin's foundational (1872) *The Expression of the Emotions in Man and Animals* (London: J. Murray) initiates a new period in the study of biology and the development of biological sciences. To some degree, Darwin's book could also be considered one of the first scientific or empirical studies of gesture, as he proposes the distinction between inherited and conventional gestures. Darwin's work can also be considered the first ethologic approach to gestural behavior, and subsequent ethological work considers Darwin its illustrious precedent.

---

13 Duchenne, Guillaume B. 1862. *Mecanisme de la physiognomie humaine ou analyse électrophysiologique de l'expression des passions. Avec un atlas composé de 74 figures électrophysiologiques photographiés.* Paris: Ve Jules Renouard, Libraire.
14 Gratiolet, Louis Pierre. 1865. *De la physiognomie et des mouvements d'expression.* Paris: Hetzel.

Garrick Mallery (1881a, 1881b),[15] on the other hand, also distinguishes two types of gestures, instinctual and conventional, and argues that meaning is created either starting from words and gaining autonomy later, or directly and independently. Mallery also discusses the relationship between the study of gestures (the study of signs) and of philology (particularly the study of etymology). He is the first author to relate explicitly the study of philology and the study of gestures. His knowledge of previous treatises on gesture is also remarkable, since it allows him to discuss from Quintilian's classic work to Andrea de Jorio's. Furthermore, Mallery's research on the sign languages of American Indians (1881a) could be seen as a forerunner of anthropological studies of non-verbal communication. Indeed Mallery's (1891) work is one of the first studies of a cultural pattern such as greeting.[16]

Other contributions published at the end of the 19th century include Kleinpaul's (1888)[17] examination of different types of communication and gestural language; Pitrè's (1889)[18] commentary on Sicilian gestures; and Sittl's (1890)[19] review of classical Greek and Roman gestuality. In addition, we have a number of handbooks, such as Bacon's (1875)[20] of oratory gestures; Adams' (1891),[21] and specially Hacks' (1892).[22] Hacks is the author of a treatise of over 500 pages, in which he discusses different gestures grouped as *natural* (professional gestures, as well as everyday gestures), *cultivated / cultured / sophisticated / refined* (artistic as well as from mimicry), and pathological (produced by ill people). In many ways, these treatises are the first conventional (although not prototypical) handbooks of gesture, which appear right at the transition between the 19th and 20th centuries.[23]

---

15 Mallery, Garrick. 1881a. The gesture speech of man. *Proceedings of the American Association for the Advancement of Science* 30. 283–313. Mallery, Garrick. 1881b. *Sign language among North American Indians (compared with that among other peoples and deaf-mutes)*. Washington, Annual Reports of the Bureau of American Ethnology (Reprint: [1972] The Hague: Mouton).
16 Mallery, Garrick. 1891. Greeting by gesture. *Popular Science Monthly* Feb.-March, 1891. 477–490.
17 Kleinpaul, Rudolf. 1888. *Sprache ohne Worte. Idee einer allgemeinen Wissenschaft der Sprache*. Leipzig: W. Friedrich [Reprint, The Hague: Mouton, 1972].
18 Pitrè, Giuseppe. 1989. *Usi, costumi, crecenze e pregiudizi del popolo siciliano*. Palermo: Pedone-Laurel. Reprint, Bologna: Forni, 1961.
19 Sittl, Carl. 1890. *Die Gebärden der Griechen und Römer*. Leipzig: Teubner.
20 Bacon, Albert M. 1985. *A Manual of Gestures in Oratory*. Chicago: S. C. Griggs.
21 Adams, Florence A. F. 1891. *Gesture and Pantomimic Action*. New York: Edgar S. Werner.
22 Hacks, Charles. 1892. *Le geste*. Paris: Marpon et Flammarion.
23 On the other "side" of the 19th–20th chronological boundary, we also have the 1902 handbook by Edward Amherst Ott: *How to Gesture*. New York: Hinds and Noble.

1.2 The 20th century

From a synthetic panoramic viewpoint, the rhetoric approach that predominated during previous centuries disappears or dissolves at the beginning of the 20th century into the more progressive and contemporary approaches of psychology and anthropology (Payrató 2009). Wundt's work is the first significant work with a psychological approach, right at the beginning of the 20th century. A few decades later we find Efron's (1941) anthropological groundbreaking work, which is the first study to use the term emblem. For reasons of clarity, we rely on the some of the main studies of the 20th century to group authors into three sets: (a) from Wundt (1900) to Efron (1941), (b) from Efron (1941) to Ekman and Friesen (1969), and (c) from Ekman and Friesen to McNeill's (2000) edited volume that opens the 21st century.

1.2.1 Initial period (1900–1941)

Wundt[24] significantly modifies the classification set forward by the rhetoricians. He leaves aside the expressivity reflected in movement, which is a central aspect of Engel's and Gratiolet's classifications, and focuses instead for the first time on semiotic nature of gestural elements. Wundt proposes a three-part classification (which is *de facto* a five-part one):
1) *Demonstrative* gestures, which are the basis or primary ones, as they are the simplest ones in regards to communication intent. The most basic form of a demonstrative gesture involves drawing attention to a co-present object.
2) *Mimetic* and *descriptive* gestures, which are the most common and diverse, and which result from the direct evolution of movements that were originally imitative and can be sub-divided in:
   2a) *Mimetic* or *indicative,* which are essentially descriptive gestures: "the outline of the object is drawn in the air by the index finger" (78)
   2b) *Plastic,* where "the image of the object is drawn in the air by the index finger" (78), as for instance, in the cases of gesturing a sphere and the horn gesture for cuckold
   2c) *Connotative*: which refer to a part or a secondary trait of an object that becomes its referent, as for instance, imitating the lifting of a hat to refer to a man in a deaf sign language

---

24 Wundt, Wilhelm. 1900. *Völkerpsychologie. I. Die Sprache*. Stuttgart. An English translation of Chapter 2 was included in *The language of gestures* [1973]. The Hague: Mouton.

3) *Symbolic*: "this kind of gesture refers indirectly to the idea it represents" (88), in contrast to the direct referencing in the other gestures. Symbolic gesture evoke ideas by association, as for instance, the association of yes and no with head movements).

Wundt's classification categorizes gestures more appropriately because its basis of argumentation. In fact, if we examine closely the three main groups that Wundt proposes we discover a pre-configuration of the essential trichotomy of the character or nature of the sign. In his semiotic foundational work, Charles S. Peirce (1931–1958), discusses precisely three types of signs, which he defines as "something that represents something to somebody in some respect or capacity" (244), according to the established relationship between the substituting object (the *vehicle* sign) and the substituted object:

A) *Indexicals*, where the relationship is *contiguity* (as between smoke and fire, the finger and the object pointed at, or as the deictic system in verbal language).
B) *Icons*, where the relationship is *resemblance* (as between a photograph and the photographed person, a quantity and the number of fingers used to count it, or as onomatopoeias in the verbal language).
C) *Symbols*, where the relationship is *conventionality* (a red light as a sign to stop or not to enter, a raised thumb with a closed fist as a display of perfect or agreement, and most of the linguistic signs in natural languages).[25]

Wundt's categorization is a genuine precedent of this semiotic trichotomy, which will be subsequently taken up also by Hécaen (1967), and constitutes the first explicit statement that there is a symbolic class of gestural units.[26] Furthermore, Wundt's classification gives us a glimpse of the long-standing controversy between *iconicity* and *symbolism*. His connotative gestures in the group (2b) represent an inflection point between the 2nd and 3rd gestural categories, but at the same time, group (2b) brings into question these categories themselves: there is not a sharp distinction – a jump – between the 2nd and 3rd categories but a transition. The confirmation of the gradual differentiation in the relationship between iconicity and symbolism will lead to an intense investigation of Wundt's distinctions and to the establishment of more flexible and functional categories throughout the entire 20th century. Such prolonged

---

[25] Conventionality must be understood in the sense of arbitrariness, or as "non-natural meaning" (as put by Grice 1957, 1975), the one we find in emblems (see Wharton 2009: 5).
[26] A possible exception to the assertion here about Wundt being the first scholar to talk about symbolic gesture is Gratiolet's use of this term in his classification mentioned earlier (cf. 1.1.2, Table 1.2 and 1.1.3). However, Gratiolet's use is debatable and somewhat peculiar.

investigation will take place within the more ambitious and the more epistemological productive framework of non-verbal communication, and more recently, of multimodality.

After Wundt's work, Efron's (1941) work and Ekman and Friesen's (1969) work can be easily identified as the two other milestones that lead to our contemporary categorization of gesture. But before we get to their work, several other works are noticeable for their contribution to defining gesture. In a chronological order, we find:

(i) Reinach's (1924) contribution in the form of a transcribed conference presentation, which constitutes the first study of the history of gestures. One year later and relying on an ethnographic approach, Leite de Vasconcellos (1925) publishes the first monograph of an emblem, the fig, in *A figa. Estudio de etnografia comparativa [...]*. Also, Bühler (1933) proposes the basis for the study of deixis.

(ii) New proposals of gesture classification: Delacroix (1924), for instance, distinguishes between the *agitation of systematic movements, representative* gestures, and *logical* gestures. However, Van Ginneken (1939) distinguishes between *lexical* (meaningful) and *indicative* gestures, while Hayes (1940) provides a very general classification:
   a. *Folk gestures*: nodding the head, shaking hands in greeting, shaking fist in defiance, pouting, biting the lips in vexation, lifting the eyebrows, etc.
   b. *Technical gestures*: the sign language of the North American Indian [cf. Mallery 1888b!], or that of the deaf and dumb; semaphor signaling, umpire signaling, etc.
   c. Autistic (or nervous) gestures: "doodling", opening and closing objects carried in the hand, swinging watch chain, etc. (Hayes 1940: 245)

(iii) In the Hispanic tradition, for instance Marañón (1937) considered that "gesture is any expression of passions and feelings, whether done by the face, the hand, or the body", he applied a potential distinction in Spanish (*visaje, mueca* and *mohín*) and finally he noted that "we consider 'gesture' as the material translation of an emotional state through habitual means of emotive expression, whether executed or imagined, in light of a specific social attitude" (Marañón (1937: 5–8). The Catalan tradition is started to an important degree by Rosell (1930), who within a racial-spiritualist theoretical framework, emphasizes also the expression of an internal state found in gesture:

> Gestures – and by this term one must understand any corporeal expression with the exclusion of the word [sic!] but indeed the tone [sic] – are the expression of the internal life of an individual that is manifested outwardly. Translated from (Rosell 1930: 123)

Flachskamp (1938) makes another attempt to define gesture with precision, relying, like Marañón, on the terminology of the time. He defines gesture as "a movement that takes place in the layer of the outward poise." Based on the lexical distinction in German between Gebärde and *Geste*, Flachskamp observes that:

> In German *'Gebärden'* refer to gestures such as of fear, of horror, as well as those of joy, of delight [...]. In all these cases, *'Gebärde'* refers to the Spanish 'poise,' 'habit,' 'individual peculiarity.' Translated from (Flachskamp 1938: 3)

On the other hand, the German *Gesten* refers, for instance, to the movements of a person who does not speak a foreign language and tries to communicate with a speaker of this language, and also to the signs used by the dead to communicate.

> The *'Gebärde'* occurs spontaneously; is symptomatic; instead gesture *is made*, it can be directed, prevented, or reproduced, it is available, it functions. It is simply a psychological issue to discern whether a given movement involves a spontaneous *gesture* [*ademán*, in Spanish] (*'Gebärde'*) or a gesture respectively. Translated from (Flachskamp 1938: 4)

(iv) We find also proposals in other traditions. In the British tradition, Critchley (1939) puts forward his own proposal that, like Marañón's and Flachskamp's, does not lead to subsequent studies:

> It would be better to restrict the word 'pantomime' to that variety of dumb-show which aims at expressing an idea, while 'gesture' or its diminutive 'gesticulation' should be made to connote those movements, particularly of the hands and face, which accompany speech for the purpose of emphasis. Pantomime is silent acting, while gesture is merely a kind of italicized speech. (Critchley 1939: 12)

It is important to point out that Critchley is part of a tradition of expression studies that distinguished between *mimicry* (facial expressive movements) and *pantomimics* (expression in the rest of the body), although the latter etymologically indeed refers to the totality of the body.

In the Italian tradition, Cocchiara (1932) is interested in two types of gestures, those of *aggregation* and those of *neutralization*, but does not make any changes to Wundt's classification, which he discusses at length. Cocchiara also emphasizes the distinction between *gesture* and *emotive reaction*, which links him to the classical categorization discussed earlier and that will be taken up by subsequent studies.

> While the gesture, in fact, according to us, "is an intentional movement for the purpose of expression," the emotional reaction, which is only improperly called a gesture, lacks, precisely, an intentional meaning.
>
> Translated from (Cocchiara 1932: 32)

This initial period of the 20th century is best represented by the publication that indeed closes it: David Efron's *Gesture and Environment* (New York: King's Crown Press) published in 1941, and re-issued as *Gesture, Race and Culture*, 1972, with a preface by Paul Ekman (The Hague: Mouton). At the risk of abusing the stereotype, the publication of Efron's book does indeed constitute a before and after in the study of emblematic gestures or emblem. The subtitle of the book is certainly very explicit, following an early tradition of long subtitles:

> A tentative study of the spatio-temporal and "linguistic" aspects of the gestural behavior of eastern Jews and southern Italians in New York City, living under similar as well as different environmental conditions.

Efron's (1941) anthropological study on gestures is still very relevant today. He compared the gestures of Italian and Jewish immigrants in New York with those of their original countries, and the evolution of such gestures over successive generations in the city. His work demonstrates the fallacies of some theories or fictions of certain anthropologists who associated the concept of race with certain non-verbal patterns.

Efron's work is the actual start of emblem studies, since for the first time the concept of emblem is established and investigated systematically, though established in a highly restrictive way to refer only to symbolic gestures. His proposal of gesture classification is the first one based on a rigorous and extensive empirical study. In this light, Efron's classification could be considered as the first scientific classification (rather than simply a programmatic or descriptive one) of gesture. Efron limits his analysis to the examination of hand and head movements, and develops it along three axes (cf. Ekman 1970):

a) *Spatio-temporal*: Efron studies in the first place the spatial and temporal features of gesture, considering it in terms of its characteristics as movement:
   1) *Radius* (size, movement axis).
   2) *Form* (straight, elliptical ...).
   3) *Plane* (in regards to the speaker and the hearer).
   4) *Bodily parts* (used: head, finger ...).
   5) *Tempo* (transition types).
b) *Interlocutional*: the interactive aspects of gesture are studied in this second level:
   1) *Familiarity* (with the interlocutor).
   2) *Simultaneous gesticulation* (by interlocutors).

3) *Geography of conversation* (use of space and distance between interlocutors).
  4) *Gesticulation with objects*.
c) *Linguistic*: lastly, Efron considers the referential meaning of gesture, and establishes the following classification:
  1) *Logical-discursive*: gestures that refer to the course of an ideational process:
     a) *Baton*: they mark the successive stages of mental activity.
     b) *Ideographic*: they sketch the direction of thought in the air.
  2) *Objective*: they have independent meaning from discourse and can be sub-divided into:
     a) *Deictic*: they point to a present object.
     b) *Pictographic*: they display visually what they signify:
        I) *Iconographic*: they describe the form of an object.
        II) *Kinetographic*: they describe a bodily action.
     c) *Emblematic* or symbolic: without a morphological relation to what they represent.

For the first time, Efron makes available a categorization that brings together the physical, contextual, and signification aspects of gestural units, and that can easily apply to the organization of empirical data. Ekman and Friesen (1969) build on this classification and resituate it in the wider context of non-verbal communication. Ekman and Friesen's contribution is exactly that: recontextualizing Efron's classification makes possible a more empirically grounded and functional categorization, something that was absent in previous classification and that is still not fully formed in Efron's own work.

1.2.2 Intervening period (1942–1969)

In terms of the specific work towards delimiting the category of emblems, but certainly in many other aspects, one could go directly from Efron's (1941) work to Ekman and Friesen's (1969). However, a number of less significant contributions help to understand changes in the research milieu of the intervening period:
(a) In the French tradition, La Barre's (1947, 1964) contribution, although rarely cited in general and even less in the English-speaking world, is important in terms of establishing the cultural foundations of gesture studies. La Barre's contribution together with Efron's work paved the way for the later analysis of gestures in terms of their cultural roots.

(b) In the Hispanic tradition (cf. Payrató 2008), a good number of studies also appear during this period, which are even less known and cited than the ones in the French tradition. However, they are worth mentioning because they are original contributions and precursors of later work. Cardona (1953–54) compiles and classifies some everyday gestures in Venezuela. Rabanales (1954–55) proposes his own gesture classification, but with a strange and unsuccessful terminology ('Somatolalia'). Meo-Zilio's study of gestures in Uruguay and Río de la Plata (1961a, 1961b) is a clear precursor to geographical studies of gesture and Hayes (1959) creates for the first time an explicit guide to collect emblematic gestures (or folkloric gestures, as he calls them in his research (see 3.2.1).

(c) Ruesch and Kees (1956) not only write the first handbook of non-verbal communication, but the first book with the words "non-verbal communication" on its title. Increasingly, an "epistemological" – if it can be called that – context emerges, where research is placed within the interdisciplinary framework of non-verbal communication. In this period, Hayes (1957) publishes the first bibliographic review of gesture studies.

In regards to the gesture classification controversies, Ekman and Friesen's (1969)[27] proposal can be located as a point of consensus despite the multiple diverging categorizations. Their classification in based on three explicit criteria: origin, use, and codification of non-verbal acts. The three criteria in this classification could be considered as pertaining to *etymological, physical*, and *semiotic* aspects of gesture. Therefore, Ekman and Friesen's criteria of classification are broader than the criteria that underlie Efron's. The broader criteria make possible a more appropriate – and flexible – framework to classify empirical evidence. The combination of the three criteria leads the authors to differentiate five basic categories, as found in the original proposal and reproduced in Table 1.3.

Ekman (1980: 98) will complete this table with a more sophisticated subcategorization of illustrators, in which he takes up and widens Efron's classification. In Ekman's conceptualization, illustrators are the closest category to

---

[27] This piece of work is a classic among non-verbal communication studies. Although it is usually cited as published in 1969, a preliminary version was presented as a communication at the symposium "Teoría de la comunicación y modelos lingüísticos en ciencias sociales" that took place in October 1967 at the Centro de Investigaciones Sociales del Instituto Torcuato di Tella, Buenos Aires. A Spanish translation, entitled "Origen, uso y codificación: Bases para cinco categorías de conducta no verbal" accompanied by an appendix and commentary sections, appeared in Eliseo Verón et al.: *Lenguaje y comunicación social*. Buenos Aires, Nueva Visión, 1971, 51–105.

Table 1.3: Classification of Ekman and Friesen (1969).

	EMBLEMS	ILLUSTRATORS: Batons, Ideographs, Deictic, Spatial, Kinetographs, Pictographs	REGULATORS	AFFECT DISPLAYS	ADAPTORS: Self-, Alter- & Object-
USAGE: external conditions	Most frequent when verbal channel blocked; also related to demographic variables	May vary with enthusiasm or excitement; varies with setting and demographic variables	Vary with and partially define roles, orientation of interaction; vary with demographic variables	Culture, social class & family define affects appropriate for certain settings; display rules incorporate social norms about affect displays	Self adaptors inhibited by conversations, but still prevalent. Adaptors triggered by feeling, attitude
relation to words	high agreement about verbal definition; can be replaced by word or phrase	directly tied to speech, illustrate message content, or rhythmically accent or trace ideas	maintain and regulate back-and-forth conversational flow, not tied to specifics of speech	can repeat, augment, contradict or be unrelated to verbal affective statement	can be triggered by verbal behaviour in a present situation which is associated with conditions when adaptive habit first learned
awareness	usually as aware as choice of words	within awareness, not as explicit as emblems	periphery of awareness; difficult to inhibit	often highly aware of affect once displayed, but can occur without any awareness	typically not aware of adaptors, although tend to conceal and inhibit

(continued)

Table 1.3 (continued)

	EMBLEMS	ILLUSTRATORS: Batons, Ideographs, Deictic, Spatial, Kinetographs, Pictographs	REGULATORS	AFFECT DISPLAYS	ADAPTORS: Self-, Alter- & Object-
intention to communication	usually intended to communicate	intentional to help communicate, not as deliberate as emblems	over-learned habits that are almost involuntary	often not intended to communicate but can be; subject to inhibition; can be dissimulated	rarely intended to communicate
receiver feedback	visual attention and direct comment	visual attention and some direct comment or response	other interactant very responsive to, but rarely directly comments on	greater receiver attention; can or cannot be direct comment on	other interactant rarely comments on, and politeness implies lack of attention to
type of information	more shared than idiosyncratic, typically communicative, informative & interactive	more shared than idiosyncratic; informative, often interactive & communicative	more shared than idiosyncratic; by definition interactive, usually informative, not often communicative	both shared & idiosyncratic; informative, can be interactive, communicative only in simulations	both shared & idiosyncratic; often informative, not usually interactive, rarely communicative

	Col 1	Col 2	Col 3	Col 4	Col 5	Col 6
CODING:	Some arbitrarily; some iconic (pictorial), kinetic, spatial usually not intrinsic. Iconic can be decoded, at least in part, by a foreign culture	Batons & ideographs: rhythmic/iconic; pictographs; pictorial/iconic; deictics; spatial & kinetographs; iconic or intrinsic. Vary with culture, social class, etc.	Arbitrary, iconic or intrinsic; we have not clearly specified. Vary cross-culturally and source of misunderstanding which is often not recognized	Some intrinsic, may be iconic as result of display rules; perhaps some arbitrary. Some evokers, blends, display rules & consequences vary within and between cultures	Relationship between facial musculature & affect and some of the evokers neurophysiologically programmed. Dome evokers, blends, display rules, consequences socially learned	Intrinsic/kinetic or tend to be iconic when fragmented by time. Some similar, some differ across cultures
ORIGINS:	Culture specific learning; specifiallly taught as verbal language taught	Socially learned by imitation; vary with ethnicity; cultural and social class differences in type and frequency	Learned but we have not specified when			Habits first learned to deal with sensation, excretion, ingestion, grooming, affect; or to maintain prototypic interpersonal relationships; or to perform instrumental task
OVERLAP:	Can be based on affect display, or adaptors	Kinetographs can include an adaptor	All other categories can serve as regulators; but we call acts regulators only if they are not part of another category			

emblems, but unlike them, illustrators are directly linked to the verbal message. Illustrators can be classified as:
- *Batons*: movements that accentuate a particular word.
- *Underliners*: movements that emphasize a phrase, clause, sentence, or a group of sentences.
- *Ideographs*: movements that indicate the path or direction of thought.
- *Kinetographs*: movements that represent an action of the body or a non-human action.
- *Pictographs*: movements that draw the shape of a referent in the air.
- *Rhythmics*: movements that represent the rhythm or the pace of an event.
- *Spatials*: movements that represent a spatial relationships.
- *Deictics*: movements that point to a referent.

Since the 1970s, Ekman and Friesen's table has become the main point of reference for most non-verbal communication research. Despite later modification of some details – some by the authors themselves – and Kendon's 2004 sharp critique, the categorization of non-verbal units in *emblems, illustrators, regulators*, and *displays of internal states*, continues to be today one of the most lucid and clear classifications among the many that have been proposed. Ekman and Friesen's categorization, by providing a wider theoretical framework, opens the possibility of a new gestural category, *autonomous* gestures, that have semiotic characteristics very similar to those of verbal communication items, that is, the spoken verbality of natural languages (see Kendon 2004 and the following sub-section).

1.2.3 Final period (1970–2000)

From the 1970s until the end of the century, emblem studies become normalized and have developed in different ways, particularly in the field of gesture studies and more generally in the fields of non-verbal communication and multimodality, the latter term appearing indeed at the end of the century. In a very synthetic way, we can list here the most important contributions of this period:
- Birdwhistell (1970) attempts to build a structure for the non-verbal domain to parallel the verbal one, with similar units and a conceptualization inspired by linguistic structuralism (see Kendon 2004).
- The year 1972 becomes a very significant year, since many important research studies and essential theoretical work are published: Wiener et al. (1972) clarify the distinctions between the concepts of non-verbal behavior and of non-verbal communication. Lyons (1972) makes an explicit proposal

of what the limits of *linguistness* may be, since what can be considered as linguistic is not as easy to define as it may appear at first. For the first time, Kendon (1972) and Condon (1976) produce very explicit research studies about the coordination and synchronization of gesture and talk.

- Poyatos (1970, 1976, 1980, 1983, inter alia) stands out with his very extensive but seldom cited work, with an interesting proposal to conceptualize human communication as having a triple structuration: verbal language, prosody or vocal paralinguistics, and kinetics. Other authors will adopt Poyatos' proposal or will develop similar ones (see for instance Ardnt and Janney 1987 and their "intergrammar" proposal with verbal, prosodic, and gestural aspects).

If we focus specifically on emblematic gesture studies, we find theoretical and foundational studies, as well as studies from different traditions that are expositive in nature, and that aim to group or classify emblems:

- Ekman and Friesen continue to develop their classification proposal with a second study (1972). Saitz and Cervenka (1972) create one of the first comparative repertoires using Ekman and Friensen's methodology. Kendon (1981a) analyzes comparatively several repertoires for the first time, and Hanna (1996) develops an extensive and explicit attempt to classify emblems as a semiotic category.
- We find most contributions in the Italian tradition, at least of the historical nature. We highlight different compilations and dictionaries (see below subsection 3.5.1., in which we analyze lexicographic repertoires) and more importantly, the descriptive as well as theoretical work by Poggi (1983, 1987).
- In the French tradition, often excluded from the English-speaking tradition, (in fact, as it happens with the Hispanic and Italian traditions), we can note many studies on the French repertoire and on the conceptualization of emblems (Dahan and Cosnier 1977, Calbris 1980, 1981, 1990), multimodal interaction and the interrelationships between orality and gesture (Santi et al. (eds.) 1998).
- In the Hispanic tradition, Meo-Zilio's research on gestures in Spain and Latin American stands out (see Meo-Zilio 1983, 1987, 1990, inter alia). Payrató (1993), combining the Hispanic and Catalan traditions, proposes a pragmatic approach to the study of emblems.
- Finally, Morris et al. (1979) write what is perhaps the best-known book about emblematic gestures, although the authors do not use that term. Instead, they use the term *symbolic gesture*, which is partially explained by the fact they do not analyze emblems with a high iconic value. Morris et al.'s opus contains a very significant amount of information about gesture, while at the same time, suffers from some important methodological problems. In addition, Sherzer (1973, 1991, 1993) expands ethnographic approaches to emblems.

1.3 The 21st century

The beginning of the 21st century brings with it the definite constitution of an interdisciplinary domain of gesture studies, even though there remains work to be completed in terms of its theoretical foundations, as well as in how gesture studies may be integrated into larger theoretical frameworks and established disciplines such as pragmatics, semiotics, communication studies, psychology, anthropology and sociology. The larger theoretical issue at stake is the degree of "epistemological autonomy" that gesture studies can achieve, or expressed the other way around, the degree to which gesture studies are (theoretically) contingent and dependent on other disciplines and in need to be integrated in a larger theoretical framework.

Unquestionably, gesture studies have become institutionalized during the 21st century: more conferences, the creation of professional associations (GeVoix, ISGS, iGESTO), journals (*Gesture*, since 2001), gesture laboratories (Aix-en-Provence, Berlin, Chicago, Frankfurt-Öder, Njemegen), projects, bibliographies/handbooks, online studies and compilations, and so on and so forth.

To some degree we can also talk about a paradigm change. Until the middle of the 20th century (1941) the most widespread term used is gesture, and later emblem, a period during which we see how these concepts are included in the more general term of non-verbal communication. During the 21st century, in turn, we see how the concept of non-verbal communication is used alternatively with the concept of multimodality, which is increasingly substituting the former, at least when it comes to the main or predominant term (see Payrató 2009). Kress and Van Leeuwen's book *Multimodal Discourse*, which can be regarded as the beginning or official "christening" of the term, is published in 2001.

Among the most remarkable publications of this period we find the book edited by McNeill (2000) and Kendon's monograph (2004). In the edited volume, McNeill (2000) proposes again the gestural "continua" in his particular contribution (see 2.2.2). This edited volume, taken together as a collection of different authors, can be interpreted as the symbolic opening of 21st century. McNeill's collection is followed and complemented by Cavé, Guaitella and Santi (eds.) (2001), Rector, Poggi and Trigo (eds.) (2003), Müller and Posner (eds.) (2004) – despite the fact that it contains earlier work from 1998 – and Kendon's monograph (2004), which is a study of reference for all research related to gesture and its types (cf. also Kita (ed.) 2003 and Enfield 2009). In regards to emblem research in particular, the work by Poggi, Calbris, and Brookes deserve a special mention.

To conclude this chapter, we must mention the monumental work in two volumes edited by Müller et al. (2013) and Müller et al. (2014), in which they analyze in greater depth the concept of emblematic gesture and of other types of gestures (such as pragmatic gestures), though there continue to exist some variation (cf. Tessendorf 2013, Payrató 2014a and Poggi 2014). In regards to repertoires, which we examine in more detail in subsequent chapters, Galhano-Rodrigues's 2014 and Payrató's 2014b both set forward a pragmatic categorization and characterization of emblems.

2 Emblems and other gestures

2.1 Gestures and emblems

In the first section of chapter 2, we briefly describe the different pathways that have led to our current understanding of gesture and the prototypical features associated with it. Readers will be familiar with some of these features, since they have been discussed in the historical overview in chapter 1. In the following section, we focus on the concept of emblematic gesture, and present three theoretical approaches to its categorization. In the final section, we outline the types and functions of emblematic gestures, as well as the relationship between emblems, other gestures, and non-verbal acts.

2.1.1 Pathways towards a definition of gesture

The definition of gesture as *an expressive and meaningful bodily movement* is the most commonly used one in the literature discussed in the previous section/chapter, and corresponds to the etymology of the word gesture (from the Latin GESTUS, in the sense of "posture" or "poise," see Haviland 2004: 200).[1] Although there are numerous variants that qualify this definition, most of these variants do not modify it substantially. Some early variants have attempted and failed to provide a more technical definition. The basic characterization is also the one included in contemporary definitions and dictionary entries, as for instance in the Merriam-Webster Dictionary:

---

[1] Haviland (2004: 200) points out that "the origin of the English word "gesture" is to be found in Latin *gerere* 'bear, carry, carry on, perform' (via medieval Latin *gestura*), and its earliest usage accordingly meant a "manner of carrying the body; carriage, deportment" – a very broad notion which only later comes to be narrowed to "(a) movement of the body or limbs, now only as an expression of thought or feeling; the use of such movements as an expression of feeling or a rhetorical device," and still later to the typical twentieth-century meaning: "[a]n action performed as a courtesy, formality, or symbol to indicate an intention or evoke a response." Recent theoretical treatments question several aspects of these common usages: "manner" (which may imply something stable or established, as opposed to the apparent ephemeral nature of much gesture), "expression of thought or feeling" (which may conflate what might be presumed to be very different cognitive underpinnings), and perhaps most problematic, "intention" with all the attendant difficulties about the nature of the person, the will, and the emergent character of interpersonal interaction."

https://doi.org/10.1515/9781501509957-003

(1) Gesture
   1: archaic: carriage, bearing
   2: a movement usually of the body or limbs that expresses or emphasizes an idea, sentiment, or attitude; "raised his hand overhead in a gesture of triumph"
   3: the use of motions of the limbs or body as a means of expression
   4: something said or done by way of formality or courtesy, as a symbol or token, or for its effect on the attitudes of others

Definitions of gesture that carry a higher degree of specialization – as to be expected in any scientific approach – are first introduced by Efron (1941) and developed more comprehensively by Ekman and Friesen (1969). The latter authors widen the analytic paradigm with the more general concept of "non-verbal act," which they classify according to the categories of emblems, illustrators, affective displays, regulators and adaptors. Ekman and Friesen's categorization represents moving the field from studies of an everyday language term such as "gesture," to studies of the technical term "non-verbal act," which is accompanied by other specialized technical subcategories. Despite the theoretical breakthrough that Ekman and Friesen's non-verbal communication analysis represents, the term "gesture" has continued to be used extensively.[2]

Following other theoretical pathways to define gesture, Poyatos (1976) distinguishes *gestures, manners,* and *postures,* and define the former as:

> [...] A conscious or unconscious body movement made mainly with the head, the face alone or the limbs, learned or somatogenic, and serving as a primarily communicative tool, dependent or independent from verbal language, either simultaneous or alternating with it, and modified by the conditioning background. Examples: smiles, eye movements, a gesture of beckoning, a nervous tic, etc. (Poyatos 1976: 128–9)

The concept of gesture differs from *manner* in that manner is a learned and socially coded preferred bodily attitude, such as sitting at the table, greeting another person, or sneezing. Gesture also differs from *posture* in that the latter involves a static bodily positioning that results from a previous gesture or a previous manner (about such distinction, see also Poyatos 1988: 41).

Over several decades, Adam Kendon is the scholar who has devoted more efforts and developed more qualifications in his pursuit of an adequate definition

---

2 Indeed, as we note below, Kendon has proposed a similar move in his later work, substituting the everyday term "gesture" with the technical term of "utterance visible action" (Kendon 2013: 8).

of gesture. In his first work, Kendon defined gesture in the following terms, with the notion of *action* at its core:

> A *gesture* is usually deemed to be an action by which a thought, feeling, or intention is given conventional and voluntary expression. Gestures are thus considered to be different from expressions of emotion, involuntary mannerisms, however revealing, and actions that are taken in the pursuit of some practical aim, however informative such actions may be. (Kendon 1981b: 28)

A problem of precision can be seen in the term *conventional*, which disappeared in Kendon's subsequent definitions. A possible explanation for the disappearance of the term could be found in complex issues around criteria, mostly connected to still-to-be-clarified concepts of (emotional) expression and of pantomime (devoid of practical action). At the same time, the term action becomes specified as a *visible action*:

> The word 'gesture' in this chapter will be taken to mean any visible action by which meaning is given voluntary expression. 'Gesture' is to be considered separate from emotional expression; it also does not include those various minor tics, mannerisms, or 'nervous movements' which, though informative to the eye of another, are not treated in interaction as part of the individual's intended 'official' or 'given' expression. Practical actions will also not be considered as gestures, even if, as is sometimes the case, such actions have an expressive purpose. Only if a person is seen to pantomime a practical action will this be considered a part of gesture. (Kendon 1983:13)

In subsequent work, Kendon further specifies the definition of gesture, arguing that gestures have a function or intent as *explicit communicative acts*:

> I use the term "gesture" to refer to any instance in which visible action is mobilized in the service or producing an explicit communicative act, typically addressed to another, regarded by the other (and by the actor) as being guided by an openly acknowledged intention, and treated as conveying some meaning beyond or apart from the action itself.
> (Kendon 1984: 81)

In Kendon's later definitions, gesture is framed as a *communicative act* to be understood as the deliberate and intentional transmission of information. Kendon underscores here the importance of intentionality as well as of interactional participation, including the participation of recipients:

> The term 'gesture' will be used to mean any distinct bodily action that is regarded by participants as being directly involved in the process of deliberate utterance. Gesture, in my use of the term, comprises visible bodily action that is regarded by participants having 'given' (Goffman 1963) or intended communication as its primary function. [...] Bodily actions that are deemed to be produced in the service of such deliberate or intended

communication – whether or not they are produced in association with spoken utterance – will be referred to here as 'gesture'. (Kendon 1985: 215–216)

More recently, general but also diverse definitions of gesture have appeared, for instance, in the encyclopedic work edited by Müller et al. (2013) and Müller et al. (2014). The multiple nuances that have incrementally been added to Kendon's initial definitions of gesture now multiply and we find a noticeable diversity of conceptualizations and attempts to find a relatively brief and simple definition of gesture. McNeill, who constitutes the other main figure in gesture studies together with Kendon, explains how he accepts Kendon's 2004 definition but ends up modifying it in two aspects (McNeill 2013: 29):

> Adam Kendon placed gestures in the category of "actions that have the features of manifest deliberate expressiveness" (2004: 13–14). I adopt this definition; it is the best I have seen but do so with one qualification and one proviso.[3]
>
> The qualification is that gesture cannot be deliberate; as we define them, "gestures" are unwitting and anything but deliberate. (Kendon may have meant by "deliberate" non-accidental, and whit this I agree; but the word also conveys "done for a purpose," and with that I do not agree.)
>
> The proviso concerns "action." If by action we understand movements orchestrated by some significance created by the speaker, this is accurate but (again) are not actions to attain some goal.
>
> So our definition, based on Kendon's but excising "deliberate" and specifying the kind of action (and far from tripping off the tongue), is this: A gesture is an unwitting, non-goal-directed action orchestrated by speaker-created significances, having features of manifest expressiveness.
>
> Very often I use "gesture" still more restrictively to mean all of the above, plus:
>
> An expressive action that enacts imagery (not necessarily by the hands or hands alone) that is part of the process of speaking. (McNeill 2013: 29)

McNeill puts forward these definitions from the standpoint of a psychological perspective. It is remarkable that he excludes the term "deliberate," which has been a recurrent aspect of definitions of gesture historically, as well as that he qualifies gestures as unconscious. All together, McNeill's definition seems to

---

3 To be exact, Kendon (2004: 13–14) states the following: "It is proposed that movements may vary in the extent to which they can be said to have those features which we shall here refer to as the *features of manifest deliberate expressiveness*" (emphasis in the original). Later in the same publication, Kendon (2004: 15) provides a full definition: "'Gesture', we suggest, then, is a label for actions that have the features of manifest deliberate expressiveness. They are those actions or those aspects of another's actions that, having these features, tend to be directly perceived as being under the guidance of the observed person's voluntary control and being done for the purposes of expression rather than in the service of some practical aim." Wharton (2009: 151–152) develops a very similar argument to the one postulated here by McNeill.

move away from Kendon's, because it is more restrictive, and comes closer to the concept of *gesticulation*, which Kendon, others, and even McNeill (cf. McNeill 2013: 30) himself, have used occasionally.

To conclude our overview of gesture definitions, Kendon himself, lists a series of reasons to account for his objection to the term *gesture* and his proposal to substitute it with the term *utterance visible action* (Kendon 2013: 8):

> [...] I shall call utterance visible action, and it corresponds to what is often referred to by the word "gesture". However, because "gesture" is also sometimes used to refer any kind of purposive action, [...] because it is also used as a way of referring to the expressive significance of any sort of action [...] and because, too, in some contexts the word "gesture" carries evaluative implications not always positive, it seems better to find a new and more specific term.

With the substitution of *gesture* by *utterance visible action*, an everyday term is opposed to a technical term, as it is often the case in the language and communication sciences: word/morpheme, utterance/sentence, or sound/phoneme. In any scientific endeavor, technical terms are a necessary practice, but the ease and frequency of everyday terms often lead to these enduring lexical doublets, in which the common term denotes a general notion and the technical one a much more specific notion. Taking into account this circumstance and what has been reviewed so far, is it possible then to come to a single definition of gesture? Any notion of gesture is inescapably polysemic,[4] since it must capture both meanings, the general and the specific, as we illustrate in Table 2.1 and Figure 2.1 below. In Table 2.1 we hightlight the basic and optional features of a notion of gesture, some of which are physical (morphological) and others pragmatic. In Figure 2.1, on the other hand, the polysemy of a notion of gesture is illustrated with a general notion, defined by Feature a.1 "Bodily action or movement" (higher circle), and with a specific notion, defined by both Feature 1.a "Bodily action or movement" and Feature b.1 "Meaningful and relevant action" (lower circle).

Also illustrated in Table 2.1 and Figure 2.1, we propose and argue that a definition of gesture (and the same for each one of its subcategories, including emblems) will stand as long as it is understood as an instance of a prototypical category, in line with the theory of prototypes.[5] Accordingly, a category has an

---

[4] Cf. Burgoon et al. (2013: 611): "as a last prefatory classification, the term gesture is open to a wide range of interpretations, ranging from the full gamut of nonverbal communication codes [...] to the more narrow and familiar intepretation referring to displays performed by the limbs (usually hands or head)."

[5] See, inter alia, Rosch (1978), Geeraerts (1989), Taylor (2003 [1989]), and Croft and Cruse (2004). On the relationship between (linguistic) polysemy, prototypes, and radial categories, see Lewandowska-Tomaszczyk (2007). Apart from the polysemy of the word gesture, which we discuss

Table 2.1: Basic obligatory and additional optional features for a categorization of gesture as a prototypical category and for a description of the concept of gesture, from the most general level of definition (A), to an intermediate level (B), and to a specific level (C and D).

'GESTURE' AS A PROTOTYPE

(A) BASIC PHYSICAL/MORPHOLOGICAL FEATURE
    a.1 Bodily action or movement

....

(B) BASIC PRAGMATIC FEATURE
    b.1 Meaningful and relevant action ("ostensive") accompanied by verbal language or in absence of verbal language

....

(C) ADDITIONAL OPTIONAL PHYSICAL/MORPHOLOGICAL FEATURES
    c.1 Action or movement involving only hands and arms
    c.2 Action involving head movement
    c.3 Action involving facial movement
    c.4 Action involving eye movement
    c.5 Action involving other body parts

....

(D) ADDITIONAL OPTIONAL PRAGMATIC FEATURES
    d.1 Illocutionary action
    d.2 (Sociocultural) conventional action
    d.3 Deliberate (non-accidental) action
    d.4 Unconscious action
    d.5 Meaningful and relevant action in absence of verbal language
    d.6 Meaningful and relevant action only if accompanied by verbal language
    d.7 Intended as a message (action addressed to a copresent recipient in an interactional setting)
    d.8 Action involving natural meaning
    d.9 Action involving non-natural meaning
    d.10 Action involving procedural meaning

---

ideal or idealized representative or exemplar[6] that meets a series of criteria, but at the same time, numerous other examples do not, and instead, move away in

---

here, we also assume that the polysemy of the emblems is comparable to or equivalent to verbal *polysemy*, which makes the lexicographic treatment of emblems particularly challenging (see 3.4).

6 Because of space limitations, we do not discuss here the differences and similarities between prototype theory and exemplary theory, which complement each other in several aspects, cf. Ross and Makin (1999) and Smith (2014), inter alia. A thorough and comparative analysis of both theories applied to the categorization of gestures and emblems, as well as their learning, remains to be done.

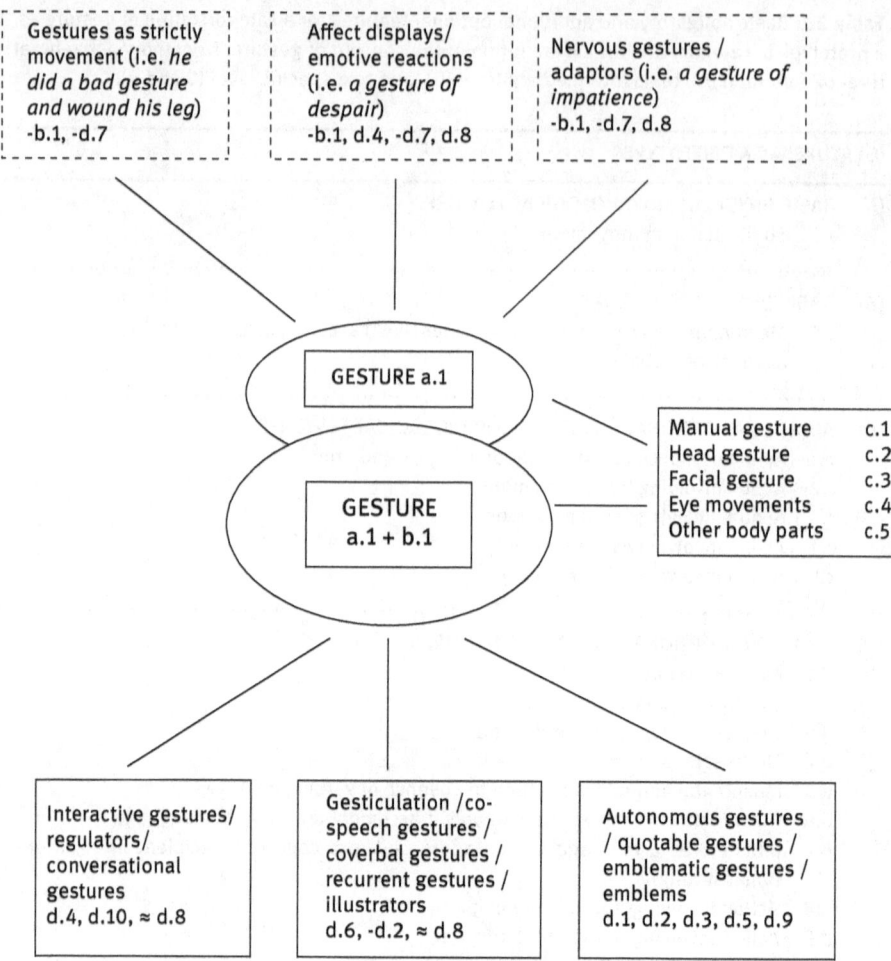

Figure 2.1: Conceptualization of gesture as a prototypical radial category, with specified subcategories that are more or less prototypical.

radial fashion from the prototype because they do not meet all the requisites/ criteria. These instances that fulfill the criteria only partially determine the subtypes or subcategory of the base (proto)type.

Geeraerts (1989) points out four features that are frequently considered characteristic of prototypicality:

(i) Prototypical categories cannot be defined by means of a single set of criterial (necessary and sufficient) attributes [...]

(ii) Prototypical categories exhibit a family resemblance structure, or more generally, their semantic structure takes the form of a radial set of clustered and overlapping meanings [...]
(iii) Prototypical categories exhibit degrees of category membership; not every member is equally representative for a category [...]
(iv) Prototypical categories are blurred at the edges (Geeraerts 1989: §2)

Lewandoska-Tomaszczyk (2007) reorders the four points in a perhaps more significant and intuitive way: (iii) – (iv) – (i) – (ii). In fact, features (iii) and (iv) "both involve the members (exemplars or subclasses) of a concept: some members are more typical than others, and sometimes membership status may be unclear" (Lewandoska-Tomaszczyk 2007: 145). On the other hand, feature (i) has to do more with the structure of the definition than with the structure of the affiliation (membership) in a category, and that is precisely what makes it impossible to define a category in a classical way. Instead, it is necessary to turn to a model of family similarity, which is included in feature (ii).

As far as our concern here with a definition of gesture, all four features are perfectly applicable to the category of *gesture*. In fact, the four features are applicable to all gesture subcomponents or subcategories, particularly to emblematic gestures, as we will see below: different degrees of membership, blurry edges, cannot be defined by simple criteria, and display a family resemblance structure (see 5.2.2 for a more detailed explanation).

By identifying the most important and recurrent features in the definitions reviewed above, we propose a description of the notion of gesture as a prototype in Table 2.1. This description consists of a set of prototypical features that categorize the concept of gesture, with basic and obligatory features and additional and optional features organized in different levels of definition. From the most general possible definition (level A), corresponding to a supraordinate level, and through a basic level definition (level B), technical or particular definitions of gestures (corresponding to a subordinate level) are to be found only in specific levels (C) and (D), taking into account that these last levels presuppose levels (A) and (B).[7]

The two most basic features are, firstly, a physical or morphological one, a.1, that determines the supraordinate or most general level of definition (the

---

[7] Obviously, a more general assumption could be that it is impossible to represent all the complexity and details of the notion of gesture (and gestural subcategories) in a single schema. Therefore Table 2.1 must be seen as a general and introductory proposal. For a comparison with the classifications discussed above and the reviews and proposals by Schönherr (2014), see Bohle (2014) and Maricchiolo et al. (2014).

hyperonym of gesture is *bodily action* or *movement*), and a pragmatic one, b.1, that determines the basic or intermediate level. This main pragmatic feature characterizes gestures as meaningful and relevant, in the sense of manifest and pertinent ("ostensive," using relevance theory terminology, see chapter 5), and whether accompanied by speech or not. Prototypically, a message is addressed to some copresent recipients in an interactional setting.

Once we focus on the additional and optional features of Table 2.1, the diversity of subcategories increases rapidly. Having to make a selection among the wide range of features discussed in the previous chapter, we limit our definition to two sets of additional optional features in a specific level, grouped in a physical (C) and in a pragmatic (D) domain. Physical or morphological features include the body part involved in a gesture, from hands and arms to other less prototypical parts. Pragmatic features include features such as illocutionary action (d.1, according to speech act theory), conventionality (d.2, as a sociocultural base), deliberation (d.3), consciousness (d.4), need of concomitant talk (d.5/d.6), and meaning type (d.7/d.8), according to usual parameters (as natural/non-natural meaning and conceptual/procedural meaning).[8] These pragmatic features also include whether the action involves emotional displays (d.9) and information about the sender (d.10).

Categorizing the subcategories of the gesture concept, that is, specifying them, is the next step to make the concept more precise. In the next section, we will do so particularly in reference to the subcategory of emblematic gesture or emblem. Now, in Figure 2.1, we introduce the subcategories in a radial fashion according to the prototype mode, in which each subcategory is specified closer or farther away from the nucleus of the prototype. Each subcategory is presented with its most characterizing or defining features (the notation "–" before the feature indicates negative value, and the notation "≈" indicates that the value is gradual). Boxes and circles with solid lines indicate very stable or highly stable gestural (sub)categories. Boxes and circles with intermittent lines indicate more "blurry" (sub)categories that stand at the boundaries of the very definition of gesture.

In the reminder of this chapter, we focus on one subcategory of gesture, the emblem or emblematic gesture, which we define, examine its types and functions, and compare it to other subcategories of gesture and other non-verbal actions.

---

8 See sections 2.3 and 2.4 for a detailed categorization of the different (sub)types of gesture, which we briefly discuss here to illustrate the conceptualization of gesture as a prototypical category. For a discussion of the types of meaning, particularly in reference to non-verbal communication, see Wharton (2009). Non-natural meaning involves what is (strictly) said plus what is implicated (intended); procedural meaning gives indications to interpret inferences (and not conceptual meaning).

2.1.2 Pathways to a definition of emblematic gesture

As described in the historical overview of chapter 1, David Efron (1941) is the first scholar to provide a rigorous definition of emblem. He defines it as an "either a visual or a logical object by means of a pictorial or non-pictorial form which has no morphological relationship to the thing represented" (Efron 1941: 96). Ekman and Friesen (1969: 63) take Efron's definition and widen it to include iconically codified gestures – gestures that have resemblance to its referent – which come to be simply named as *emblems*: "those non-verbal acts which have a direct verbal translation, or dictionary definition, usually consisting of a word or two, or perhaps a phrase. A few years afterwards, Ekman and Friesen (1972: 357) slightly modified their definition of emblem as:

> Those nonverbal acts (a) which have a direct verbal translation usually consisting of a word or two, or a phrase, (b) for which this precise meaning is known by most or all members of a group, class, subculture or culture, (c) which are most often deliberately used with the conscious intent to send a particular message to other person(s), (d) for which the person(s) who sees the emblem usually not only knows the emblem's message but also knows that it was deliberately sent to him, and (e) for which the sender usually takes responsibility for having made that communication. A further touchstone of an emblem is whether it can be replaced by a word or two, its message verbalized without substantially modifying the conversation. (Ekman and Friesen 1972: 357)

A series of authors have also used the terms *emblem* or *emblematic gestures* following Ekman and Friesen's definition, many for instance in the English tradition. McNeill (1992) also uses the term *emblem* and places it within several gestural continua that we analyze in the section 2.2.2 below. In the French tradition, Dahan and Cosnier (1977) use *quasi-linguistique*, and Calbris (2003, 2011) has alternated between general terms such as *French Gesture, symbolic gesture*, and *emblem*. The term emblem has seldom been used in the Hispanic tradition. Payrató (1993, 2008, 2013a) has used it within a cognitive and pragmatic perspective in the Catalan tradition.

Some other authors have discussed the same type of gestures but have used different terminologies. Only a few years after Ekman and Friesen's (1969) article, Wiener et al. (1972) propose that emblems should be included in the category of *pantomimic gestures*, a category that they formulate, together with improvised and non-conventionalized pantomimic gestures. Morris et al. (1979) use instead the term *symbolic gestures*. In the Italian tradition, Poggi (1981, 2007) also uses the term *symbolic gesture* and distinguishes two types, *holophrastic* and *lexical/articulated*. Poggi (2007: 71) defines a gesture as holophrastic "if it is a unique signal that conveys the meaning of a whole communicative act, both its performative and its propositional content" and as articulated "if it conveys only a part of the communicative signal". Tessendorf (2013) provides a welcomed panoramic overview of such terminological divergence, and synthesizes accurately the different perspectives and analytic approaches.

Among the authors that have put forward different terms – and definitions and conceptualizations – Adam Kendon occupies a preeminent position. On the one hand, Kendon proposes to use the term *autonomous gesture* rather than emblem, based on his efforts to find the most precise definitions of the subtypes of gestures:

> *Autonomous gestures* have been termed *emblems* by Ekman, and this usage has been widely followed in recent years. I prefer the term here proposed, however, because it is purely descriptive. Unlike the term 'emblem', it implies nothing about the semiotic character of such gestures. Furthermore, the word 'emblem' has a well-established use in common parlance, and it seems inappropriate to make a technical term out of it (Efron's 'emblematic gesture' would have been better). In addition, by referring to such gestures as 'autonomous' the possibility that some gestures may be more autonomous than others is admitted. The term 'emblem' is categorical. Terms that suggest the positioning of phenomena along dimensions of variations are, in general, to be preferred.
>
> (Kendon 1983: 40)

In subsequent work, Kendon (1984, 1986) has widened his terminological proposal to add the concept – perhaps less clear – of *quotable gestures*. In the quote above, Kendon rejects the term emblem because of its categorical dichotomous nature i.e. either it is an emblem or it is not, without the possibility of a gradualness. However, he uses quotable gestures categorically to distinguish quotable gestures from gestures that must be accompanied by talk, which he includes under the term of *gesticulation* and which we examine below as coverbal or co-speech gestures and pragmatic gestures (cf. 1.1.1 and 1.1.2). It is important to note that the concept of quotable gesture is more restricted than the concept of autonomous gesture, which leads Kendon (1984: 94) to admit he has come back to a definition that is similar to Ekman and Friesen's original definition of emblem:

> I suggest the term "quotable gesture" to refer to just those gestures which can be "quoted" and have been listed by various writers as stable forms. Not all "autonomous gestures" can be quoted. A "quotable gesture" is in many ways very similar to Ekman's concept of "emblem."

In principle, it remains unclear which autonomous gestures would not be quotable or emblematic according to Kendon's terminology. One can assume that non-quotable autonomous gestures would involve emblems that have a low degree of conventionalization and a reduced ability to be autonomous from talk.

In fact, non-quotable autonomous gestures would occupy a bordering zone between illustrators and emblems according to Ekman and Friesen's terminology. The bordering zone that is occupied by non-quotable autonomous gestures could include conventional illustrators. Illustrators, under rare and exceptional circumstances, can be used without words, as for instance, to indicate measurements, or in question/answer sequences. In other words, illustrators can undergo *emblematization* (see 4.1.1), understood as a process for items that are located along a continuum. This process seems analogous to that of sporadic synchronic grammatical habilitation (i.e. a category change between different types of words, for instance between nouns and adjectives) and can also be seen as analogous to the historical processes of changes of category.

Despite some categorization gray areas, the terms *autonomous gesture* and *quotable gesture* have been used in subsequent studies (see Brookes 2001, 2004, 2005, 2011). More recently, Kendon has proposed the notions of *autonomous gestures* (Kendon 1983) and *quotable gestures* (Kendon 1984, 1990) "to refer to any gesture that makes its way into an explicit list or vocabulary" (Kendon 2004: 335). Throughout this book, we will not generally distinguish between autonomous and quotable gestures, unless we explicitly do so, as we have noted above in this discussion of potential autonomous gestures that are not quotable. From our perspective, Kendon's terminological proposal of autonomous and quotable gesture is relevant, although we also take notice that the term emblem (and emblematic gesture) is decidedly the term most often used currently, while it coexists with the terms that we have discussed earlier.

Most importantly, the advances made over the last forty years of gesture studies imply that any categorization of gesture, any definition of gesture, and any attempt to delimit a class of autonomous gestures has to begin with a set of functional parameters and a degree of flexibility and prototypicity, as shown in Table 2.1 and Figure 2.1. Different "gestural entities" have the ability to carry out an action as a representation of different categories depending on the specific context in which they are used. This (contextual) (multi-) functionality is basic in the case of emblems, since we propose that an emblem becomes an autonomous gesture precisely because it constitutes a functional act – a speech act with illocutionary value – and not because of the particular morphology of that gesture (or its holophrastic/lexical character or use, in Poggi's terms mentioned before). The functionality factor also accounts for the preeminence of pragmatic over morphological classifications of gestures, as well as the fact that considering a degree of flexibility in any definition of gesture moves us towards prototypical categories instead of 'airtight sealed" compartment ones.

2.2 Emblem as a category

Early on his career, Kendon himself acknowledged that for gestures, "[a]n exact definition is not possible" (1983: 13). Indeed, the same could be stated about emblems. As is the case for many non-verbal phenomena, the definitional boundaries of emblems are often blurry. Thus, it becomes difficult to define them with any additional precision beyond what the various attempts previously discussed in this chapter have accomplished. However, it is possible to rethink the definitional challenge if it is formulated as an issue of prototypical categorization and not so much as one of traditional, orthodox definition. That is, rather than delimiting rigid boundaries of what an emblem is, establishing a prototypical category of emblems makes possible a step forward towards a more nuanced and precise definition. We aim to do so in this section. After reviewing in the previous sections the theoretical pathways that have led to current definitions of the term gesture, we examine now three proposals to define emblem as a gestural category. We begin with Hanna's (1996) theoretical conceptualization of emblem as a semiotic category, followed by McNeill's (1992, 2000) definition of emblem with a specific position within four gestural continua, and close the section by revisiting Payrató's proposal to define emblem relying on a cognitive theory of prototypes based on parameters of gradual application.

2.2.1 Emblem as a semiotic category

Hanna (1996) provides the most important theoretical discussion of the category of emblem, in which she includes Efron's and Ekman and Friesen's previous definitions. Hanna's article, although not often cited or simply ignored in a field like non-verbal communication with a very short memory, closes many debates over the "epistemological" value of the emblem as a sign and over its conceptualization.

Hanna argues against a "verbocentric" definition of emblem, that is, a categorization of emblem in terms of its (independent or dependant) relationship to talk. Instead of focusing on the emblem's relationship to talk, Hanna examines two non-verbocentric semiotic theories that focus on communication, Peirce (1931–1958) well-known division of signs and Eco's (1976) model of signification. After reviewing them critically, Hanna proposes to define emblems according the aspect of convention and the fact that the foundation of the category must not rely on its condition of (non-)dependency on verbal language. She proposes "a definition which treats it as a sign amongst other signs, rather than a behavior pattern distinguished by a typical relationship with words" (Hanna 1996: 352–353):

> I propose that the emblem be considered as a sign of which the interpretants in a given cultural group fulfill at least the following tasks:
> (a) Set up a piece of human gestural activity as a sign
> (b) Set up a sign in such a way that it is usually interpreted as having been deliberately produced, and communicative intention is generally [?] attributed to the immediate producer of the sign.
> (c) Set up the sign as the replica of a type already known, that type being fairly precise as regards the physical shaping and the interpretation of significance. Strong conventions govern emblems so that the tokens of the one type closely resemble each other.
> (Hanna 1996: 289–290)

In regard to Hanna's proposal to define emblems in relation to other signs, it is worth recalling Pierce's (1931–1958) well-known classification of signs in indexes, icons, and symbols (see 1.2.1). It is clear that the emblems stand with symbols, together with items from sign languages and words. However, emblems may nonetheless include indexical and iconic elements, and non-emblematic gestures may include symbolic components. These parameters are not applied in terms of their presence/absence, but are gradual and distributed along continua, which have been modified and retouched by several authors, as we examine next.

Furthermore, we consider Hanna's point (b) to be valid and indeed it is included in our proposal as feature d.3 in Figure 2.1, together with communicative intention (feature b.1), with the proviso that communicative intention is attributed in every case in our proposal, rather than the vague "generally attributed" in Hanna's. As noted in section 1.2.1, we consider Hanna's point (c) to be contingent on the application of exemplar theory to emblematic gestures, as a complement to prototype theory. Our proposal is the combination of prototype theory (complemented with exemplar theory) and relevance theory (feature b.1, cf. also 5.4), which makes it possible to explain the recognition and interpretation of emblematic gestures from a pragmatic perspective, that is to say, from an integrated explanation of the communicative use of these gestures. Both theories presuppose, in fact, a principle of economy in the cognitive treatment of the countless stimuli that we receive continuously, and therefore, an optimization of the resources that we as communicators have at our disposal. This fact, in turn, allows converging the two theories with a pragmatic theory of optimality (see Blutner 2013), as a broader and more general theoretical framework: communicative items evolve historically and are chosen synchronously according to an optimatily criterion.

2.2.2 Gestural continua

Another proposal of emblem definition has been provided by McNeill (1992) in his formulation of "Kendon's continuum," later re-formulated as four continua. According to Gullberg (1998: 38), "[t]he term does not appear in Kendon's own writings, but seems to have been invented by McNeill (McNeill, Levy and Pedelty 1990). It is based specifically on the discussion in Kendon (1988a) on lexicalisation processes in gestures."[9] Gullberg (1998: 38) gives the illustration included in the Figure 2.2 and after her analysis proposes a subsequent expansion of Kendon's continuum (Figure 2.3, Gullberg 1998: 97):

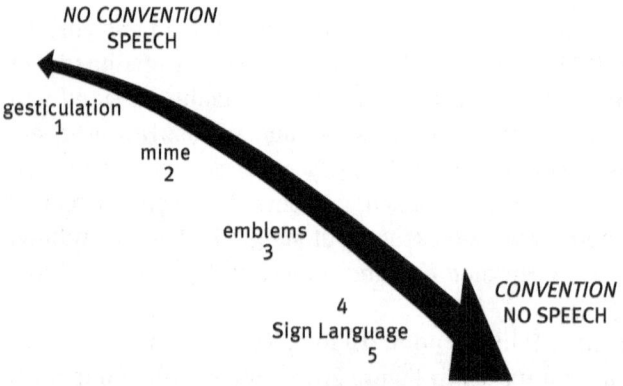

Figure 2.2: "Kendon's continuum" (Gullberg 1998: 38).

Gullberg's proposal, as shown in the two figures, implies developing, subcategorizing, or further specifying McNeill's initial categories, especially in relation to the iconicity trait.[10] Kendon (2004) argues that Gullberg's expansion is not useful, in the same way he argues that Ekman and Friesen's criteria for classification are not useful. For his part, McNeill (2000: 2–6) has re-formulated the four continua, as illustrated in Table 2.2.

---

9 Gullberg (1998: 38) adds that "[t]he gradual transition between gesture categories was suggested already by Wundt (1973), later by Hécaen (1967), and has been dealt with specifically for representational gestures by Feyereisen, van der Wiele and Dubois (1988b)." Note that Gullberg refers to the 1973 English translation of Wundt (1900).

10 The O-VPT abbreviation refers to gestures produced while adopting the point of view of an obserser or third person, and C-VPT to gestures produced while adpoting the point of view of the character or first person. This classification is originally from McNeill (1992); see also McNeill (2013: 6.2).

2.2 Emblem as a category — 45

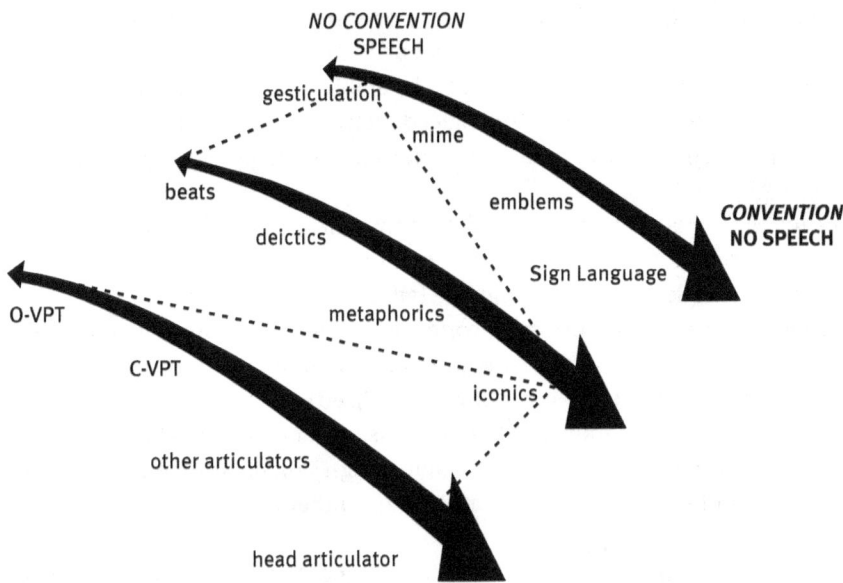

Figure 2.3: Kendon's expanded continuum: a mimesis scale. The area between gesticulation and mime expanded, and the area between iconics and mime expanded (Gullberg 1998: 97).

Table 2.2: McNeill's formulation of "Kendon's continua" (McNeill 2000).

	GESTICULATION ->	EMBLEM->	PANTOMIME->	SIGN LANGUAGE
1: Relationship to Speech	Obligatory presence of speech	Optional presence of speech	Obligatory absence of speech absence	Obligatory absence of speech
	GESTICULATION ->	PANTOMIME ->	EMBLEM ->	SIGN LANGUAGE
2: Relationship to linguistic practice	Linguistic properties absent	Ditto	Some linguistic properties present	Linguistic properties present
3. Relationship to conventions	Not conventionalized	Ditto	Partially conventionalized	Fully conventionalized
	GESTICULATION ->	PANTOMIME->	EMBLEM ->	SIGN LANGUAGE
4. Character of semiosis	Global and synthetic	Global and analytic	Segmented and synthetic	Segmented and analytic

In subsequent work, Payrató (2014a: 1475) has summarized the positions of emblems in the continua proposed by McNeill as follows:
(i) Regarding their relationship to speech, emblems (performed with the optional presence of speech) are placed between gesticulation (obligatory presence of speech) and pantomime and sign language (obligatory absence of speech).
(ii) As for their relationship to linguistic properties, emblems (with some linguistic properties) are between gesticulation and pantomime (without linguistic properties) and sign language (with linguistic properties).
(iii) Regarding their relationship to conventions, emblems are partly conventionalized, compared with gesticulation and pantomime (not conventionalized) and sign language (fully conventionalized).
(iv) Finally, as for the character of the semiosis, gesticulation is global and synthetic, pantomime is global and analytic, sign language is segmented and analytic, and emblems are segmented and synthetic.

The first and foremost point of McNeill's proposal is that the features of Table 2.2 – and consequently, the very concept of emblematic gesture – cannot be analyzed in a dichotomous way, in the sense of separating (sub)categories completely into yes/no presence. The concepts of gesture and emblem cannot be categorized in a traditional sense because the features that characterize them cannot be defined or delimited in such a way. The features are expressed in a continuum (such as gradations), without any breaks in continuity. Although emblems have standard and consistent forms more often than other gestures, the differences observed between the units are still gradual and treatable in terms of greater or lesser frequency, but not of absolute values. As we discuss in the next section 2.2.3, these circumstances make a pragmatic and prototypical conception of the emblem better suited and more explanatory, as it often happens in many other linguistic and communicative phenomena.

In addition to the gradual character of the features, the fundamental point now is to choose the aspects that best characterize (prototypically) the category, and therefore whether the four (i – iv) proposed continua are appropriate. Let us note that Hanna (1996), as we have seen above, rejects the first continuum (i) because she dismisses a conception of the emblem on the basis of whether or not the emblem is accompanied by speech (presence/absence).

For the same reason of dependence, we could rule out (as the main and defining feature) the continuum (ii), which serves to locate the emblems along the different types of gestures, but not to define them as such. Payrató (2014a: 1476) argues, "the possibility of breaking emblems into minimal units and identifying their morphological variants are complex and controversial issues." It is also the reason for why we have not included it in Table 2.3, above. While the standards of "good formation" for emblems are much more rigid than those for co-speech gestures, the argumentation in favor of their articulation in minimal components seems questionable and detached from theories on production and interpretation. In fact, McNeill (2000) considers them synthetic. An analysis of emblems according to the presence/absence of distinctive features, as in the analysis of linguistic sounds, is also fraught with problems (see Meo-Zilio's 1961a attempt). Although it is evident that one can find "distinctive" features in a repertoire of emblems, they do not collectively constitute a real language, and the established relationships between them do not resemble phonological relationships by any means. From a cognitive perspective, an emblem can be seen as a symbolic construction or association between a gestural form and a signified (see 5.2.1), as it is the case in the verbal domain of any lexical term, syntactic construction and more particularly in the case of an interjection (see 2.4.3).

The feature in continuum (iv), the type of semiosis, effectively characterizes the emblems, but neither defines nor identifies them. Finally, we have the feature in continuum (iii), conventionality, which we have already accepted as per Hanna's proposal (1996). However, conventionality alone or together with the other three features does not adequately characterize emblems, since there are other non-emblematic gestures that are also conventional.

McNeill (2005: 41–42) has cogently described the challenge of trying to select features and organize them hierarchically in a consistent and persuasive manner:[11]

> I wish to claim, however, that none of these 'categories' is truly categorical. We should speak instead of *dimensions* and say *iconicity, metaphoricity, deixis, 'temporal highlighting'* (beats), *social interactivity*, or some other equally unmellifluous (but accurate) terms conveying dimensionality. The essential clue that these semiotic properties are dimensional and not categorical is that we often find iconicity, deixis, and other features mixing in the same gesture. Falling into multiple headings is not impossible in a system of categories, but simultaneous categories imply a hierarchical arrangement. We cannot define such a hierarchy because we cannot say in general which categories are dominant and which are subordinate.

We propose to find an operational solution to this challenge by taking a step back and returning to two aspects of the emblem that we consider to be more basic and elementary than the previous ones discussed in this section: (1) as a gesture, its

---

[11] See also Schönherr (2014), which raises the same problem of categories and reproduces McNeill's quote.

character of movement that is significant and relevant, shared with other gestures, and (2) its illocutionary value, not shared with other gestural categories.[12]

2.2.3 Emblematicity criteria: Emblem as a prototypical pragmatic category

Drawing from a theory of prototypes, we argue that the category of emblematic gesture can be best defined as a (pragmatic) prototypical category, in a similar fashion to our proposal of a prototypical definition of gesture in section 2.1.1. Emblematic gestures, like gestures more generally, are not based on Aristotelian categories that can be understood in a dichotomous way. Instead, they are entities with a set of characteristics or features that may be present partially or completely. As we discuss below, the more features an entity fulfills, the more prototypical it is, and the closer it comes to an "ideal" or "perfect" example of the category. In some instances, the perfect or ideal example does not exist: it is an idealized case. In some other instances, perfect examples do exist. In general, prototypical exemplars are used more often, and are the first ones learned by children and non-native speakers and the last ones to be forgotten.

Payrató (1993, 2003, 2008) synthesized recurrent features of prior definitions of emblem and redefined the category with the following list of features: (a) autonomy from speech, (b) communicative goal (intentional and deliberate), (c) illocutionary force, (d) social nature, and (e) semantic core.

According to this characterization, emblems are gestures that can – and usually, do – take place independently of verbal language, and which are made deliberately, with a full communicative intention. They have an illocutionary value analogous to that of pragmatic speech acts, are typical of sociocultural groups or communities, and maintain a semantic core or nucleus that is specified in every concrete context, depending on situational factors and functional values. This semantic core is symbolically coded (as non-natural meaning),[13]

---

[12] We develop this proposal in a synthetic manner in the following subsection 2.2.3, and more extensively in sections 5.2, 5.3 and 5.4. Some parts of this subsection first appeared as Payrató (2014a), while other parts are either reformulated or original.

[13] Non-natural meaning is to be understood in Grice's sense (cf. Grice 1957, 1985), and contrasting with the natural meaning of many other prosodic or gestural actions (see Wharton 2009). Wharton (2009:4) describes Grice's distinction between natural and non-natural meanings in the following terms: "For Grice, 'means naturally' is roughly synonymous with 'naturally indicates,' so in the same way that black clouds might be said to mean that it will rain or spots mean someone has measles, Lily's smile might be said to mean she is happy, or Jack's frown to mean he is displeased."

although the emblem may also have indexical and iconic components (see Ekman and Friesen 1969).

A prototypical emblem has all these features, and its prototypicality increases depending on how close or distant it comes to the essence of each feature. However, at least from a pragmatic perspective, there is one trait that stands out and from which the other features can be derived: the illocutionary force, i.e., the ability to materialize an act (a speech, communicative act, for instance an assertion, a promise, a request, etc.) via the performance of the gesture. The fact that a gesture has acquired illocutionary force explains other features (and not vice versa): it is conventional – as any illocutionary act – and, therefore, social and typical of a group in which the process of conventionalization has been (gradually) carried out; it is autonomous (it does not need verbal language) and may be more or less easily quotable; it involves a core of basic meaning (like any other illocutionary act), and it can be translated (relatively) easily into verbal language (with a statement, precisely the one that identifies it as a speech act). In short, a gesture such a greeting or an insult can be considered a prototype emblem not because of its relation to verbal language, but rather because the non-verbal act is itself significant and relevant, and is by itself an illocutionary act, which Austin (1962) pointed out (see 5.6.2) can be defined by felicity conditions and good formation.

As in the prototypical categorization of gesture provided in Table 2.1, we incorporate now in Table 2.3 physical (or morphological) and pragmatic features, obligatory or optional, that characterize our proposed prototypical category of emblems, and we reformulate the wording of the parameters according to the previous table.[14]

Traditionally it has also been said that emblems are fully aware non-verbal acts, which are used as deliberate tools of communication and which are recognized immediately. These features show, on the one hand, the high degree of salience or prominence of these units, and, on the other, their relevance (in the sense of Sperber and Wilson 1986 [1995]): emblems greatly increase the information about our mental, cognitive context, and at the same time are processed at a very low cost; therefore they are diametrically opposed to movements that a speaker would interpret as totally irrelevant (cf. 5.3 and 5.4).

In what follows, we examine different types of emblematic gestures and some of their most common functions as non-verbal communicative acts, equivalent to speech acts, one of the most basic concepts and more examined in the field of pragmatics.

---

[14] For a practical application of the concept of emblematic prototypical category, see the next analysis of greeting emblems in 2.3.2.

Table 2.3: Basic and additional optional features to characterize emblematic gestures as a prototypical (physical/morphological) and pragmatic category.

'EMBLEM' AS A PROTOTYPE

(A) BASIC PHYSICAL/MORPHOLOGICAL FEATURES
    a.1 Bodily action or movement

....

(B) BASIC PRAGMATIC FEATURES
    b.1 Meaningful and relevant action ("ostensive," intended as a message), even in absence of verbal language, addressed to a copresent recipient in an interactional setting
    b.2 Illocutionary force
    b.3 Sociocultural conventional action
    b.4 Semantic core of non-natural meaning (symbolic)
    b.5 Deliberate (non-accidental) action
    b.6 Conscious action

....

(C) ADDITIONAL OPTIONAL PHYSICAL/MORPHOLOGICAL FEATURES
    c.1 Action or movement involving only hands and arms
    c.2 Action involving head movement
    c.3 Action involving facial movement
    c.4 Action involving eye movement
    c.5 Action involving other body parts

....

(D) ADDITIONAL OPTIONAL PRAGMATIC FEATURES
    d.1 Attachable to verbal language
    d.2 Quotable
    d.3 Translatable easily to verbal language
    d.4 Equivalent to a verbal speech act

2.3 Types and functions of emblems

Regarding the (sub)types of emblems and their functions, a first way to classify emblems is to separate those found in everyday contexts – and associated with informal, colloquial or ordinary talk (see 2.3.1) – from those in communicative situations that can be associated with specific linguistic varieties, such as technical or specialized registers (see 2.3.5.). We review the characterizing features of the first (sub)group in more detail according different degrees of emblematic prototypicality: greeting emblems (2.3.2), deictic emblems (2.3.3), and insult emblems (2.3.4).

2.3.1 Current speech and current emblems

What is the meaning of *"colloquial/casual" emblems*? Or what is the meaning of *everyday emblems*? Payrató (2004) relates this type of emblems to the colloquial or everyday linguistic variety:

> As a simple, and final, example, the variation framework designed may be useful to define current notions such as that of *everyday gestures*. What is the exact meaning of this notion? I suggest that it can be defined in much the same way as *colloquial, casual, everyday speech*, i.e. as a non-specific, spontaneous, interactive, and informal variety (regarding field, mode, tenor, and tone, respectively). This functional, contextual or stylistic variety is as ever associated with a threefold dialectal base: geographical, historical and social.
> (Payrató 2004: footnote 9)

In regard to emblems associate with everyday language, Johnson, Ekman and Friesen (1975) conducted one of the first analyses of emblem types, and identified eight domains:[15]

(1)
- Interpersonal directions or commands
- Own physical state
- Insults
- Replies
- Own affect
- Greetings and departures
- Physical aspect of persons
- Unclassified

Although Johnson et al. do not discuss it, their classification relies on a combination of thematic/semantic and of usage/pragmatic features. An additional problem is the lack of specificity of the domains, particularly "replies" and "unclassified." Indeed, it is difficult to avoid some vagueness in both semantic and pragmatic classifications, as a result of the features of the (emblematic) communicative acts and of their multifunctionality. The general meaning of an emblem, which initially might be considered lexical (Kendon 1988a),[16] only refers to

---

[15] Examples of each domain are provided in the repertoires of the appendices and the section 5.6.
[16] The title of Kendon's contribution (1988a) is explicit enough: "How Gestures Can Become Like Words." Indeed, particular gestures, through a process of conventionalization or emblematization, come to acquire a meaning and functional value similar or identical to those of a word or sentence. A trivial, but indicative example of this phenomenon can be found in a television commercial in Catalan – specifically, an institutional public announcement. In the commercial, a closed hand with a raised thumb is shown, accompanied by the verbal text:

some core or central meaning that is mostly decontextualized and lacking specificity. However, it cannot capture the specific meaning that an emblem will have in a particular context. When it comes to the usage, an emblem may be used to carry our different communicative acts again in various particular contexts. For this reason it seems more appropriate to characterize the meaning of the emblem as "non-natural", as reflected in Feature b.4 in the table (see note 42). Wharton (2009) already uses this characterization. Dahan and Cosnier (1977: 2096–71) introduced another classification that attains more precision for "quasi-linguistique" gestures, the term they employ for emblematic gestures. The classification consists of four main groups with multiple subtypes according to a combination of semantic and pragmatic criteria:

(2) I. Expressive
   1. Affective expressions
      - Detachment
      - Disorientation and reflection
      - Annoyance
   2. Appreciations and comments
      - Declarative with negative connotation
      - Declarative with neutral or positive connotation
  II. Conative
   1. Hostility and ill will
   2. Commands
   3. Politeness and congratulations
 III. Phatic
   1. Appreciations and comments
      - Interactional modulators
   2. Greetings
   3. Deictics
   4. Others
  IV. Operational
   1. Actions

"The thumb is used to say 'very good.'" The distinction between an emblem and a typical illustrator (see 4.1.1.) locates them on an axis that goes from *substitution* to *contiguity*. Moreover, the consideration of emblems as *verbal* or *non-verbal* is rather questionable because, among other reasons, of the controversies surrounding the ambiguity of the term *verbal*. Emblems are not quite verbal if we understand verbal to be synonymous with *word* and *linguistic system*. However, in terms of signification and use, emblems come much closer to a word, idiomatic phrase, or a sentence than most other non-verbal signs.

2. Appreciations and comments
3. Quantitative deictics>

Dahan and Cosnier's classification is more precise and adequate, particularly in terms of usage. A classification that takes usage criteria as its starting point would certainly facilitate the comparison of emblem repertoires. Kendon (1981b: 141) and (1984: 95) has observed that the range of functions that emblems carry out is in fact very limited:

> In the great majority of cases they are concerned with the regulation of interpersonal relationship, with displays of one's own current mental or physical condition, or with an evaluative response to another. Forms that function simply as labels for objects or actions are very rare. (Kendon 1984: 95)

In his comparative analysis of quotable gesture repertoires, Kendon determines that 80% of the items refer to (a) regulation of interpersonal relationship, (b) displays of one's own current mental state or physical condition, and (c) evaluative response to the actions or appearance of another. On the other hand, the analyzed repertoires include very few (d) nominal gestures with the function of *labels* for objects and actions. Morris et al. (1979) and Washabaugh (1986) also report similar findings.

In addition to classifications that include pragmatic criteria, emblematic gestures can also be classified according to morphological and semantic criteria. Such classifications are useful to highlight how gestural units originate. Kendon argues that a distinction between *location* and *referent* of the gesture must first be established:

> The *base* of the gesture is the object, action, or (in some cases) abstract entity that the gestural form may be regarded as being modeled upon. The *referent* of the gesture is whatever the gesture is used to refer to. (Kendon 1981b: 152)

In the case of the widely recognized emblem for victory (see reference in Appendix <I, 103>), in which the index and middle fingers are raised to form a V, the letter would be the base of the emblem and the concept of victory would be its referent. On the basis of this distinction, emblems can be classified in terms of (1) base type from which is derived, (2) relationship between gestural form and base, and lastly (3) relationship between base and reference. Criterion (1) seems to be the most productive to specify emblematic subclasses. Kendon (1981b: 153) distinguishes six types of base:

(3) (1) Specific interpersonal actions
    (2) Intention movements

(3) Actions patterns that can be observed in other
(4) Concrete objects
(5) Symbolic objects
(6) Abstract entities

Payrató (1993) proposed a classification established completely on pragmatic criteria and based on the illocutionary value of communicative acts. Following Searle's (1979) classic formulation of speech act subtypes, Payrató (1993) distinguishes five non-verbal emblematic acts, which we discuss in more detail in sections 5.6.1 and 5.6.2:

(4) (1) Assertives
   (2) Directives
   (3) Expressives
   (4) Commissives
   (5) Declarations

Lastly, everyday emblems can be divided into two broad groups, depending on whether an emblem's origin has a more markedly cultural or linguistic component: "While some emblematic gestures are linked exclusively to idiomatic expressions in one language (or to only a variety of that language), others have a broader range, spreading over different languages" (Payrató 2008: 11). For example, emblems used to refer to coffee or tea – or to ask for a coffee or a tea– only make sense for languages in which the words "coffee" and "tea" begin with the letter "c" and "t" respectively. A similar situation takes place in the case of idiomatic words and expressions. However, emblems such as the fig, the finger impudicus, and the forearm jerk are found in much wider cultural areas that cut across multiple languages (see for instance Figure 2.8 in 2.3.4).

2.3.2 Greeting emblems

Greetings, such as the greeting that the man performs by raising his hand palm out in Figure 2.4, are examples to illustrate numerous aspects highlighted in previous sections, particularly in our proposal for a definition of emblem as a prototypical category (see Table 2.3 in 2.2.3). First, greetings can be considered prototypical because these basic features characterize them: (a.1) they are bodily actions, (b.1.) they are meaningful and relevant ("ostensive"), even in absence of verbal language (autonomous), (b.2) with illocutionary force – expressive, in this particular case–, (b.3) they are conventional and they have sociocultural nature, which

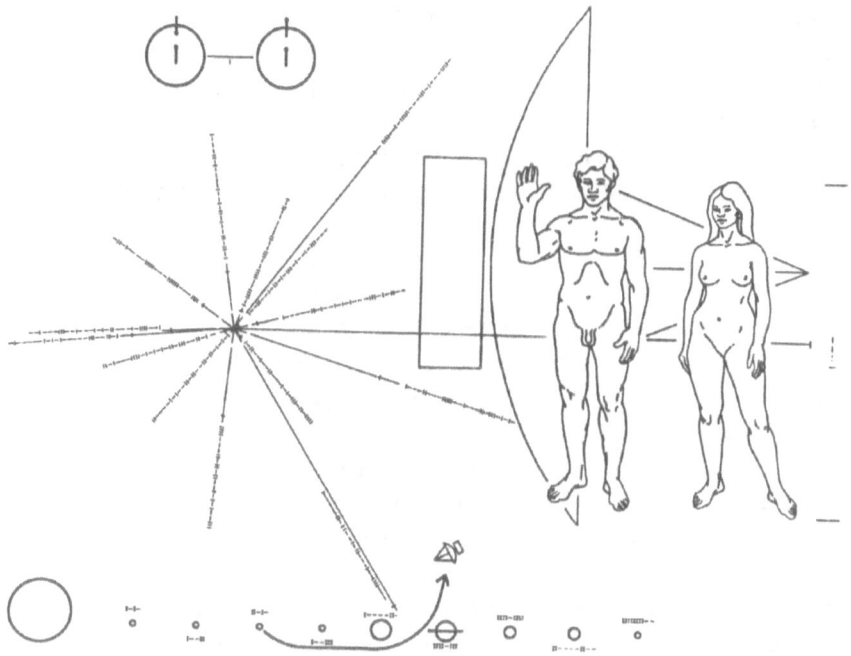

Figure 2.4: Placard of the spaceship Pioneer 10, designed by Carl Sagan and Frank Drake, and drawn by per Linda Salman Sagan.
Source: https://commons.wikimedia.org/wiki/File:Pioneer_plaque_(transparent).svg

comes from groups or communities that use this particular gesture to greet people (in the case of Figure 2.4, it is presented as used by the earth inhabitants). The greeting reproduced here is also characterized by: (b.4) basic semantic content around the notion of greeting as 'contact' or 'social connection', (b.5) deliberate (non-accidental), and (b.6) conscious action. In sum, the emblem is clearly intended as a message (an action addressed to a copresent recipient in an interactional setting, i.e. with a communicative goal), although in this case, it is image printed to be seen by unknown audiences. In regard to the optional features (d.1–d.4), greetings are also characterized by the fact they can be "attached" to talk, are quotable, fairly easy to translate,[17] and are equivalent to a verbal speech act.

---

[17] This is a debatable feature, both in the case of greeting emblems as well as in others. In general we could state that greeting emblems are translatable, but there are particular instances, such as blowing a kiss from a distance by moving the fingers or the hand away from the mouth, or simply using the lips, that are not so easily translatable. Rather than describing them as translatable, it would be more accurate to state that emblems may be the non-verbal equivalent of a verbal act. Thus, greeting a person by waiving one's hand is the equivalent of saying "Hello!"

Greetings have long been considered as a prototypical instance/example of what we consider an emblem today. This perspective can be tracked as far back as Garrick Mallery's work ("Greeting by gesture", *The Popular Science Monthly*, published in 1891). Relying on examples from across the world, Mallery distinguishes between salutations with contact, including those involving touch, smell, and taste, and those without contact. Krout (1942: 19–22) analyzes salutations from a symbolic ritual and makes a strong case showing the gestural diversity of greetings due to cultural variation (see Table 2.4).[18]

Some of these practices include physical contact with the recipient. More recently, Lynn (2011, 2014) has created the first dictionary of "physical contact gestures", based on research conducted in the Mid-Atlantic Region of the United States, and inspired by the Berlin Dictionary of Everyday Gestures (see Serenary 2003, 2004, and Posner at al. (eds.), in preparation). Morris et al. (1979) have also noted how greetings seem to be related to emblematic gestures of beckoning or summoning, and how there appear to be specific types of couplings, depending on the position of the hand (palm up or down), illustrated in Figure 2.5.

In Morris et al.'s work across Europe and Turkey, we find "Category A" in the British Isles, Scandinavia, Holland, Germany, Austria, Belgium, France and (the former) Yugoslavia. "Category B", secondly, "was found in Spain, Malta, Tunisia, S. Greece and Turkey. In other words, this was confined to countries bordering the Mediterranean, but excluding Italy, Corfu and N. Greece" (242). "Category C" in third place "was confined to the Italian-speaking region, including not only the mainland, but also the islands of Sicily and Sardinia" (242). "Category D" was limited to Portugal and Northern Greece and "Category E" only to the island of Corfu. N. Greece. The authors note that "there is only one clear-cut combination missing" (242), which is palm-up beckon with the palm-hide wave.

In conclusion, greetings are a very good example of why a pragmatic (and prototypical) conception of the emblematic gesture is necessary. An emblem does not have to be conceptualized in relation to speech and should not be defined either by negative features (what it is not, often also in comparison with verbal language), but rather by positive features: the act that it constitutes and its felicity conditions or good formation.

From the pragmatic and interactional analysis perspective, greeting emblems are used in clear, limited, and specific phases of interaction, such as the beginning and end of an interaction, and welcoming and leave taking. The interactional and pragmatic specificity of greetings contributes to their visibility and

---

[18] These examples are a selection from the extensive list (approximately three pages of his book under the epigraph "The Symbolic Rituals of Various Groups").

Table 2.4: Behavior patterns among cultural groups in salutation and welcome practices according to Krout (1942: 19–22).

ATTITUDE EXPRESSED	BEHAVIOR PATTERN	CULTURE GROUP
Salutation	Clapping hands [...]	People of Loango
	Clapping hands and drumming ribs with elbows	People of Balonda
	Yielding up one's clothes	Assyrians [...]
	Unclothing to the girdle	Abyssinians
	Doffing hat or merely touching it; handshake	Eur-Americans
	Grasping hands and pressing thumbs together	Wanyiika people
	Grasping hands and separating them with a pull so that a snapping noise is made by thumb and fingers	Nigerians
	Engaging in a sort of scuffle in which each tries to raise to his lips the hands of the other; kissing beards	Arabs
	Drawing hands from the shoulders and down the arms to the fingertips of the person greeted, or rubbing hands together	Ainus of Japan
	Blowing into each other's hands or ears	Some preliterates
	Stroking own face with other person's hands	Polynesians
	Smelling each other's cheeks and joining and rubbing each other's noses	Mongols, Malays, Burmese, Lapps
	Snapping fingers	Dahomeans and others
	Silence for a time; then ceremonials varying in complexity	Australian preliterates

[...]

Table 2.4 (continued)

ATTITUDE EXPRESSED	BEHAVIOR PATTERN	CULTURE GROUP
Welcome	Spreading arms	Europeans
	No sign of outer expression (when meeting after long separation	Ainus of Japan, Australian Blackfellows
	Hand-clapping	Certain Africans
	Jumping up and down	Natives of Tierra del Fuego
	Weeping	Australian tribes

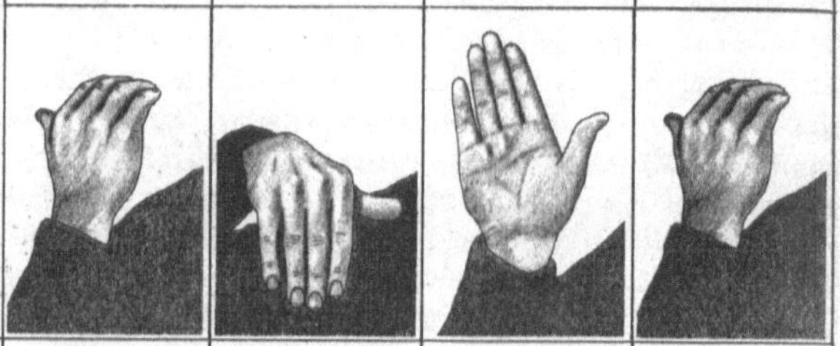

	Palm-up beckon	Palm-down beckon	Palm-show wave	Palm-hide wave
A	COMMON	rare	COMMON	rare
B	rare	COMMON	COMMON	rare
C	rare	COMMON	rare	COMMON
D	moderate	moderate	COMMON	rare
E	rare	COMMON	moderate	moderate

TABLE I

Figure 2.5: Beckon/wave combination in different geographical zones according to Morris et al. (1979: 242).

salience, as they appear at the initial and final boundaries of an interaction. In the case of greeting emblems – like in strictly verbal greetings– we find a very significant phatic component that apparently pairs up with the great feebleness of the referential dimension. In other words, the informative function is highly reduced in the benefit of the interactive function, or the referential content in the benefit of social contact and expressivity. However, it does not mean that these elements cannot be analyzed from an optimal relevance perspective (see section 5.4. and specially Padilla 2003). They are fully pertinent in relation to their informativity and the modification of the (cognitive) context that they provoke, as well as in relation to the low cost of (interpretation) processing that they require.

2.3.3 Deictic emblems

Deictic gestures can be considered emblems, but with the particularity that their referential content is tied to the identification of speakers, as individuals and agents (personal deixis), or their circumstances or conditions of production (space deixis and temporal deixis). In the case of greetings referential content is fulfilled in benefit of the phatic dimension, however in the case of deictics it is fulfilled in benefit of the indexical dimension.

Also as with greetings, the subcategory of emblematic deictics is highly salient and easily recognizable, which has resulted in its frequent inclusion in gestural typologies. The strong association between speech and gesture is evident in the case of deixis, as illustrated in Sherzer's (1973) pioneering ethnographic, pragmatic, and multimodal analysis of lip pointing among the Kuna of the San Blas islands (see 4.4.1). Building on Fillmore's classification, Levinson (1983: 65) includes gestural deictics in his seminal handbook of pragmatics, and defines them as gestures that "require a moment by moment physical monitoring of the speech event for their interpretation." With the known example of "Meet me here a week from now with a stick about this big," Levinson shows how the linguistic meaning is crippled without a concomitant gestural reference. In fact, the reverse seems more appropriate. The issue is not whether the gesture can be used without words – as is the case emblems– but the opposite: the deictic (word) cannot be used without its accompanying gesture, which is most often a hand gesture but can include other gestural types (cf. Sherzer 1973, 1993 and 4.4.1).

More recently, Kita (ed.) (2003) has meticulously studied different aspects of pointing, and Enfield (2009) has studied the relationship between speech and talk in "composite utterances," many of which have a clear deictic value. In regard to specific forms of gestural deictics, Efron (1972 [1941]) had already collected multiple examples of personal deixis in his research:
(a) "Me", "a distinctly Italian gesture in form and quality" (Efron 1972 [1941]: fig. 76); see also Efron (1972 [1941]: 209, number 54) and Figures 2.6a and 2.6b.
(b) "You – This – That" (Efron 1972 [1941]: 224); see Figure 2.6c.

Figures 2.6a, 2.6b and 2.6c: Emblems for "Me" and "You" / "This" – "That" (Efron 1972 [1941]).

Relying on a multimodal perspective, Nogué and Payrató (2007) describe some of the mechanisms and speech-gesture couplings in ordinary conversations in Catalan. Figure 2.7 illustrates some of these couplings.[19]

Kita (2003) and Enfield (2009) highlight the importance of intercultural analyses of gestural deictics, and Müller et al. (eds.) (2013, 2014) reproduce many references for this type of research. Indeed, the analysis of multimodal deictics should have an important focus on pragmatics, especially intercultural pragmatics. By pointing, gestural deictics assess or function as assessments; very often, though, they are in agreement and occur simultaneously with verbal elements. This means that the degree of detachment of deictics from verbal elements in actual practice – and therefore in terms of frequency and probability – is lower when compared to other prototypical emblematic gestures such as greetings, which we examined above, and insults, which we examine next. Furthermore,

---

19 The sample analyzed here comes from a TV show on language use (*Caçadors de paraules*, Televisió de Catalunya, 2007). In the examples deictic linguistic forms are shown in bold, and the discourse fragments coinciding with the central part of the gesture are underlined. Generally, in Catalan deictic personal gestures, "I" is marked with the index finger pointing to the chest (or with the palm on the chest), and the rest ("you", "he", "we", etc.) with the pointing index finger away from the body of the speaker (see for instance Appendix <II, 12>: "He"). The basic space deictic item for "here" is usually marked with the index finger pointing to the ground, and "there" with the index finger up, also away from the body. For other examples of deictic emblems, see the discussion of the differences between deictics to indicate the height of people versus deictics to indicate the height of animals in Colombia in section 4.3.1. Spanish examples are included in Appendix <VIII, 3, 5, 56, 83, 86, 89>.

(I)

FOREFINGER: EMPHATIC IDENTIFICATION OF THE SPEAKER (1 Singular)
The speaker accompanies a deictic linguistic first person form (singular), stressed or unstressed, with the forefinger pointing at his chest.

A: *Això es diu aquí, que **sóc** un carallot?*
(A: 'Is that what it says here, that **I'm** stupid?')

(II)

FINGERS OF BOTH HANDS: REFERENCE TO THE SPEAKER'S GROUP (METONYMIC VALUE) (1 Plural)
The speaker points at herself with the four fingers of both hands when she includes herself in a group

A: *Ses al·lotes, digam, **estàvem** damunt ses voltes i **esperàvem** es joves que passaven.*
(A: '**We girls**, let's say, sat on the porches, **waiting** for the boys passing through.')

(III)

TWO FOREFINGERS: REFERENCE TO THE ADDRESSED RECIPIENTS (AUDIENCE) (2 Plural)
The speaker – in this case the presenter of a TV program — refers to the audience by pointing at it (more exactly, pointing at the camera) with both forefingers, spreading the hands forward.

A: *Us deixo una reflexió.*
(A: 'I'll leave *you* with something to think about.')

Figure 2.7: Multimodal deictic units in contemporary Catalan (Nogué and Payrató 2007).

the illocutionary force of deictics is probably the least salient among the various types of emblems. These two factors may account for why deictic gestures are sometimes not seen as emblematic gestures, but solely as "deictic." Despite these remarks, deictic gestures have been usually included in emblem repertoires since Efron's and Ekman and Friesen's works.

2.3.4 Insult emblems

In this sample of emblems that we are discussing, and taking into account their high frequency in many repertoires, we include a subsection about insult emblems, which are more or less related to threats, obscenities, euphemisms, and taboos (see Brookes 2014b for a recent review). The analysis of insult emblems illustrates how ethnographic research is necessary to understand the meanings and uses of emblems by a specific community (see 4.4.1). Emblems are closely linked to culture, and in this case, they are related to the issues of taboo and politeness, for which ethnographic and cultural analyses are unavoidable.

We can find common examples of insult emblems in many contexts and regions. The Figure 2.8 illustrates the most common insults in the cultural areas where Catalan and Spanish are spoken respectively, but they are also present in cultural areas where French, Italian, and English are spoken. Figure 2.8 includes a visual representation of each emblem, together with the corresponding name for each language as well as the most common verbal expression with which these emblematic insults are found. This figure includes only the use of

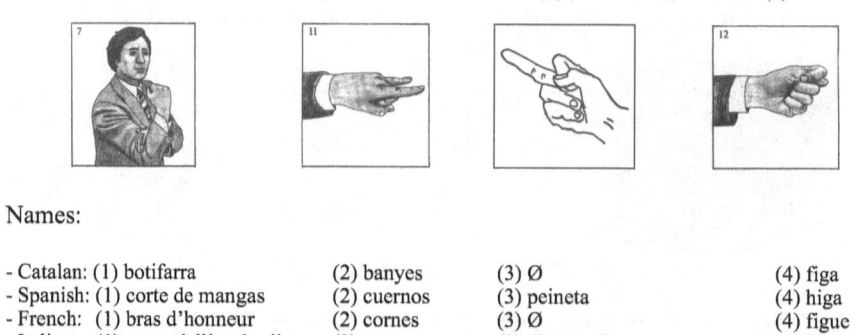

Names:

- Catalan: (1) botifarra (2) banyes (3) ∅ (4) figa
- Spanish: (1) corte de mangas (2) cuernos (3) peineta (4) higa
- French: (1) bras d'honneur (2) cornes (3) ∅ (4) figue
- Italian: (1) gesto dell'ombrello (2) mano cornuta (3) dito medio (4) fica
- English: (1) forearm jerk (2) horn (3) finger (4) fig

Verbal translations/verbal expressions in current speech:

(1) fer botifarra / hacer un corte de mangas / faire le bras d'honneur / fare il gesto dell'ombrello / ∅
(2) fer banyes / hacer cuernos / fare le corna / ?? / ∅
(3) hacer un corte de mangas / hacer una peineta / ∅/ fare il dito / to put/stick two fingers up at somebody (UK), to give somebody the finger (US)
(4) fer la figa / hacer la higa / faire la figue (arch.) / fare la fica / ∅

Figure 2.8: Sample of insult gestures that can be associated to a casual Catalan register (see Appendix I) and to other languages and cultures (illustrations (1), (2), and (4) are from Morris et al. 1979, illustration (3) from Payrató 1989/1991).

these emblems as insults. Items (1) and (3) can also be used as negation (aggressive and more or less offensive), and items (2) and (4) as spell or conjuration gestures (rejection of bad luck). When item (2) is used with this meaning, it is usually done by placing the hand horizontally (see Morris et al., 1979).

Emblematic gestures of insult constitute one of the best examples to illustrate families of resemblance gestures and the structuring of units within repertoires (see 5.2, with examples). They also illustrate processes of continuity of use, obsolescence, and even "rebirth" of specific emblems.

Examples of very frequent insult emblems in Catalonia and Spain are (1), Cat. *botifarra* or Sp. *corte de mangas* (the forearm jerk in Morris et al. 1979); (2), Cat. *banyes* or Sp. *cuernos* (the horizontal horn-sign in Morris et al. 1979); and (3) the finger impudicus, a classical Roman gesture that has survived until today (see Fornés & Puig 2008). Gestures (1) and (3) have clear sexual references. Gesture (2) is interpreted as Cat. *cabró* (cuckold) through the association between having horns and having an adulterous wife with a probable explanation through mockery or sarcasm (cf. Morris et al. 1979 and section 5.5 on multimodal tropes). The most widespread gestures in the Western world are undoubtedly (1) and (3) with significant cultural and regional variation, which is well documented in many popular dictionaries of emblems and gestures.[20]

An instance of obsolescence is the fig gesture in Catalonia and Spain (number 4), which is no longer used by younger generation of speakers and sometimes is confused with other emblems. In contrast, the finger impudicus has experienced a kind of rebirthing or rebranding in Spain, perhaps helped by Anglo-Saxon influences. The finger impudicus was often used but did not have a name, at least not in everyday language use. Starting ten years ago, it is now usually referred as *hacer la peineta* ('to insert a hair comb' such as the large decorative combs worn by Flamenco dancers) presumably because the movement of the gesture resembles the action of inserting and pinning a comb into bun of hair.

Hayes (1957) already provided a first extensive bibliography of this line of research. More recently, Müller (2013: 214) has described the finger impudicus

---

20 These emblems are often included in dictionaries for general audiences. Items (1) and (3) are also very frequent in "media" samples and it is very easy to find them online. For example, the Polish pole vault jumper Władiysław Kozakiewicz addressed gesture (1) to Russian audiences of the Moscow Olympic Games (1980), after they whistled at him disapprovingly during his jumps. The action resulted in a diplomatic complaint. It is also necessary to conduct in-depth studies that examine the confusion between this gesture and other similar ones (such as those that are mentioned in 4.3.2 and 5.3), and especially between emblems (1), (3) and (4), which can be combined with each other and also with (2) (see the family resemblance model in 5.2.2). All four emblems are easily found mixed together online.

in an instance of a conductor of offensive behavior (with its subsequent punishment). It is undoubtedly the best example of the illocutionary value of emblems, of their ties to culture, and of the need of carrying out ethnographic research and intercultural pragmatics analyses to understand what they mean and how they are used by specific communities (cf. 4.4.1, 4.4.2, and 4.4.3).

2.3.5 Technical emblems or emblems for special purposes

We can find different examples of emblems in technical or specialized repertoires, including:
(a) Sports: the codes used by referees of numerous sports.
(b) Professional codes (harvesters, airport workers ...).
(c) Codes of secluded communities, for instance, codes used in monasteries.

The difference between technical emblems and everyday emblems runs in parallel to the difference between specialized languages or technolects and everyday registers. A technical emblem functions as a technical term, with the specific goal of having one single meaning, precise, and unequivocal. In the same manner that technical lexical items avoid homonymy and polysemy and instead rely on a single signified-signifier correspondence, there is no room for a degree of vagueness and imprecision that may occur in everyday emblems. Thus, a technical emblem is a symbolic association between one meaning and one gestural form that can only have *one single* meaning within the technical domain it appears. Like with technical words, some technical emblems have ended in everyday registers. "Dead time" with the emblem of a capital T with both hands is a widespread example of the transfer from the technical domain (i.e. sports) to everyday language, which has also been accompanied by a semantic extension. Whereas the original technical meaning is precise and limited to time, pause, and break without additional connotations, the everyday meaning is extended to contiguous conceptual domains such as demanding for an action to stop, cancelling an activity, and shutting up. Also regarding the domain of sports, Figure 2.9 includes a small compilation of technical emblems used by fencing referees.

Numerous cases of technical repertoires that have been included in professional codes (the class (b) above) have been collected in dictionaries (see 3.3.2). Within these areas we can distinguish, among others, the following: harvesters, airport technicians, underwater divers, firefighters and police officers. Furthermore, numerous studies of emblems have described different systems of signs used by monastic orders (the class (c) above), such as Barakat (1975) and Umiker-Sebeok and Sebeok (eds.) (1987).

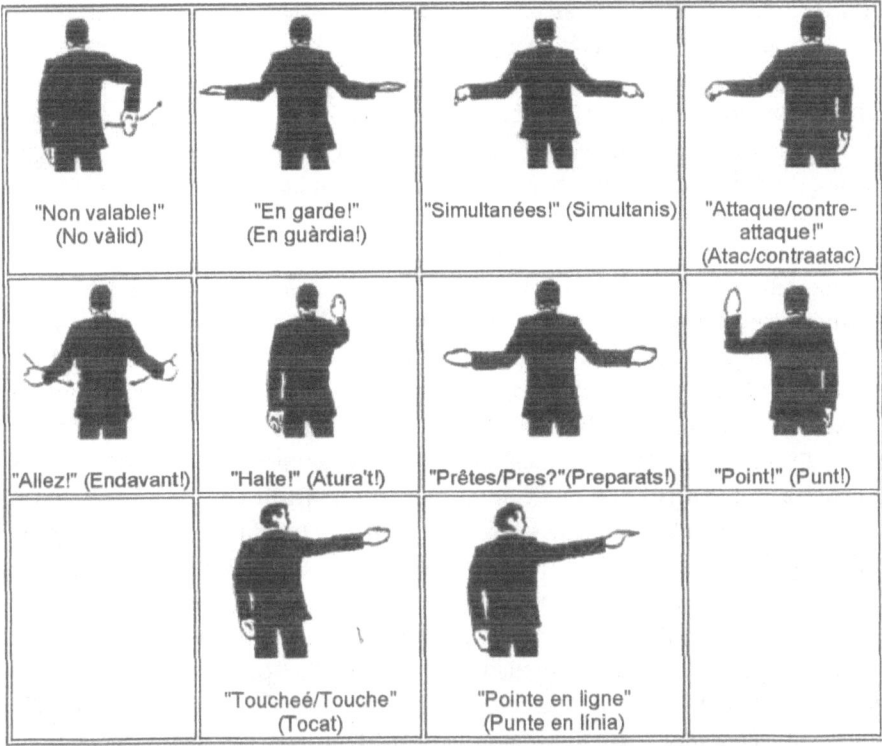

Figure 2.9: Emblematic technical gestures used by fencing referees (after Payrató 2013a: 82).

A final instance of technical emblems differs from the ones just discussed in that it is halfway between prototypical technical and everyday repertoires. We are talking about emblem repertoires used by different ethnic, cultural, or linguistic groups in special circumstances, particularly to communicate about taboos. Kendon (1988) provides an excellent analysis of Australian aboriginal people and another one of Native American groups, which Mallery (1881b) had previously studied (see 2.4.4).

2.4 Other gestures and non-verbal acts

As illustrated by the historical overview in chapter 1, the terminological richness and diversity of gesture subcategories often lead to great confusion. We do not attempt to carry out an exhaustive and encyclopedic discussion of these categories in this section, but instead we propose to examine the relationship between emblematic gestures and other gestural subcategories. As part of this examination, we also specify as much as possible how the emblematic gesture, defined as a prototypical category established according to the criteria discussed in section 2.2, differs from other gestures.

In this examination, we first note that like emblematic gestures, other gestural categories, and even more generally the category of gesture itself, can often be defined satisfactorily if one resorts to prototypical terms. The gesture category and subcategories have blurred and fuzzy boundaries, and are applied to gestures that have significantly different origins, forms, uses, and contexts. Furthermore, there is no one-to-one correspondence between gestural form and function. Identical or highly similar gestural units can carry out a multiplicity of different functions and therefore, they evade any straightforward definition; conversely, morphologically different gestures can function in similar ways. Secondly, non-verbal communication and in particular gestures carry out psychological functions in terms of the presentation of self and the expression of identity, and sociological functions, in terms of the regulation of social interactions – for instance, the importance of gestures in turn-taking –, and in terms of the normative control of public behavior. Thirdly, in addition to the prototypical pragmatic (semiotic or communicative) functions described in this chapter so far, emblematic gestures can also be used to create, complete, and modulate meaning as items with a procedural (non-conceptual) meaning, i.e. as discourse markers (see inter alia Kendon 1995). Fourth, they create, recreate, or reinforce the context via contextualization cues, and express a person's identity stylistically vis-à-vis (in)formality, politeness, and conversational implicature (Payrató 2009). Fifth, they can deploy full illocutionary force, as they do in the greetings and insults discussed above. Finally, we can find a biological background to all these functions. Emblematic gestures unquestionably contribute to many communicative functions, and do so in ways that complement the functions carried out by verbal elements and by other types of gestures.

2.4.1 Co-speech gestures

In general terms, a co-speech gesture is a gesture that only appears when accompanying talk. It differs from an emblematic gesture in that an emblematic gesture can co-occur with talk, but also can occur without it. A co-speech gesture is dependent on talk, otherwise the meaning of the gesture cannot be understood.

Underlying the definition of co-speech gesture, we find the notion that these gestures are produced simultaneously and narrowly with the linguistic or verbal utterance. Co-speech gestures are also called *illustrators* in Ekman and Friesen's (1969) classification, and *gesticulation* in some of Kendon's work (see Kendon 2004). Other terms used that come close or very close to the meaning of co-speech gesture but have not always been used as synonyms are *co-expressive gesture* and *coverbal gesture* (see Müller et al. (eds.) 2013, 2014).

McNeill has often classified these gestures as iconic and metaphoric gestures (see inter alia McNeill 1992: 12–14), which constitute in many later studies the two main groups that have been proposed for these types of gestures. It is worth noticing that gestures are classified as having following features according to continua that he established:
(1) Obligatory presence of speech
(2) Linguistic properties absent
(3) Not conventionalized
(4) Global and synthetic

In terms of feature (2), co-speech gestures are the gestures farthest away from verbal items (words), something that explains the first – by making it required – and the fourth. The degree of conventionalization of a co-speech gesture is often the most disputed and variable feature. Different degrees of conventionalized can be assumed, in such a way that the least conventionalized are improvised, and the most conventionalized are the ones that come close to emblems. The latter ones could become actual emblems if they underwent a process of becoming increasingly autonomous from talk (see 4.1.1).

2.4.2 Pragmatic gestures

Although not used as often as the term co-speech (or coverbal) gesture, *pragmatic gesture* is a term used to refer to a specific class of gestures that are difficult to delimit with precision. While the terms *co-speech/coverbal* invoke the less vague concept of co-existence, the term *pragmatic* has a history of a tremendous variable usage. In regard to gesture, the first difficulty emerges when trying to determine when a gesture would not be pragmatic. Within a wide interpretation of the term, all gestures are pragmatic. The only exclusions would perhaps involve "functional" gestures in the sense that they have a practical goal but not a communicative one, for instance the object adaptor of grabbing a pen; expressions of the speaker's emotional state (mostly facial expressions of emotion); and purely "physiological" gestures in the sense of mere movements of the body. Common to these gestures is the fact that they only fulfill Feature a.1 in Figure 2.1, which we discussed in section 2.1.1.

Within the understanding that almost all gestures are pragmatic in the sense that they contribute to making communication possible and that they have a semiotic component that relates them to their users, Payrató and Tessendorf (2014) present different groups of gestures that are susceptible of being called "pragmatic gestures":

(a) Interactive gestures, as defined by Bavelas et al. (1992, 1995). Among their functions, there is the marking of information to distinguish new from old, citing contributions by other speakers, looking for an answer, looking for agreement, and turn-taking coordination. These functions involve similar functions to *verbal pragmatic* markers, and we can also include *beats* and *batons* that mark the pace or rhythm of speech. All these functions could be considered associated with a *procedural* (non-conceptual) meaning, as illustrated in Figure 2.1 and in Table 2.1. (see section 2.1.1). The classification of *beats* and *batons* in this category contrasts with Ekman and Friesen's (1969), who consider them as illustrators (see 1.2.2). The contrast is perhaps indicative of the dual functional aspect of these and other gestures: its interactive nature and its chacterizing/specifying of the verbal and prosodic chain.

(b) Pragmatic markers, according to Kendon (2004). These gestures have solely pragmatic content and have no referential or propositional content. They can "serve in a variety of ways as markers of the illocutionary force of an utterance, as grammatical and semantic operators, or as punctuators or parsers of the spoken discourse" (Kendon 2004: 5). Therefore, we find ourselves again with gestures with a *procedural* content, intended to facilitate the interpretation of the content without being part of it.

(c) Speech-handling or pragmatic and meta-pragmatic gestures, according to Streeck (2005). These gestures mark the communicative interaction, regulating the conduct of the participants. A pragmatic gesture "encompasses all actions of the hands (and a variety of other body parts, notably the face, head, and shoulders) by which aspects of the communicative interaction are displayed" (Streeck 2005: 73).

(d) Recurrent gestures, according to Ladewig (2014a: 1559), like emblems, "show a stable form meaning relation and can be distinguished from "singular gestures" (Müller 2010b) or "iconic" and "metaphoric gestures" (McNeill 1992) due to their conventional character. Singular gestures have been described as spontaneous creations, which are used co-expressively with a certain speech segment and, as such, are part of the propositional content of an utterance. Recurrent gestures often fulfill performative functions, act upon speech, and form a repertoire of gestures that is shared within a culture". Ladewig (2014a: 1560) provides several reasons to justify the use of the term 'recurring,' and also highlights some differences between emblems and recurring gestures: "although recurrent gestures have undergone processes of conventionalization they cannot be considered as emblems since their meaning is schematic rather than word-like." Moreover, Ladewig (2014a: 1560) adds that "the link between form and meaning in emblems can in many cases not be reconstructed anymore and is very often considered to be opaque." Some gesture families[21] are good examples that illustrate the concept of pragmatic or recurrent gesture, as in:

(d.1) Families of precision grip gestures (Kendon 1995, 2004, with the *grappolo* or *mano a borsa* and the ring-gestures).
(d.2) Palm up open hand (Kendon 2004; Müller 2004; Streeck [2009] 2011).
(d.3) Brushing aside (Müller and Speckmann 2002; Tessendorf 2005, 2008, 2014).

In these cases we find "traditional" illustrators (as defined by Ekman and Friesen 1969) where an instrumental action has become ritualized (as in the concept of biological display), for example: grabbing an object with precision, displaying something, or sweeping or putting aside something, respectively. The gesture acquires what we could call pragmatic functions in reference to the development of an interaction and the relationships among participants. As found earlier in co-speech gestures, the progressive transformation of a pragmatic or recurrent gesture into an emblem may take place if the following processes occur:
(1) definitive development of standards of form and stable meaning,
(2) full acquisition of illocutionary value (that will give it full autonomy from speech), and
(3) social conventionalization (that will lead to the diffusion, familiarity, and use among the members of a sociocultural group).

As shown in the studies collected in Müller et al. (eds.) (2013, 2014),[22] the frontier between recurring and emblematic gestures is very blurred, and should be considered as a continuum or a gradation, as a clear example of the effects of

---

[21] Kendon (2004: 227) refer to families of gestures "as groupings of gestural expressions that have in common one or more kinesic or formational characteristics" (see also section 5.2.2).
[22] For an overview of pragmatic and recurrent gestures, cf. Payrató and Tessendorf (2014) and Ladewig (2014a). For particular cases of recurrent gestures, cf. Bressem and Müller (2014a, 2014b); for a repertoire of German recurrent gestures, see Ladewig's (2014b); and finally, see Tessendorf's (2014) research on the cyclic gesture of the brushing aside gesture. For the integration of gesture types within the speech continuum, see Ladewig (2014c).

prototypicity (see 2.1.1). In fact Ekman and Friesen (1969) had already conceived the relationship between illustrators and emblems in terms of a gradation, both in the sense that illustrators can become emblems as well as in the sense that emblems can be used at certain moments as illustrators. If, as we have proposed, emblems are understood as a prototypical gestural category, recurring gestures represent the last step before full emblematization. Leaving the terminological question aside, what matters is that recurrent and emblematic gestures are analyzed in their situational and sociocultural context, and their properties are described in relation to the interaction and its pragmatic characteristics (illocutionary force, conventionality, non-natural meanings and relation with speech).

2.4.3 Vocal items: From sounds to interjections

Leaving aside the concept of prosody because of the current multiplicity of definition proposals, the separation between the verbal (understood as linguistic and made up of words) and vocal (produced by the phonation system) is the basis for the establishment of four large groups: vocal and verbal (oral language), non-vocal and verbal (written language), vocal and non-verbal (vocal paralinguistics), and non-vocal and non-verbal (kinesics and proxemics).

Paralinguistics can be understood as the set of vocal resources that go beyond the phonological repertoire of a specific language. Within paralinguistics, we also find the conventional and cultural repertoire of each linguistic community, which varies by linguistic community and results in intercultural diversity. For instance, English speakers request silence by using the sound [ʃ] whereas Catalan or Spanish speakers use the sound [s]. These usages are conventional and culturally based, and the sounds can be understood as vocal emblems. They have the same features as the ones we described in Table 2.3, but with the difference that they consist of a sound, a vocal item produced by the phonation system, rather than of a bodily movement. Du Bois et al. (1992) provide a list of examples in their oral language transcription system (and treat them as "marginal words" or sounds).

The illocutionary value of these vocal sounds can be easily observed in conversation, for instance in assent and backchannel sounds and in communication channel or phatic sounds. At the borders of interaction, emblematic gestures are also used for these purposes, occupying the same space within a prosodic unit and with clear interactive functions. Indeed, some sounds have become so conventionalized that their meaning is found as dictionary entries, for instance in the examples (1) and (2), translated from the *Gran Diccionari de la Llengua Catalana* (s.v.):

(1) *tocar l'ase [lit. to touch the donkey]* To make the tongue touch the front of the palate, to lower it quickly producing a sound that expresses annoyance (GDLC, s.v.)
[Example of an explosive sound with the tongue, "fer petar la llengua" (in Catalan or Spanish)]
(2) *xiular* (tr) *[to whistle]* 1 To play a tune by whistling 2 To call a person or animal by getting their attention with a whistle 3 To display disapproval of something or somebody by whistling.

In example (1), the expression of "touching the donkey" refers to the sound made with the tongue as a sign of negation or annoyance, which is identical to the sound that was used to instruct working animals that carried a load. The sounds used to give commands to animals are also conventional and constitute a repertoire.[23] Whistling, as found in the last two entries for the transitive form of this verb, can be used to call somebody (second entry) or as a sign of disapproval (third entry).

The process from sound to interjection is particularly interesting because it represents the conventionalization of phonic sounds, and is therefore similar to the processes of emblematization of gestures and of lexicalization (or grammaticalization) of verbal elements. Whereas sounds do not need to follow the phonetic norms of a specific language as we have seen in the examples (1) and (2) above, interjections involve the first step towards verbality, which is the same step found in onomatopoeias and ideophones. In all these cases, sounds are filtered through the phonological system of that specific language. In this light, interjections, as well as onomatopoeic words and ideophones, are verbal elements, but with a high degree of iconicity, much higher than the rest of the verbal or linguistic elements.

Poggi (1981) and Cuenca (2011) offer a semantic and pragmatic approach to interjections. Stange and Nübling (2014) examine interjections as multimodal forms of expressing motions, and analyze their forms, functions, and their verbal, nonverbal, and bodily aspects. On the other hand, Wharton (2009) examines them from the perspective of relevance theory (see 5.4). Wharton's classification proposes different groups with distinct properties for each group. In all this research, it is easy to find parallelisms between features of interjections that we have highlighted and those of emblems discussed above. The

---

[23] For the Catalan language, the repertoire is fairly extensive, and can be checked in Bernadó and Prat (1980). In fact, we find here a mixture of sounds and interjections; cf. for interjections in Catalan Cuenca (2011).

main common feature is – at least from a linguistic and pragmatic perspective – that both interjections and emblems display illocutionary force, and that the element can be treated as having the value of a sentence. Interjections and emblems are autonomous units: interjections constitute an independent phonic and prosodic group, and emblems often have clear boundaries vis-à-vis prior and subsequent units or gestural phrases. Notice that the etymology of the word interjection comes from the Latin INTERJECTIONEM, with the meaning of 'throwing between', that is making a clear reference to the frontiers that delimit it.

From an intercultural pragmatic perspective, future studies should include a thorough analysis of the interjections and vocal repertoires of each culture, including their interactive functions. Furthermore, they should also examine the multimodal verbal-vocal-kinetic constructions that become conventionalized in different sociocultural groups. For instance, Ferguson had already pointed out that "[i]n a large part of the Mediterranean there is a negative reply form which consists of a click accompanied by a sharp lift of the head and eyebrows" (Ferguson 1964: 175). It is in an emblem of denial or rejection that is commonly used in Catalan, Spanish and other languages (see Morris et al., 1979: 161), in which the head and eyebrow movement is combined with the vocal item. The same phenomenon can be done by combining gestural emblems with the vocal equivalent. For instance, whistling, blowing or vibrating the lips can be used as an exclamation or emphasis sign (often transcribed as 'pfff' and very easy to document online). All these constructions contribute to characterization of these sociocultural groups in terms of their communicative and expressive styles, and therefore, to their identity and distinctiveness.

2.4.4 Sign language items

McNeill locates sign language gestures as the closed to the characteristic verbality of the human (spoken) language:
(a) Obligatory absence of speech
(b) Linguistic features
(c) Fully conventionalized
(d) Segmented and analytic

The gestures of sign languages have clear linguistic properties, much more clearly than any other gesture, and they are fully conventionalized. They are, therefore, the last step in the continuum that starts with gesticulation, and with emblems following. In this light, we can consider emblems as the last step before the gestures of sign language.

However, the relationship between emblematic gestures and sign gestures is more diverse and complex that the continuum may suggest, particularly if one looks to the development of complex languages, as well as the emblematic origins of part of the lexicon of sign languages. Indeed, many communities have developed complex languages in special circumstances. Deaf communities are the best-known and studied cases. Other sign language systems do not achieve such complexity, but are nonetheless very interesting. Some of these have been mentioned in section 2.3.5. For instance, Mallery (1881b) compiled the sign languages developed by Great Plains Native American communities, and provided precise findings on intercultural communication. Mallery structures his compilation around a specific meaning that corresponds to different signifiers depending on the village and culture, as illustrated (fragmentarily) by example (1) below:

(1) NO, NOT. (Compare NOTHING.)
The hand held up before the face, with the palm outward and vibrated to and fro. (*Dunbar.*)
The right hand waved outward to the right with the thumb upward. (*Long; Creel.*)
Wave the right hand quickly by and in front of the face toward the right. (*Wied.*) Refusing to accept the idea or statement presented.
Move the hand from right to left, as if motioning away. This sign also means "I'll have nothing to do with you." (*Burton.*)
A deprecatory wave of the right hand from front to right, fingers extended and joined. (*Arapaho* I; *Cheyenne* V.)
Right-hand fingers extended together, side of hand in front of and facing the face, in front of the mouth and waved suddenly to the right. (*Cheyenne* II.) [...]
The hand waved outward with the thumb upward in a semi-curve. (*Comanche* I; *Wichita* I.) [...]
Wave extended index before the face from side to side. (*Apache* III.) [...]

Deaf-mute natural signs:
Shake the head. (*Ballard.*)
Move both hands from each other, and, at the same time, shake the head. (*Hasenstab.*)

Deaf-mute signs:
French deaf-mutes wave the hand to the right and downward, with the first and second fingers joined and extended, the other fingers closed. This position of the fingers is that for the letter N in the finger alphabet,

the initial for the word *non*. American deaf-mutes for emphatic negative wave the right hand before the face.

Turkish sign:
Throwing head back or elevating the chin and partly shutting the eyes. This also means, "Be silent." (*Barnum.*)

Japanese sign:
Move the right hand rapidly back and forth before the face. [...] (Mallery 1881b: 440–443)

Kendon (1988b, 2004) has provided perhaps the most detailed analysis of these types of signs in his studies of Australian Aboriginal sign languages:

> These sign languages have developed as an alternative to speech, which is needed since there are taboos on the use of speech that must be observed by people when in certain ritual states. [...] These sign languages are quite rich – for example, for Warlpiri sign language well over 1500 lexical items have been recorded, and there are undoubtedly many more. [...] Particularly interesting is the way in which Warlpiri sign language and the other central Australian sign languages are related to spoken language. It was found that there is an extensive relationship between the morphological structure or words and the structure of signs. (Kendon 2004: 301–302)

Washabaugh's (1986) examination of the deaf community in Providence, Rhode Island, US is also particularly interesting. Unlike what it may have been expected in similar circumstances Washabaugh argues that the Providence deaf community did not develop and adopt a fully formed sign language, but instead used a system or set of emblematic gestures, more rudimentary than the sign languages generally used by deaf communities. In this language (Providence), *regulator* emblems (A), which originate from interactive gestures, are the ones who have achieved the highest degree of conventionalized, whereas *nominal* emblems (B), which result from labeling, have the lowest.

In fact, in regard to the emblematic origins of part of the lexicon of sign languages, many signs originate or are based on everyday emblems found in spontaneous and ordinary colloquial registers. Among these, we can find signs based on metaphors, metonymy, or other processes (see 5.5.). These processes may go in the opposite direction when compared to the processes discussed in section 2.3.5, such as, for instance, in the case of "dead time" with the technical gesture and the everyday gesture. Three examples (see Figure 2.10) from the vocabulary of the Catalan Sign Language illustrate this process of sign languages originating from everyday emblems: to zip one's mouth ('to shut up'), to show a closed tight fist ('to be stingy with money'), and to throw a kiss ('excellent'):

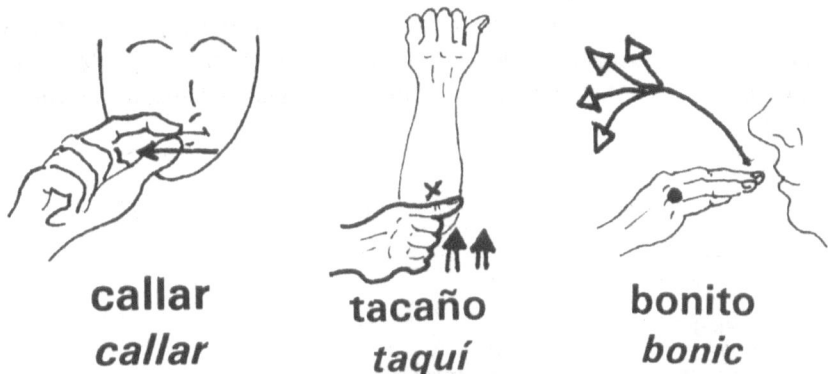

J. Perelló; J. Frigola (1987): *Lenguaje de signos manuales.* Barcelona: Editorial Clentifico- Médica.

Figure 2.10: Sign languages items in LSC (Llengua de Signes Catalana or Catalan Sign Language) that originate from everyday emblems (illustrations from Perelló and Frigola 1987).

Delaporte and Shaw (2009) point to a similar case in the history of the development of the French sign language:

> One group of signs in French Sign Language (LSF) is described in the Dictionnaire des sourds-muets at the end of the 18th century as having in common the form of a cross, placed in front of the face. All of these signs have negative connotations. We identify the etymon of the signs as an emblematic gesture of hostility used by hearing people since the 15 th century. Inherited from the hearing milieu, the gesture evolved into an important lexical family in use by the deaf in both LSF and its sister language, American Sign Language. (Delaporte and Shaw 2009: 35)

Sherman Wilcox has analyzed in detail these pathways between everyday gestures and emblems on the one hand, and sign language items on the other hand, as well as the presence of gestures in sign language communication (see a synthesis in Wilcox 2014). In fact, these pathways are not limited to lexical items, but also include the emergence of grammaticalized evidential and modal forms that have gestural bases (Wilcox 2004). The Catalan Sign Language forms "evident, "clear" "to presage/foreshadow" and to "seem/appear" illustrate this point:

> The Catalan Sign Language forms EVIDENT, CLAR, PRESENTIR, and SEMBLAR develop from gestural sources having concrete meanings, which through grammaticalization have developed more subjective and epistemic or evidential senses. (Wilcox 2014: 2173)

Ladewig (2014a) has also proposed to consider the concept of recurrent gestures (see 2.4.2) as a dimension with different transitions from (spontaneous) singular gestures to (fully conventionalized) sign language items as shown in Figure 2.11.

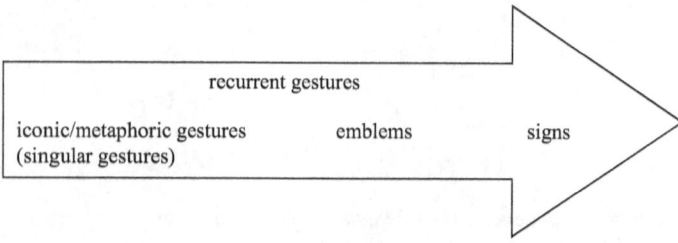

Figure 2.11: Type of gesture in relation to the concept of "recurrent gesture" according to Ladewig (2014a: 1570).

A detailed and multicultural study of the interrelations between everyday emblem repertoires and items in sign languages of the corresponding culture may reveal remarkable pragmatic and semiotic processes, which is another area of the study of emblems that needs to be developed.

3 The taxonomical task: Methodology and repertoires

In any scientific endeavor, there exists an indispensible taxonomic phase that is preferably descriptive. On several aspects, gesture studies are still in this phase, and the study of emblem is not different from that. Beyond the fact that gesture studies are still an incipient research domain, progress is certainly hampered by the heterogeneity of the research and of the research approaches. To overcome this problem, there is a need to agree on common empirical bases, with standard notation systems and shared methodologies that facilitate the comparison of repertoires, and the contrastable analysis of the values and functions of emblems in interaction.

3.1 Notation and transcription: Visual representations

To begin with, there is no reason why the notation, description, and transcription of emblems should be any different from those of any other type of gesture. Consequently, if we apply well-established conventions (see Müller et al. 2013, 2014), we can highlight the following aspects:

(1) Recording: the most reliable method is video-recording, that is, the audiovisual recording of interactions. In Appendix VIII we include several links to video-recorded excerpts of interactions in which the use of several Spanish emblems can be observed. Video-recording has the clear advantage that it makes it possible to reproduce an emblem throughout all it phases, not only during the most significant phase, known as the stroke, the completion of which tends to be the only the phase reproduced in photographs and drawings.

(2) Description and exposition/display: video-recording is also the most reliable and appropriate method, although it is not always feasible. For instance, the use of a large emblem repertoire with a great number of recordings makes its use difficult. In such instances, the more adequate means of reproduction are drawing and photographs. Drawing is the most traditional method (and the one used for a long time): from medieval treatises, to de Jorio (1832) and Efron (1941) to the present time, drawings are used in many dictionaries (see 6.3.1.). Photographs in emblem repertoires appear in the middle of the 20th century (see Meo-Zilio and Mejía 1980–1983 for instance), and are easily found in many online repertoires (cf. 3.4).

(3) In the representation along speech in oral language transcriptions, emblems can be included as any other type of gesture and vocal expression (non-verbal), and the specific way of representation will vary according to the system. For instance, if the usual version of the ethnomethodological system of transcription is used, the gesture is simply added to the text (as any other non linguistic element). If the system developed by John Du Bois et al. (see Dubois 1991; Du Bois et al. 1992) is used, the gesture tends to take the place of an intonation/prosodic group. In regards to the possible synchronization of gesture and verbal elements, Kendon and other authors use a system in which the three typical phases of the gesture production (preparation, stroke, and retraction) are noted above the linguistic items (see Kendon 2004). Emblems can also be incorporated to the notation and transcription system depending on the grammatical model being used, for instance the discursive-functional model (see Alturo et al. 2016: 24, where a greeting emblem is incorporated as a speech act, and as a head of a illocution) or formal models (see Fricke 2013).

As a rule of thumb, the most convenient system – audiovisual or written – should be chosen with specific purposes in mind. Kendon (2004) has listed a number of reasons for the use of drawings. Müller et al. (2013) includes a wide range of techniques and recommendations of different methods, which are similar to the ones that pragmatics and the ethnography of communication use to describe everyday communicative interactions among members of a speech community.

3.2 The compilation of an emblem repertoire: Conception, types and methodology

Emblems are part of "soft" repertoires, more or less blurry and prototypical, which can be associated with linguistic communities, cultures, and particular sociocultural groups. There are two basic types of repertoires: colloquial or everyday ones, associated with the informal everyday varieties of each language and cultural context (see 3.4.1.), and specialized or technical (discussed in section 2.3.5. as well as some examples shown in section a 3.4.2.). Here, we focus on the first type of repertoires, since they include the pragmatic and multimodal resources that are found in everyday interactions.

As pointed in Payrató (2014b), the morphological variation of many emblems, their (partial) synonymy and polysemy, and the modalization they can receive (in facial expression) make it advisable to treat the repertoires not as closed categories and simple lexicographic lists, but in terms of family resemblance networks with radial frames (see 5.2.2). In these networks, related items, with varying degrees of prototypicality, link with each other sharing formational features and through metaphorical or metonymic extensions (or both simultaneously, see 5.5.3), sometimes also through the more or less literal or figurative meaning of verbal expressions (see 5.5.5).

Similarly, as the degree of conventionalization of each unit is different, often clear boundaries between emblems and co-speech gestures (*illustrators*, to use Ekman and Friesen's term) or recurrent gestures (see 2.4.2) cannot be established, so the repertoires of emblems should also be conceived in this sense as open sets with fuzzy boundaries. In fact many emblems arise from processes of ritualization of actions which initially did not have a communicative purpose (cf. especially Posner 2003 and 4.1), or they rely on other gestures such as affect displays or illustrators (Ekman and Friesen 1969, cf. 1.2.2, 4.1.1 and 4.1.2), or they appear from particular behaviors, concerning extra-linguistic or linguistic phenomena (cf. Morris et al. 1979; Brookes 2001, 2004; Payrató 2008 and 4.1.3). The combination of this set of processes with social, gender, regional, and generational variables makes the repertoires even more open and changeable. Consequently, an emblem repertoire should not be understood as a "depot" or depository for gestural units with the capability of signification (such as in a dictionary), which is fully diffused socially but also, in a creative sense, as a pragmatic tool of production of new meanings in interactional contexts, where some of which will spread socially and be shared by the entire speech community.

3.2.1 Traditional repertoires and methods

Until Efron's study (1941), there are no rigorous approaches to data collection and emblem repertoire creation. Studies and work that discuss emblems present these items with little information included about them (e.g. who uses them, what for, when, and where) and often without any information on how they have been collected. Gestures are presented as "material" that do not require verification, that are validated by themselves, and by the testimony of the scholar who discusses them. Efron is the first one to conduct recordings and take photographs, and not just figures or drawings. Efron introduces video-recordings, interviews, and exhaustive observation of the gestural behavior of a large number of informants; indeed, much larger than in the dialectological research conducted during Efron's time (see 4.3.2). Efron's interest is not so much in the establishment of repertoires; his interest is in the analysis of gesture styles of different ethnic and social groups that he studies, as well as in the adaptation of these styles to the North American context.

The concern with the methodological problems and challenges of emblem data collection is raised for the first time in the work of the anthropologist and folklore scholar Francis C. Hayes, that publishes "Guía para el que recoge ademanes o gestos" (*Folklore Americas*)[1] in 1959. The title of the publication is significant, as it highlights how it advances an application of rather traditional system data collection, even naïve, with obvious dialectological parallelisms: fieldwork with informants, whose answers are compiled in a questionnaire, to be transcribed and analyzed. This extensive quote illustrates Hayes' conceptualization of data collection:

> ¿Cómo se recogen los ademanes? Es relativamente fácil. Uno se encuentra con pocos tropiezos. El método de recoger gestos es distinto del de la recolección de (digamos) canciones folklóricas. [...] No hay que viajar en mula a los lugares campestres ni buscar a gente del campo analfabeta. Se puede prescindir de máquinas, aunque sí puede ser útil una cámara fotográfica. No hay problemas de timidez en la persona como sucede en el caso cuando se recogen canciones y cuentos folklóricos. [...] Generalmente lo que necesita el que está a caza de gestos [sic!] es habilidad en entablar conversaciones casuales con gente extranjera, un esfuerzo de refrescar la memoria de éste hablando de ademanes familiares ya al recolector ("un clavo saca otro clavo, si no tiene revuelto el rabo"), y un lápiz y un cuaderno. Claro, es afortunado el que sabe dibujar. Pero es posible tomar notas rápidas y breves y después de la entrevista corregirlas y aumentarlas.
>
> Naturalmente una actitud de simpatía y paciencia hace milagros [sic!], y frecuentemente es necesario decirle al interlocutor cuatro palabras sobre cómo se clasifican los ademanes en el estudio total del folklore; a saber, que se deben clasificar como subsección del *habla popular*. (Hayes 1959: 3–4)

How does one gather gestures? It is relatively easy. One finds oneself with few stumbling blocks. The method of recognizing gestures is different from that of collecting (let's say) folk songs. [...] It is not necessary to travel on mules to rural places or to seek illiterate country folk. One can do without machines, although a photography camera can be useful. There are not problems because of the shyness of people when one collects folk songs and stories. [...] Generally what someone hunting for gestures [sic!] needs is the ability to engage in casual conversions with foreign people, an effort to refresh the memory of the person by talking about familiar gestures that are already known to the collector [researcher collecting the gestures] ("One nail removes another nail, if it does not have a twisted tail"), and a pencil and notebook. Indeed, one is fortunate if one needs how to draw. But it is possible to take quick and brief notes and to fix and develop them after the interview.

---

[1] Hayes had already published a compilation of emblematic gestures in 1951, and as discussed in chapter 1, he is also the author of the first gesture bibliographic study (Hayes 1957). Even earlier, he published a pioneering article about the need to make gesture dictionaries available (Hayes 1940).

> Of course, a sympathetic and patient attitude works miracles [sic!], And it is often necessary to tell the speaker a few words about how gestures are classified in the overall study of folklore; namely, that they should be classified as a subsection of *popular speech* [*everyday talk*]. (Hayes 1959: 3–4)

It is important to recognize Hayes' pioneering work and approach, even though the approach to data collection of gestural material reminds one of guides to hunt mushrooms or to catch butterflies. In fact, "catching" gestures requires at least – in addition to consideration and patience – specific types of questionnaires, with a transcription system and specific criteria of informant selection.

Hayes' work is a product of his time and his research emerges in the context of traditional dialectology. As noted subsequently by Contarello (1980), during Hayes' period, emblem research is considered not requiring anything special but the existing linguistic methodology, more specifically the dialectological interview and method:

> [...] i gesti emblematici, provvisti di significati condivisi dai membri di un gruppo, possono essere indagati allo stesso modo che gli elementi di una lingua [...]
> (Contarello 1980: 18)

> [...] the emblematic gestures, provided with meanings shared by the members of a group, can be investigated in the same way that the elements of a language [...]
> (Contarello 1980: 18)

Certainly, although at a first look linguistic data collection methods may seem applicable to emblem data collection, emblems have features that make them, after all, different enough to require their own methodology. As demonstrated comprehensively by pragmatics and sociolinguistics, traditional dialectological research is too limited to deal with complex linguistic phenomena in cities and metropolitan areas, and too limited to analyze the complexity of communicative interactions. At present, in-depth emblem research requires the application of methods that are similar or analogous to corpus linguistics. Creating an emblem repertoire must be regarded as a task that requires measures of representativeness of the community being studied. Consequently, a socially stratified sample and a statistical or quantitative analysis are often needed, but generally these requirements have not been achieved even in the most contemporary repertoires.

3.2.2 Contemporary repertoires and methods: A sample

The first work to analyze the problems of establishing an emblematic repertoire is by Poyatos (1975) in his review of Efron's (1941), Green's (1968) and Saitz and

Cervenka's (1972) publications. Poyatos discusses theoretical issues, such as the sources of data, the suitable informants, recording techniques, and data presentation while examining these three publications. Poyatos (1975) may also be among the first authors to have an explicit reflection of contemporary repertoires, perhaps with the exception of Green, who was more focused on education.

Multiple studies published during the second half of the 20th century use for the first time questionnaires and different types of tests. For instance, in the production of a first repertoire of American emblems, Johnson, Ekman and Friesen (1975) applied encoding and decoding tests, as well as percentage rates with respect to decoding, the awareness of the naturalness of the usages, and the degree of certainty about message and usages. These types of tests have been repeated and modified in subsequent works (cf. Sparhawk 1978; Payrató 1993; Brookes 2004).

In the case of French, Calbris (1980, 1981, see Calbris 1990) carried out intra-cultural and intercultural experimental studies. Intra-cultural studies were designed to determine the relevant features of a gestural expression, while the intercultural ones to determine the cultural and iconic nature of gestures. The repertoire used can be accessed in dictionary format in Calbris and Montredon (1986).

In the case of Italian, with Spanish, the languages with the highest number of repertoires, Poggi stands out for her work towards creating a repertoire that has even developed its own name: the *gestionario*, the "gestionary", in which emblems are examined in a lexicographic manner (cf. Poggi 2004, 2014 and 3.4).

A very valuable case to include here is Brookes' work (cf. Brookes 2014a, Brookes and Nyst 2014), who has recently put together multiple repertoires of African cultures and languages (see Table 3.1). Brookes (2014a) incorporates the first repertoire of emblems from South Africa with Zulu and South Sotho speakers, that she had previously created using rigorous and contrastable methods (Brookes 2004). A last example of a repertoire that can be used as a model is the emblem dictionary of the city of Berlin, which was initiated by Roland Posner at the Berlin research Center for Semiotics. Unlike previous repertoires, it is not associated with a language but with a location, and with a multicultural and multilingual environment (mostly German and Turkish). Serenari (2003) give some specific examples, which are the only available ones until the entire work is published (see Posner et al. in preparation).

Table 3.1: Current emblem repertoires (books are highlighted in italics) and related works.

African languages	Mathon (1969). Creider (1977) (Kenya). Eastman & Omar (1985) (Swahili). Schneller (1988) (Ethiopia). Brookes (2014a) (South Africa). Brookes & Nyst (2014) (Sub-Saharan region). Meyer (2014) (Wolof)
Amerindian languages	Devereux (1949). Brown (2014) (Mexico and Central America: The Mayan cultures). Reiter (2014) (South America: indigenous cultures). Devereux (1949). Ussa & Ussa (2001) (U'wa, Colombia)
Arabic	Goldziher (1886). Brewer (1951). Hamalian (1965). Barakat (1973). Safadi & Valentine (1990)
Armenian	Gevorkian (2001)
Catalan	Amades (1957) (Catalonia). *Payrató* (1989/1991). Payrató (1993, 2014b) (Barcelona)
Chinese	Hou & Sou (2014)
English	*Saitz & Cervenka* (1972) (U.S.A.). Johnson, Ekman & Friesen (1975) (U.S.A.). *Harrison* (1983) (U.S.A.). Safadi & Valentine (1990) (U.S.A.). Lynn (2011, 2014) (Mid-Atlantic Region, U.S.A.)
French	Brault (1963) (France). *Wylie & Stafford* (1977) (France). Dahan & Cosnier (1977) (France). *Calbris & Montredon* (1986) (France). *Calbris* (1990) (France), Boutet & Harrison (2014) (France)
German	Kirch (1987). Merz (2010, 2011), *Posner et al.* (in prep.)
Greek	*Danguitsis* (1943) (Démirdési). Papas (1972)
Italian	*De Jorio* (1832) (Naples). *Pitrè* (1889) (Sicily). *Efron* (1941). Munari (1963, 1994). Lamedica (1982). Diadori (1990). Ricci Bitti (1992). Paura & Sorge (2002) (Naples). Poggi (2002, 2004, 2014). Bonaiuto & Bonaiuto (2014)
Japanese	Saint-Jacques (1972). *Johnson* (1985). Tumarkin (2003)
Persian	Sparhawk (1978)
Portuguese	Basto (1938a, 1938b). Leite de Vasconcellos (1938). *Harrison* (1983) (Brazil). *Rector & Trinta* (1985) (Brazil). Rector (1986) (Brazil). Rector & Trigo (2004). Nascimento (2008) (Brazil). Galhano-Rodrigues (2014) (Portugal). Rector (2014) (Brazil)
Russian	Eismann (1983). *Monahan* (1983). *Grigorjeva, Grigorjev & Kreydlin* (2001). Kreidlin (2001, 2004)

Table 3.1 (continued)

Spanish	Kaulfers (1931, 1932). Flachskampf (1938). Cardona (1953–4) (Venezuela). *Kany* (1960) (Spanish America). Meo-Zilio (1961a) (Uruguay). *Meo-Zilio* (1961b) (River Plate). *Green* (1968). Poyatos (1970). *Saitz & Cervenka* (1972) (Colombia). *Torrego* (1974) (Madrid). *Meo-Zilio & Mejía* (1980–3) (Spanish America and Spain). Meo-Zilio (1986, 1987) (Spanish America and Spain). *Coll et al.* (1990) (Spain). Martinell & Ueda (1990) (Spain). Meo-Zilio (1990) (River Plate). *Cestero* (1999). Pérez (2000) (Santo Domingo). Nascimento (2008). Rector (2014) (South America)
Swedish	Andrén (2014)
Turkish	*Posner et al.* (in prep.) (Germany)
Yiddish	Efron (1941). *Broide* (1977). Safadi & Valentine (1988)
Other languages/areas	*Sittl* (1890) (Ancient Greece & Rome). *Morris et al.* (1979) (Europe & Tunisia). *Gruber* (1980) (Ancient Near East). Aldrete (1999) (Ancient Rome). *Fornés & Puig* (2008) (Ancient Rome). Kreydlin (2014) (Northeast Europe: Russian, Poland, Croatia, Czech Republic, and Slovakia)
Contrastive works	Efron (1941). *Saitz & Cervenka* (1972). *Calbris* (1981/1990). Kendon (1981a). Lamedica (1982). *Harrison* (1983). Creider (1986). Safadi & Valentine (1990). Forment (1996). Ussa & Ussa (2001). Tohyama (2003). Rector & Trigo (2004). McClave et al. (2007). Nascimento (2008). Merz (2010, 2011)
Other monographs and works about emblems or related works	Leite de Vasconcellos (1925). Hayes (1940). Schuler (1944). *Wolff* (1945). Davidson (1950). Hayes (1951). Taylor (1956). *Feldman* (1959). Hayes (1959). *Laikin* (1963). Brun (1969). Sherzer (1973). *Bäuml & Bäuml* (1975). Givens (1977). Zamora (1983). *Axtel* (1991). Sherzer (1991). Krüger (2004). Seyfeddinipur (2004). Núñez & Sweetser (2006) (Aymara). *Lefevre* (2011). Bressem & Müller (2014a) (German). Graziano (2014). Essegbey (2014) (West Africa: Ghana). Sandoval (2014) (Arapaho bimodal talk). Shapero (2014) (Ancash Quechua)

3.2.3 Past and future: Comparisons between repertoires

The elaboration of specific repertoires of emblems has a clear value by itself, but it is a descriptive and ethnographic task that should lead into more interpretive, explicative, and ethnographic types of analysis, such as the comparative repertoire studies, and ultimately, the explication of its universal and regional features. Saitz and Cervenka (1972) provide the most likely first systematic comparative study, examining a Colombian and a U.S repertoire. Their book includes both repertoires and compares them systematically, highlighting the differences and similarities between gestures (morphologically) and their use. As we noted above, Poyatos (1975) follows with his comparison of the work by Efron (1941), Green (1968) and Saitz and Cervenka (1972), with a special methodological emphasis. Kendon (1981a) is the first author to compare systematically all the repertoires that had been published until that point. Kendon's comparison is particularly interesting because he examines the functional and pragmatic features of the emblems in each repertoire, and therefore, he considers for the first time the degree to which differences may exist between specific cultures (see chapter 4).

However, the progress of this type of work depends greatly on the degree of comparability of research, of corpus design, questionnaires and data collection techniques. As long as there are significant differences, the reliability of the findings makes it difficult to develop intercultural comparisons similar to the ones carried out by international projects in the parallel field of pragmatics, as for instance, the analysis of speech acts, politeness, and pragmatic connectors.

3.3 Elaborated repertoires

We illustrate in this section a list of emblem studies, particularly associated with everyday communication in a specific language (3.3.1). In subsection 3.3.2 we present a short review of technical emblem repertoires, associated with technolects or functional varieties for specific tasks, for instance professional repertoires of sport referees, of workers (reapers, truck drivers, croupiers, firefighters), of divers and hunters, and of monastic communities. In section 3.4, we will examine the lexicographic features (as dictionaries and compilations) of some of these studies (whether everyday or technical).

3.3.1 Current repertoires

Table 3.1 includes a list of publications, organized by the language that each repertoire may be associated with, and in a few cases, the cultural areas surveyed, such as at the end of the table. Italics indicate the work is a full-length book, instead of an article, an appendix, or a book section. More concrete geographical or linguistic location is sometimes given after the reference.

Furthermore, the list in Table 3.1 only includes publications that compile everyday gestures, associated with the informal register of the respective languages, and with the denomination of emblems, symbolic gestures, or simply gestures. Many compilations and dictionaries of "gestures" are, in fact, almost exclusively emblem dictionaries because emblems have forms that are highly recurrent and standard, and their meaning remains constant even outside of situational contexts of production and interpretation.

The list does not include compilations of gestures of different local rituals, nor studies or compilations of gesture in the arts or history (see next section, Table 3.2). We do not include what are considered full sign languages such as the sign languages of the deaf, for instance, those of Native Americans and Australian aborigines (for more on these cases, see Kendon 2004 and Müller et al. (eds.) 2013, 2014). The full bibliographic information of the publications listed is found at the end of the book, in the chapter of references.

Table 3.2: Technical emblem repertoires (books are highlighted in italics) and related works.

Monastic repertoires	*Barakat* (1975). *Umiker-Sebeok & Sebeok* (eds.) (1987)
Professional repertoires (sample)	Brun (1969). Meissner & Philpott (1975). Johnson (1977). Harrison (2014a)
Artistic repertoires	*Schmitt (ed.)* (1984) (art, history). Ramesh (2014) (dance, Southwest India). Pasquinelli (2005) (art, history)
Sport repertoires (sample)	Handball http://activities.eurohandball.com/hb4all/content/2BasicHB/IHFRulesoftheGame.pdf Volleyball https://www.southern.edu/administration/intramurals/docs/Volleyball/NCAAVolleyballSignals.pdf Football https://www.nfhs.org/media/1018297/2017_football_rules_book_official_signals.pdf Basketball http://www.nsbo.ca/wp-content/uploads/2016/10/FIBA-Signals-1.pdf Rugby http://laws.worldrugby.org/?signal_category=all&language=EN
Diving Signs (Sample)	https://www.pinterest.com/mmxsviaemail/scuba/ https://ambergriscaye.com/photogallery/130715.html
Other related/ contrasted works	Sport signals contrasted https://www.pinterest.com/ponching17/sports-referee-hand-signals/

3.3.2 Other repertoires

Table 3.2 above lists compilations of other emblems, particularly technical emblematic gestures, which parallel the relationship between technolects (technical registers or functional varieties used for specific purposes) and everyday varieties of a linguistic community. As in the previous subsection, we present books in italics. In addition to the ones listed here, different types of information and emblem technical repertoires can be found online (specially on Wikipedia).

3.4 Gestural lexicography

Some of the studies we have examined in the previous subsections are indeed structured as genuine dictionaries, and exemplify the fact that the study and analysis of emblem has often been carried out with methods and approaches taken from language sciences.

The first time that an explicit reflection to recreate a gesture dictionary occurs in 1940, and we find it in the work by Francis Hayes, entitled explicitly "Should we have a dictionary of gestures?" In regards to genuine dictionaries, the classical work that comes closer to them are the work by Austin (1806), De Jorio (1832) and Mallery (1881b), which were discussed in chapter 1. During the 20th century, there are numerous studies that are structured like a dictionary – most of them are found italicized in Tables 3.1 and 3.2 above – and almost all of them are structured according to semantic criteria, that is, starting from the signification core of gestures. Examples of this structuration are Papas (1972) for Greek, Calbris and Montredon (1986) for French, Meo-Zilio and Mejía (1980–83) for Spanish (in the Americas and Spain), or Munari (1963), for Italian. The title of Munari's book makes clear this dictionary making effort: *Supplemento al dizionario italiano*.

Regarding lexicographic entries, Poggi's gestionario stands out, because of its more contemporary conception, incorporating the following aspects[2] (Poggi 2014: 1492–3):

---

[2] Payrató's compilation (1993) points towards the same direction, including the following aspects (for a more detailed description, see 3.5): semantic keyword, number of cases of codification and decodification, basic physical variants, contexts of production, brief verbal description, basic meaning, verbal utterances associated with the gesture, category, relations with other items in the repertoire, usage characteristics of the gesture, designs and photographs of the item. Regarding the structuring of the Russian gestures dictionary by Grigorjeva, Grigorjev and Kreydlin (2001), see Kreydlin (2010).

(i) Verbal formulation
(ii) Context
(iii) Synonyms
(iv) Semantic content
(v) Grammatical classification
(vi) Pragmatic classification
(vii) Semantic classification
(viii) Source rhetorical meaning of the gesture
(ix) Coexisting rhetorical meaning

Simpler entries are found in many other dictionaries, with a semantic label header followed often by an illustration, either a drawing or a photograph. Some dictionaries hardly give any information about how they were elaborated, for instance Green (1968) and Meo-Zilio and Mejía (1980–83). Others are much more explicit and reliable, such as the Berlin Dictionary of Gestures (see Serenari 2003 for a discussion of its entries).

The degree of information about the included units available in dictionaries varies considerably. In general, it is scarce. An adequate emblem dictionary should include information about the use of the units, particularly indicating whether it is an everyday unit and is frequently or rarely used; whether it has a neutral vs. pejorative, vulgar, or obscene connotation; and whether it is often used for a specific type of interlocutor, for instance mostly men, mostly women, or mostly children. It would also be valuable to have available information about the verbal expressions that may frequently accompany a specific emblematic gesture.

Most studies constitute compilations of emblems and/or illustrators, organized in terms of the meaning of the units, and with a variable degree of information about its use. In fact, only a few could be considered genuine *gestural dictionaries* if we take into account their very limited scope.

The only study in which the basic criterion to organize the units is not according to meaning (though it is the secondary criterion), but to the bodily parts involved in the execution of the gesture is Bäuml and Bäuml's dictionary (1975), a compilation of "non-codified, non-arbitrary, culturally transmitted (semiotic) gestures" (1975: vii), scarcely known and rarely cited. Bäuml and Bäuml's dictionary is very original but also a risky option. The use of the dictionary is cumbersome on certain aspects, and the organization of the book ends up being somewhat arbitrary in some cases, as for instance, when two or more parts of the body are involved in the gestures. The dictionary makes it possible to scrutinize the diversity of actions that are achieved with the use of a specific body part, and as well the associated variation (of the gesture done with that specific body part) of meaning according to geographical and cultural differences. Each entry is subdivided, in turn, by the different meanings, compiled with data from gesture studies and literary sources. To illustrate a case, we reproduce below the entry for ARM, which has a long list of subsequent subdivisions, each of them with a corresponding description and references (we omit them because of space limitations):

(1) *adoration, affection, amusement, anger, apotopry, approach, assistance, attention, authority, baby, blessing, confession, congratulation, death, defiance, disbelief, emphasis, encouragement, enthusiasm, etiquette, farewell, fear, flattery, friendship, gratitude, greeting, innocence, interrogation, joy, judgment, magnitude, marriage, medico-magical, melancholy, mourning, negation, oath, pacification, plea, pointing, praise, prayer, pregnancy, pride, protection, refusal, rejection, resignation, rest, satisfaction, series, sincerity, sorrow, stop, strength, submission, surprise, surrender, understanding, victory, voting, welcome*

The full entry ends with the remaining combinations (also included in other entries) of the arm and the other parts of the body, each of them consistently specified:

(2) ARM, BREAST / ARM, BREAST, KNEE / ARM, BREAST, SHOULDER / ARM, ELBOW / ARM, FACE / ARM, FINGER / ARM, FINGER, HAND / ARM, HAND / ARM, HAND, HEAD / ARM, HAND, MOUTH / ARM, HAND, SHOULDER / ARM, HEAD / ARM, HEAD, SHOULDER / ARM, KNEE / ARM, LIP / ARM, MOUTH / ARM, NECK / ARM, SHOULDER / ARM, WRIST.

Lastly we have Meo-Zilio and Mejía's (1980–1983) work, which is probably the most ambitious, comprehensive, and extensive gesture dictionary published until now.[3] Numerous units are illustrated, although not all are accompanied with photographs. The (two) volumes are the result of research conducted in Spain and Latin America (except Brazil). The overall goal was to develop a series of gesture dictionaries of different communities. Dictionaries of Portugal, Brazil, and Italy were the next ones that would have been published. They described their goal as follows:

> reunir de una manera sistemática y detallada una primera lista provisional de gestos ordenados según su significado fundamental y acompañados de la descripción morfológica y semántica (con sus variantes). (Meo-Zilio and Mejía 1980–1983: 8)

---

[3] Giovanni Meo-Zilio and Silvia Mejía: *Diccionario de gestos. España e Hispanoamérica.* Bogota, Instituto Caro y Cuervo, 2 volumes, 1980 (I) and 1983 (II). The primary authorship corresponds to Meo-Zilio, Mejía was only in charge of the photographic documentation.

> to gather in a systematic and detailed way a first provisional list of gestures ordered according to their fundamental meaning and accompanied by the morphological and semantic description (with its variants). (Meo-Zilio and Mejía 1980–1983: 8)

Among the positive aspects of their work, we can highlight the great number of units compiled (more than 2,000 according to the author), the extensive geographical area covered, the organization of the unit, and the inclusion of verbal material associated with them. Some methodological issues are more debatable. First, the authors do not provide much information; they do not provide any details about the questionnaire and the type of survey that was conducted. In spite of their emphasis on the linguistic and dialectological parallelisms, one can assume that they only interviewed one informant per country. This is clearly insufficient and reduces the reliability of the indications given about each country in which units are collected. For instance, many gestures that are not listed as being used in Spain are in fact very common in this country. As was the case for Morris et al. (1979) (see 4.3.2), the entirety of Spain is represented culturally by a single speaker from Madrid: the extensiveness of the geographical area covered seems to have prevailed over the precision of the findings. The same can be said about the great amount of material collected and that includes different categories of gestures. In issues of more detail, the organization of the entries is not always clear, the thematic index, while useful, does not resolve all the problems, and it becomes difficult to reproduce with precision many of the units that are not accompanied with photographs. A last remark about Meo-Zilio and Mejía's work – and more generally, about many gestural dictionaries – is the fact that they do not include information about the frequency of use of the gestures, and instead mix very frequent with very rarely emblems. Furthermore, they tend not provide information about features that describe the (contextual) circumstances in which the gesture is regularly used.

We can add a note about the contemporary availability of online dictionaries and compilations, such as Martinell and Ueda's (eds.) (1990) for Spanish and Japanese, or the series of material compiled in Wikipedia that overall are of good quality. In these cases, the ease to access it and to look up entries, as well as the possibility of incorporating audiovisual materials are very significant advantages. These advantages together allow the user to have a much more comprehensive idea of what an emblem really is (when compared to compilations and dictionaries elaborated in the 20th century).

3.5 A detailed example: A basic repertoire of Catalan emblems

The methodology applied to the research into Catalan emblems (Payrató 1989/1991, 1993) draws from the one used by Johnson, Ekman and Friesen (1975) in their study of emblems in United States, and from Ekman and Friesen (1969, 1972), and adopted the following procedure:[4]

(1) A provisional repertory of 297 gestures that could be considered emblems or at least autonomous gestures (by Catalan speakers) was established. The criteria for classifying a gesture as an emblem were the criteria of emblematicity defined above (see 2.2.3.): (a) autonomy from speech, (b) communicative goal, (c) illocutionary force, (d) semantic core, and (e) social nature. Previously, direct observation and bibliographical sources, mainly concerning Catalan and Spanish gestures, had supplied a former set of 315 items that constituted the initial sample. The provisional repertoire used gestures collected by Amades (1957), who organized entries in a lexicographical manner.[5] These gestures were often checked against entries from Meo-Zilio and Mejía's dictionary (1980–1983).

(2) The use of the items mentioned was checked through a codification test applied to 10 informants with homogeneous traits: middle class men between 25 and 40 years old, born in Barcelona (as were their parents), speakers of Catalan as a first language, and educated (at least) to the high school level. On the test, informants were asked to perform gestural actions from simulated contexts, known from everyday life. A hundred and sixty contexts were prepared to elicit the gestures of the provisional repertoire (see Payrató 1989/1991). After each context had been read by the interviewer, all the performed actions were transcribed into the questionnaire, together with the informants' comments. Once the results were collected and analyzed, a few new gestures (made by the informants) were added to the first

---

[4] This section follows closely Payrató (1993), and more extensively Payrató (1989/1991), which can be accessed online with photographs and drawings of all the compiled and classified units (see note 6). A summary can be found in Payrató (2014a); for a sample of the repertoire, see also Payrató (2014b) and Appendix I.

[5] Amades' work is in fact, a compilation of gestural units presented as a repertoire of Catalan gestures in the format of a dictionary, that is to say, successive entries – organized by the popular name of the gesture or by a term that refers to its signification – that provides morphological information about the speech act and its meaning. Unfortunately, Amades' work is more valuable for reasons other than its intrinsic qualities: it is a fundamental historic study because of a simple lack of similar studies. For a detailed review and critical perspective of Amades' work, see Payrató (2013a).

repertory; the rest, including all those not performed by the informants or not clearly attested in the bibliographical sources, were eliminated. This first test also allowed the selection of more frequent morphological variants of many gestures, which were adopted as principal. The final result of this phase was called the basic provisional repertory (BPR) of Catalan emblems, composed of 221 gestures.
(3) The emblematic nature of the gestures of the BPR was checked by a second test applied to a new group of ten people (with the same characteristics as the former group). Informants were now asked to identify the preceding 221 gestures, reproduced in designs, photographs and, when necessary, by the action of the interviewer himself. The results were tabulated and a basic (definitive) repertory (BR) of 108 emblems used by Catalan speakers was set up. This repertoire is shown in Appendix I with a brief description of each emblem.

3.5.1 Exclusions, order, and repertoire entries

Besides gestures excluded from the initial selection for not fulfilling the adopted criteria, two series of gestures which might be taken as emblems were also rejected for different reasons. On the one hand, greetings, deictic gestures, and general measuring gestures were excluded, because we felt that their analyses needed a different methodology. On the other hand, gestures were rejected which were thought to be peculiar either to certain groups of speakers, or to specific activities, such as those performed (only) in certain games, sports, professions, and so on (technical gestures). Such items are not included in what was supposed to make up the basic gestural repertory associated with a language. As a matter of fact, the definitive repertory was designed to represent the gestural parallel of both a dialectal and a functional variety: the Catalan spoken in Barcelona in its current or colloquial register, that is to say, the oral, spontaneous, interactive, and informal variety of Catalan.

Concerning the order of the items, gestures were arranged like dictionary entries, according to the labeling of their semantic core. This kind of ordering was considered to be the least flawed of all those tried, and the one that allowed the clearest cross-references. Each entry is designed to include the following information:
(1) Semantic keyword (and possible specifications, as proper names or current verbal accompaniments)
(2) Situation and denomination in the provisional repertory
(3) Number of cases of codification and decodification
(4) Basic physical variants (and number of productions)

(5) Contexts (of the codification test) from which the item was elicited, and number of productions
(6) Other (complementary) contexts of production of the items, and number of productions
(7) Brief verbal description of the body action (and its variants)
(8) Basic meaning
(9) Verbal utterances associated with the gesture
(10) Category in the classifications undertaken and illocutionary value (assertive, directive, expressive, commissive, or declaration)
(11) Relations with other items in the repertoire
(12) Other information (confusions, usage characteristics of the gesture, bibliographical references, etc.)
(13) Designs and photographs of the item

3.5.2 Compilations established

The units included in the three compilations established exhibit several differences. Emblems in the strict sense form the *basic repertory* (BR). This compilation is to be understood as a basic gestural vocabulary at the disposal of (at least a defined group of) Catalan speakers. The 108 items in this compilation (see Appendix I) were both codified and decodified by a minimum of 50% of the informants. Gestures in this set are in general easily recognized and hardly ever ambiguous. Speakers are fully aware of them, so these units are considered to be frequent. Only a few cases present some problems, in that it is not clear if they should be considered different gestures (as we finally decided) or variants of the same unit (cf. numbers <14>/<15>, <69>/<70> and <88>/<89>, in contrast with <23> or <32>, in Appendix I). This is a question that is raised in all the repertoires of emblems and that must be treated as a matter of family resemblance and families of gestures (see in more detail section 5.2.2).

A group of 65 gestures constitutes the second compilation or *complementary repertory* (CR), which represents a kind of appendix to the first. The items in this set were codified by less than 50% of people and decodified by 40% or more. These less codified items cluster in two series: those that are easily recognized (and which were named *uncommon pseudoemblems*), and those which are subject to confusion and irregular decodification (*ambiguous pseudoemblems*). Confusion mainly arose because of a formal similarity between two or more gestural actions, in such a way that people interpreted an (unknown) gesture as if it were another (known) gesture (see Payrató 1989/1991 for specific cases; cf. 4.3.2).

Finally, a set of 48 other items forms the third compilation, *other items* (OI), where features such as the ambiguity and limited use hinted at with regard to the second set are much more pronounced. Items on this level also come in two groups. The first includes presumably emblematic gestures (almost) unknown by the informants, probably because they are peculiar to other languages and cultures, or because they have fallen into disuse; this could be proved by contrastive (cross-generational and cross-cultural studies). The second group contains ambiguous items with a great number of variants, none of them apparently principal. Several cases present normal, even high levels of codification, whereas others are characterized by an extremely low level of decodification. A suitable explanation for this contrast can be found in the fact that gestures of this kind are clear (and possibly) familiar to the sender (for whom the body action is a complement of (several) verbal utterances) but not to the receiver, who must decodify the gesture without the support of the verbal channel. Therefore, it is a case of pragmatic or recurrent gestures (see 2.4.2) that have not completed the process of emblematization and social conventionalization.[6]

3.5.3 Codification test

If one starts with a hypothetical and provisional repertoire of autonomous gestures used by a communicative community or social group, it is required to do as much as possible to check the real knowledge and use of these units. With this goal, it is important to elaborate a questionnaire in order to carry out a survey to codify the emblems of a group of informants (see also 5.1). The goal of this first survey is three-fold:

(a) To check the compiled units are *actually* used by informants, and therefore, are not emblems used by other groups or in other locations, and that are not rarely or no longer used.
(b) To take advantage of the opportunity to observe the production of gestures that have not been included in the provisional repertoire.
(c) To limit the number of compiled variants (that can be many for each unit), giving preference to the variants that are used most by informants (the prototypical ones).

---

[6] The gestures that form these two other repertoires can be accessed, with the corresponding illustrations, from the original source (1989/1991) at http://www.tdx.cat/handle/10803/1687;jsessionid=46B9A98A31F4448A1B0EC16CE6BEF2E0.tdx2

This third goal (c) comes before the elaboration of a second survey in order to obtain more information about knowledge – and not use – of the emblems. The completion of these objectives makes it possible, once survey results have been tabulated, to create a basic provisional repertoire.

The need of a survey of this type in emblem research is a consequence of the extreme difficulty in checking the use of the units – one by one – in naturalist observation and audiovisual recordings. Instead, a questionnaire facilitates the production of units much faster and more concretely. However, the questionnaire has two substantial limitations: the selection of informants and the decision about the most suitable survey model.

3.5.4 Informants

Taking into account the linguistic diversity found in the domain of any language, both the knowledge but even more so the use of autonomous gestural units varies greatly. It is fairly clear that an analysis of emblematic gestures has to delimit very precisely the particular research domain. In this way it will be possible to establish reliable and representative results to overcome the challenges of knowledge and use variation, the fact that the structuration of an emblematic repertoire is less rigid than that of a verbal one, and the fact that the units that make up a gestural repertoire are less systematic than linguistic units.

The solution found in the elaboration of this emblematic repertoire has been to carry out qualitative studies. They are more detailed in a restricted domain (and therefore the results are more partial but also more representative) instead of a more superficial analysis (with a very reduced repertoire) but with a domain far more extensive, for instance considering geographical variation (as in Morris et al. 1979). To achieve this goal, it would be advantageous to conduct research that would filter the results of a provisional repertoire via the selection of small groups of informants with homogenous characteristics in terms of the usual variables of sociolinguistic and pragmatic research, such as geographic, historical, social, gender, individual and contextual. In this manner, the *model* informant in the survey to codify the compiled data met the following requirements:

1. Born in Barcelona, from parents also born in Barcelona
2. Male
3. Age between 25 and 40 at the time the survey took place (born between 1950 and 1965; average age of informant was 31,9 years)
4. Native speaker of Catalan
5. A person who speakers regularly in Catalan

6. Living in Barcelona for all his life (or with stays in other locations of less than a year)
7. Middle class
8. Mid-level or higher level of education
9. No relation with any other group informant

The potential inclusion of other groups of informants depending on variables such as age, gender, and origin has to be considered carefully, because each group represents a significant increase in the number of informants and volume of data. These challenges could be resolved partially with a statistical treatment of the data, but that should not lead to an excessive simplification of the surveys. Such simplification goes against the questionnaire model that would be best suited for a study of this type, specifically, a questionnaire that is both open and detailed.

3.5.5 Questionnaires, interviews, and items

In the research design, the decision of having a small number of participants in the research project comes with the decision to elaborate a questionnaire of open answers that makes it possible to elicit and produce all the gestures incorporated in the provisional repertoire, as well as other gestures that have not been included.

The questionnaire is designed as a tool to facilitate a task of continuous simulation of different contexts, in which the informant makes a gesture (or more accurately, *may* make a gesture) if s/he thinks s/he makes it routinely, if it crosses his/her mind, or ultimately, if s/he indentifies the contextual situation with one or more particular emblems with all the variations that s/he chooses.

A survey of this kind, particularly when it comes to practical task of making gestures, requires an adequate disposition and a high degree of collaboration on the part of the informant. Otherwise, there is the risk of distorting and making the results too formal if the distance between informant and researcher is excessive, or if the former finds the presence of the latter too strange. To overcome these challenges in the study that we present here, informants who had a trusting relationship or friendship with the researcher were chosen whenever possible, and great efforts were made to create a relaxed and friendly environment in which to carry out the survey. Indeed, as is the case in surveys about delicate and taboo topics, these details are fundamental for the success of the survey. Consequently, after a variable phase of informal conversation, the researcher described the procedures and goal of the survey, and asked the informant to imagine a series of situations as examples of what s/he would be asked afterwards, during the actual survey itself. Once the survey was started, the non-verbal acts carried out during the interview were transcribed in the survey sheets, as long as they met the same criteria as the non-verbal acts included in the provisional repertoire. The verbal material produced and associated with the emblems was also transcribed.

The questionnaire for codification (see Payrató 1989/1991) contains 160 entries, all relatable *a priori* to gestures that were included in the provisional repertoire. However, there are five entries (mixed among all the others but marked with the word "bis": 32, 57, 75, 100 and 121), which are not related to a specific emblem. The goal of these unrelated entries is to scrutinize indirectly the conduct of the informant and more specifically, to ensure that the informant is not *inventing* gestures to fill in each entry, which goes against the procedures explained to the informant that s/he does not need to produce a gesture in each situation that s/he is asked. This checking mechanism worked well: all informants went though these entries without attributing to them any specific gesture.

Together with the previous measure, and to ensure also that informants did not make up gestures *ad hoc* for each entry, rather than reproducing everyday gestures of his/her own repertoire, the researcher moved on to the following contextual situation if the informant did not produce a gesture within thirty seconds. In fact, the more prototypical an emblem is, the easier and quicker it is to be recognized and produced. This second measure seems a reasonable one on the account that the goal of the research was to obtain a *basic* repertoire of emblematic gestures (correlatable, at least on the whole, with gestures that the informant was most conscious of).

In regards to the frequency of the units, the survey results display a remarkable difference; at one end, we have units that are elicited and produced almost instantly and by all or most informants, while at the other end, we have units that are only produced by a small number of informants, and produced with great insecurity and hesitation. In the data treatment, the first set has been considered as belonging to the basic emblem repertoire while the second as *pseudoemblems* or other units (as put in 3.5.2).

Finally, and in terms of the amount of responses and duration of the interviews, the average number of responses was approximately about 75% of the 160 entries, including the "bis" entries discussed above. Thus, about 25% of entries had no response. The average duration of the interview was over two hours (approximately two hours and ten minutes). The shortest interview lasted an hour and forty five minutes and the longest lasted two hours and forty minutes.

The tabulation of the decodification survey results makes it possible to establish a definitive basic emblematic repertoire contingent on the reflected knowledge/familiarity with the different units that have been included in the provisional basic repertoire. The norm followed to establish the definitive basic repertoire (Appendix I) is to include all the units that were codified by half or more of the individuals who participated in the first survey (and therefore, five or more productions of each unit), and that were decodified also by half or more of the individuals who participated in the second survey (5 or more).

The codified units with a percentage of less than 50% but decodified without important ambiguities (with a level of 40% or higher) were grouped from the definitive basic repertoire under the label of *pseudoemblems*, within the *complementary repertoire*, and the rest (units with a lower percentage) were dismissed, even though their final results from the surveys are nonetheless provided (see Payrató 1989/1991). The presentation is made according with the entry specifications discussed above in 3.5.1. The following is an example of the included entries in the repertoire (unit <1>, see Appendix I):

1) **REALIZE (SOMETHING THAT HAS BEEN FORGOTTEN)**
2) **1.3) REALIZE 3 (SOMETHING FORGOTTEN)** // <2>
3) Codification (7) Decodification (10)
4) Slap of the forehand with the palm of the hand (6) / Hand grabs the forehead (1).
5) **1.3** (6), **1.1** (1).
6) **1.1** (1), **1.3** (1), **62** (1), **96.1** (4).
7) Slap of the forehand with the palm of the hand.
8) Realize something (specially that one has forgotten something), remember something.
9) "Òstia quin *despiste*!", "Mecàgum l'olla!", "Com no se m'havia ocorregut!", "Òstia!", "Ostres!"
10) Representative / (B) / (III).
11) 174.
12) -
13) PHOTOGRAPHS / DRAWINGS.

3.5.6 Precedent repertoires and future projects

We owe the first collection of Catalan autonomous gestures or emblems to Amades (1957).[7] Notably in tune with current interpretations, Amades understood the linguistic nature of the gesture (at least in the broad sense) and its relevance

---

[7] This and the following subsections reproduce parts of Payrató (2014b).

for the ethnology of the language. His repertoire comprises 299 entries and 96 photographs of gestures which can be considered autonomous and emblematic. In fact, he speaks literally about "linguistic" gestures (and non-linguistic), on the one hand, and about "general", "individual", and "indeterminate" gestures on the other, but he does not produce an accurate characterization of the items. Neither does he establish reliable relationships between gestures (their morphological variants, for example); sometimes, variants of the same unit appear as different gestures. Many years later, in a short article, Mascaró (1981) set out the foundations of what would eventually become the study of Catalan gestures, providing specific criteria for comparison and contrast.

Payrató (1989/1991, 1993) followed the line traced by Mascaró, and Martí (1992) recorded and studied gestures from Alghero. There is still much work to be done on the differences in the gestures used throughout the Catalan-speaking territories. A project of this kind, a gestural dialect atlas compiled from an ethnological perspective, would be the best possible tool for expanding our current knowledge (see particularly Payrató 2006). A recent panoramic study recording traditional information and sketching the relationship of Catalan gestures with emblems from other cultures can be found in Payrató (2013a).

3.5.7 Selection of emblems according to pragmatic and semantic features

Below is a selection of some of the best known, traditional, and representative emblems used in the Catalan-speaking countries, grouped by subject and pragmatic function. Within the established repertoire, prototypical emblems (autonomous from speech, with a communicative goal, illocutionary force, a semantic core, and a social nature) are distinguished from pseudoemblems (which do not present all the emblematic features). In an analogy with speech acts, the most common gestures are those of an assertive and directive nature.

(a) *Emblems of mockery, insult, and threat*
Cat. *pam i pipa* (literally 'span and pipe'; the Shanghai gesture, or the nose thumb in Morris et al.'s 1979 list; cf. Appendix <I, 26>, and Appendix <III, 6>) is one of the best well-known and most widespread Catalan emblems. The name has been exported to Latin America, and especially to Argentina, where it is known as *el pito catalán* (literally 'the Catalan whistle', see Appendix <V, 28>). The gesture is often documented in Catalan literature, is included in current dictionaries, and its name appears with dialectal variants (*jutipiris* in the Balearic Islands, for example). Cat. *llengota* or *llengotes* ('to stick out one's tongue'; cf. Appendix <I, 25> and Appendix <II, 5>) is also well represented as a gesture of

derision. As it has been noted in section 2.3.4, nowadays the main emblems of insult are the horns (<I, 27>, <VII, 10>),[8] *la botifarra* (literally 'the big sausage'; <I, 56>, <II, 2>) and the traditionally called *dit impúdic* (the 'impudent finger', in Latin *digitus impudicus*; <I, 55>, <II, 3>). These gestures can be considered as separate, different items (the vertical forearm jerk, the horn-sign, and the finger, with the finger raised, see Morris et al. 1979), but they can also be understood as related items linked by family resemblance (cf. 2.3.4 and 5.2.2). Emblems of threat (or provocation) are often produced with a hand that is opened obliquely (<I, 9>), waggling the index finger (<I, 10>), or a combination of both. It is often used to admonish children but can also be used ironically. A more threatening version is produced by shaking the upraised fist (<I, 11>).

(b) *Emblems of conjuration, giving orders, or making requests*
Cat. *figa* ('the fig', Morris et al. 1979) is the gesture of conjuration *par excellence* in Catalonia and is also collected in current dictionaries (<II, 4>); also crossing index and middle fingers (<I, 39>, <II, 5>), hoping for good luck. As in Spanish and English, Cat. *tocar ferro* ('to touch iron') or Cat. *tocar fusta* ('to touch wood') are also typical expressions (both included in dictionaries, the first one more widespread) to prevent bad luck. With respect to orders or requests, the gesture performed to bring the receiver closer is normally made with the palm facing the face of the issuer (or the ground) and the fingers folding back (<I, 14>); to have the receiver move away, the gesture is usually made with the palm parallel to the ground and the fingers stretching out (<I, 6>). Similar indications can be given to make somebody hurry (stretched fingers oscillation, <I, 3>), to ask someone to speak more loudly or more softly (in the first case with the palm up, and in the second case with the palm down, as in the gesture requesting calm, <I, 28>), to obtain an answer (soft header back), or to ask somebody to be quiet (many emblems are used for this purpose: holding the lips, <II, 7>; placing the index finger in front of the lips, <I, 96>; tapping the lips lightly, or closing them like a zipper, etc.). The diversity of gestural metaphors and metonymies is evident in these cases, as well as in others requesting that something be finished or stopped (e.g. calling "time" by making a T with the hands, pretending to cut the air with scissors, etc.; see 5.5), to express that someone is talking too much in a quantitative sense (opening and closing the hand, <I, 105>) or that someone talks too much in the sense that (s)he cannot keep a secret (the index finger touches the tip of the tongue, Cat. *anar-se'n de la llengua*, literally 'to go too far with the

---

[8] Emblems found in the appendices are abreviated as <number of appendix in Roman numerals, number of the item>.

tongue', <I, 106>, cf. <VI, 5>). Other hand gestures serve to ask a favor (with the hands in the praying position, <I, 86>), ask for keys (as opening a lock on the air, <I, 35>), ask the time (the index finger touches the wrist, <I, 63>), a cigarette (making a V with the fingers, near the lips, <I, 60>), the bill (signing in the air, <I, 37>), ask if one can eat or drink something (a hand approaching the mouth with the fingers together, <I, 74>, or with a separate, stretched thumb, <I, 22>), or indicate a phone (raising the fist to the ear, <I, 101>).

(c) *Emblems to answer and to indicate states*
The non-verbal *yes* and *no* are performed by head movements (forward and sideways, respectively, i.e., nodding or shaking one's head, cf. <VIII, 74>, <VIII, 52>, <VI, 1>, <VI, 12>). Rejection can also be made moving the head back in a strong movement, and denial is expressed with the stretched index moving sideways like a metronome (cf. <I, 77>, <VI, 11>). To indicate 'good' or 'bad' the thumb is raised (<I, 21>) or lowered (cf. <I, 72>, <VI, 4>), or a circle is made with thumb and forefinger to indicate 'good' (the thumb up and the ring, see Morris et al. 1979). Warnings include the act of pulling down the skin beneath the eye ("look", <I, 5>; the eyelid pull, see Morris et al. 1979) and also tapping the nose with the index finger ('to sniff something', the nose tap, see Morris et al. 1979). Kissing one's fingers and then opening them immediately (cf. <I, 71>, <VI, 2>) has a long tradition ('delicious', 'excellent'; the fingertips kiss, see Morris et al. 1979). Some of these emblems can be traced back to Ancient Rome (Fornés and Puig 2008). Expressions of doubt or approximate evaluation ('more or less') are usually made with oscillations of the flat hand or with sideways head movements (cf. <I, 16>, <I, 17>, <VI, 6>, <VI, 7>), and expressions of indifference or ignorance are shrugging one's shoulders with a downward grimace of the lips and often by showing the palms (the three movements can be combined in various ways, cf. <I, 65>, <I, 64>, <I, 48>). Slapping the forehead manifests an oversight or that we have noticed something (<I, 1>). To swear, the fingers making a cross are kissed (<III, 1>); innocence is revealed by showing the palms (<I, 66>), and surprise by raising the eyebrows (<I, 99>).

(d) *Emblems to describe other people's traits and to describe situations, objects, or actions*
Touching one's nose with the index finger (or the thumb) denotes that someone is drunk or drinks too much (<I, 24>, <III, 2>), and rotating the index finger near the temple indicates that the person to whom the gesture is applied is crazy or talking nonsense (cf. <I, 23>, <III, 3>, <III, 4>). To indicate impertinence, there are still samples of a gesture (especially in the Balearic Islands) in which the thumb touches one side of the jaw and the rest of the hand the other, with the palm

facing inwards (Payrató 2008). The gesture is associated with the Catalan expression *tenir barra* ('to have a nerve/to have a cheek', literally 'to have a jaw'). This gesture is probably exclusive to Catalan and synonymous with another one that is also exclusive and has the same meaning: to grab one's cheeks and pull them out, Cat. *ser un galtes*, literally 'to be a cheek (see 5.5.3, Figure 5.10). However, today the most common gesture in this domain comes from Spanish and consists in slapping one's cheek (<I, 19>), corresponding to the verbal Spanish expression *caradura*, literally 'hard face' (Payrató 2008), based on another metaphor reflecting shamelessness with (hard) facial features (see 5.5.3, Figure 5.10). Another gesture that appears to be exclusive to Catalan is associated with the expression *no bufar cullera* (literally 'not to blow a spoon', meaning 'not to eat anything' or 'not to understand a word') and is performed with a vertical hand, which is closed quickly in front of the mouth.

The metaphor to indicate meanness involves showing the fist with the knuckles facing up (<II, 6>), while to indicate that someone is a flatterer, people make gestures simulating bouncing a ball or brushing or shampooing someone (<I, 2>, see 5.5.3, Figure 5.12). To denote a 'thief' or 'theft' the fingers rotate and fold (cf. <I, 93>, <VII, 13>). Extending the index fingers side by side with the palms facing the ground suggests some sort of union or complicity (cf. <I, 102>, <III, 7>). Rhythmically opening and closing the fingers of one hand (or both) signifies that a place is full to overflowing (cf. <I, 75>, <VI, 3>, <VII, 3>). If the motion is made rubbing the tips of the index and middle finger, the gesture refers to money (cf. <I, 47>, <VII, 7>, <VII, 8>). A small quantity is represented by showing a minute space between the thumb and the index finger (<I, 84>). For surprise or admiration, the hand shakes repeatedly (<I, 52>), and functions as an exclamation or an adverb of quantity.

4 An ecological view on emblems

If we applied to emblematic gestures a metaphor that is widely used in other fields and based on considering inanimate objects as being alive, that is, the metaphor that an EMBLEM IS A LIVING BEING, the central question that we would need to answer next would be the following: How are emblems born, and how do they develop, diversify, and die? From an ecological perspective, emblems are communicative elements typical of specific habitats and with many points of contact with the *displays* (ritualized exhibitions) of animal species, which ethology has studied mainly starting in the 20th century.[1] Studies within this approach lead us to ask ourselves why emblems have specialized – like communicative behaviors analogous to *displays* – and have become, after a specific historical evolution, central items of a repertoire with functions basically communicative and not of other types. Posner (2003) has emphasized the fact that there are many cases in which an emblem is based on a functional action, which is empty of contents and becomes a strictly communicative action, that is, a *display* in an ethological sense. On the other hand, Streeck (2009/2011) emphasizes that many gestures can be interpreted as schematizations of actions. Cienki (2013) synthesizes the relation between schemas and gestures in a cognitive framework, and discusses how many of these emblems have their origins in gestures of practical actions according to the recent theory of *mimetic schemas* (see Zlatev 2007, 2008 and also section 4.1.1). In brief, many emblems can be seen as the result of the ritualization or schematization of an action, which have become specialized for communicative functions and have lost their original functions.

4.1 Origins and historical evolution

The classic works by Efron (1941) and La Barre (1947) highlight the cultural roots of gestures, and thus change the idea – and in large part, the myth – of common universal gestures, which in turn relates to the old idea of the gestural genesis of human language, pointed out already in the historical review of chapter 1.[2]

---

1 See Eibl-Eibesfeldt (1972, 1977) for a well-known study on the eyebrow raise. Cf. Senft (2014) for a pragmatic perspective in one of the first handbooks of pragmatics to include fully an analysis of gesture.
2 Quintilian already discusses this idea (see quote in 1.1.1) and also several medieval authors (see Kendon 2004: 24). Kendon (1984) also discusses it, having updated his analysis more recently (Kendon 2017).

These cultural roots are evident, more than in any other gesture subcategory, in the case of emblems, intimately associated with sociocultural groups or communities. This was already visible in work such as the compilation by De Jorio (1832). The initial question, therefore, is clear: how are emblems born and, then, how are the processes of emblematization produced? And the second question that we will review along the following sub-sections is whether the historical evolution substantially or in detail changes the morphological, semantic or pragmatic aspects of emblems.

In fact, historical evolution is what justifies the diversification of many contemporary emblems, and taking that into account is the way to understand their polymorphism and their polysemy. In many cases there have been evolutions that have to do with popular etymology or with confusions by homonymy or resemblance, as in the case of the evolution of verbal items. In many cases, we must also take into account the "multi-origin" of some emblems, that is, the fact that several emblems are born in different places, coinciding or not in time (Morris et al. 1979 collect significant information about these aspects). These are "poly-births", as is the case in many phenomena of the everyday language: similar forms are developed at the same time (or not) in different cultures or linguistic varieties.

In some particular cases we have historical studies of great value about a particular emblem, for example the classic work by Leite de Vasconcellos (1925) on the fig (see <II, 4>, <V, 32>), and by Taylor (1956) on the Shanghai gesture (<III, 6>, <V, 28>). Regarding the first case, the fig is a gesture of Latin origin (*fica*, see Fornés and Puig 2008) in which the position of the fingers reproduces or at least resembles the morphology of the female genitalia. The gesture has had a very notable diffusion, and it is found throughout Europe (see Morris et al., 1979) and at least also in Spain and in Latin America (see Meo-Zilio and Mejía 1980–1983). The purpose of the gesture is varied: it can be a spell gesture (rejection of bad luck and attraction of good luck) but also a gesture of insult. Regarding the second case, Taylor's study is dedicated to the so-called Shanghai gesture (*pam and pipa* in Catalan). The origin of the gesture is related to the imitation of a fan, and with the basic purpose in this case of mockery. The Shanghai gesture is of the best documented throughout history, with multiple literary and pictorial references.

4.1.1 Illustrators or co-speech gestures and image schemas

Ekman and Friesen (1969) have pointed out that many illustrators give way to emblems (and the opposite, that some emblems can be used at certain moments as illustrators). The emblematic processes can be conceived, in many

cases, as processes of conventionalization of co-speech illustrator gestures which acquire full illocutionary force, i.e. a pragmatic value as an act based precisely on conventions and felicity conditions regarding the content of the act and the characteristics of producers and receivers (like in verbal speech acts). As the process advances, the gesture becomes increasingly autonomous, that is, more independent of the verbal language. The emblematization process would therefore involve a double subsidiary process (cf. Payrató 1993):
(a) A process of (social) conventionalization, which makes the gesture recognizable by a sociocultural group, with a particular illocutionary force, and, at the same time,
(b) A process of (semiotic) autonomy, which makes the gesture understandable without needing to be accompanied by speech.

Cases of this kind may include, for example, those for "drinking", "eating" or "smoking", which as emblems would come from the corresponding illustrator gestures based, ultimately, in the corresponding action (in the case of smoking also coincides with the adaptor gesture of holding a cigarette, see 4.1.2). As we have seen (2.4.2), gestures known as pragmatic gestures (Payrató and Tessendorf 2014) or recurring gestures (Ladewig 2014a), which can also display pragmatic functions (Bressem and Müller 2014a) are examples of items that can acquire emblematic functions and, over time, become prototypical emblems.

In many cases, it seems also clear that there are image schemes or mimetic schemas[3] that are found at the base of the origin of the emblem:
(a) In the handshape: the head as a CONTAINER (<III, 3/4>, <V, 6/7/8>, <VI, 8/9>, the fingers in PAIRING (<III, 7>, <V, 29/30>; <II, 5>).
(b) In the movement: PATH in deictic emblems and others (<I, 6/7, 14/15, 68, 80>, <II, 5>, <VII, 1/2>), CYCLE (<I, 40>, <I, 105/107>).
(c) In the forces: BALANCE (<I, 16>, <I, 17>), BLOCKAGE (<I, 8>), COUNTERFORCE (<I, 51>, <I, 91>).

---

3 Image schemes are represented in capitals. In addition to the classical work by Johnson (1987) and Lakoff (1987), see Croft and Cruse (2004) and Geeraerts and Cuykens (eds.) (2007), inter alia, for the concept of image schema. For gestures and images schemas, see Cienki (2005, 2013) and Mittelberg (2010). According to Cienki (2013: 190), "[s]chemas are an important tool we use to conceptualize, retain information about, and recognize physical aspects of the world that we perceive, allowing us to use this information for abstract thought, so it is no wonder that they figure prominently in cognitive linguistics theories and analyses". Cienki also refers to the theory of mimetic schemas (Zlatev 2007, 2008), based on bodily actions and the concept of mimesis (as representation of actions or objects using the body). Mimetic schemas are "more highly specified than image schemas in that they involve actions which human do, such as EAT, SIT, TAKE OUT, CRAWL" (Cienki 2013: 191).

(d) In usual, current body actions: some cited above (DRINK, <I, 22>; EAT, <I, 74>; SMOKE, <I, 60>), or other as CRY (<I, 82>), PHONE (<I, 101>) or those referring to stink (pinch your nose, <I, 90> or to throw a punch (<I, 11>).

Also in many cases we find combinations of various image schemes in the performance of emblems. For instance PATH and PAIRING are combined in the emblem for *caminar* ('to walk', <I, 30>) or in <II, 8> (see 5.5.3), and CENTER-PERIPHERY and CONTACT in the emblem for *molt ple* ('a lot/full', <I, 75>, <VI, 3>, <VII, 3>). Other combinations involve CONTAINER, CONTACT, and PAIRING in the emblems for *callar* ('to shut up') where the thumb and index fingers press the lips together (<II, 7>) or close them like a zipper. The emblem for *robar* ('to steal', <I, 93>, <VII, 13>) seems to be based on TO TAKE OUT and CLOSE/HIDE. In the emblem for *cardar* ('to fuck', <I, 33>, <IV, 14>) there are clear features of CONTAINER, CONTACT, FULL-EMPTY, PATH and CYCLE.

In conclusion, we can assume that image scheme and mimetic scheme can be very useful concepts to understand the origin of many emblems. Detailed cross-cultural studies of different repertoires remain to be done, in particular studies about the similarities and differences that these repertoires may present in terms of image schemas.

4.1.2 Affect displays, adaptors and regulators

Displays of internal states can become emblematic when used communicatively, that is, deliberately, ostensibly, to communicate a mood, or in pragmatic terms, with an illocutionary value of an expressive speech act. It is the citation – more or less pantomimed or theatricalized of an internal state – which turns the act from being simply emotional or expressive into an emblematic act, for example the emblem for 'crying' (<I, 82>, be it with literal or ironic meaning) from the action of rubbing one's eyes. In such cases, the concept of affect display comes together with the concept of *manner*, as established by Poyatos (see 2.1.1), and with an image schema as discussed in the previous subsection.

The best known cases in this domain are those of signs like the raising of the eyebrows and the smile. In the traditional ethological analysis by Eibl-Ebesfeld (1972, 1977), the first one is described as a universal signal that has a clear biological basis (and traceable in primates), and that later, with the historical becoming, it is particularized in different cultures, where it can signify from surprise to greetings. The smile, in turn, can be interpreted as a stylization (and as a *display*) of the gesture initially aggressive and threatening of showing one's teeth (see also <I, 25> Taunt (Tongue out), common in primates; see an illustration in <III, 5>).

The same emblematic process can take place in the case of adaptors, such as in the one for 'smoking' (<I, 60>), with the object adaptor (the cigarette) that becomes an emblem, acting recurrently as a declarative or assertive act ('to smoke', 'smoking'), or as a directive ('demand for smoking or a cigarette').[4]

It is possible that some emblems also come from regulatory gestures (according to the terminology of Ekman and Friesen 1969), but they have not been documented or cannot be proved convincingly that they are. However, the emblematic gesture of 'calm' (<I, 28>) could be a candidate, especially if we accept that, as its origin, the movement of the hands downwards could be based on taking the hands or arms of another so s/he composes him/herself, a type of regulator that is observable – at least with similar morphologies – in conversations with a high degree of involvement on the part of the partners.

4.1.3 Other sources. Gestural neologisms. Language origins

Some emblems are incorporated into the repertoires in a manner similar to loanwords or lexical calques, as genuine gestural neologisms. They may come from specialized repertoires, such as the "time" (of the "dead-time" in sport, mentioned in 2.3.5) or be based on objects and their actions ("cut", for example, imitating with the fingers the action of scissors) or in the letters of the words ("C" and "T" for coffee and tea, respectively).

Payrató (2008) presents examples of emblems linked to linguistic expressions, from which they originated (*barrut* in Catalan or *caradura* [cheeky] in Spanish, for example, see <I, 19>, <VIII, 13>), in contrast to emblems that are non-dependent of linguistic expressions (like the aforementioned "drinking" (<I, 22>, <VIII, 8>), "smoking" (<I, 60>), "eating" <I, 74>, <VIII, 15>, for example). As for the first, it is the linguistic expression that gives way to the emblem. In Spanish we have very recent examples of these processes, with expressions that have originated emblems (in groups of young people, primarily) such as *me parto [de la risa]* (literally 'I break up [laughing]', with the palm of the hand down and hitting the chest, as if

---

[4] The base of the emblem is the gesture adaptor of placing the fingers parallel in front of the mouth. It can also be considered as the "smoker" illustrator (as has been noted in the previous subsection) if one limits the movement of smoking to approaching and moving away rhythmically the hand from the lips. In the case of demand (for smoking, or for a cigarette), facial expression and head movement convey interrogation. For a different analysis, see Poggi (2014: 1485) and cf. 2.1.2 and 5.6.2.

one 'is splitting up', or *me mondo*, (literally 'I peel off myself') with a hand making some kind of twister over one's head, with the index stretching down, as if one were peeling a piece of fruit.

4.2 Variation and cultural distribution of emblems

If we extend the usual approaches of linguistic variation analysis to the domains of the knowledge and use of emblematic gestures, the factors that control it can be separated into two broad areas (see Payrató 2004):
(a) The dialectal domain, associated with permanent characteristics of the users, with three major sub-domains: the historical, the geographic and the social (or sociocultural).
(b) The functional domain, associated with variable characteristics of the users, particularly situational ones (also called stylistic). In this case, and in a simplified manner, the sub-domains involve the fields of communication (themes), the purposes (interactive or informative) and the degree of formality.

Whatever approach and background we choose in the analysis of the emblems, we must take into account that the variation of domain (a) is necessarily associated with that of domain (b), and vice versa, and that both types are given in any speech community.

Although we have seen above some references to the history of emblems, it is clear that the reconstruction of the repertoires of communities of the past is not easy, and the empirical samples that we have are very fragmentary and based only on written or artistic sources (pictorial ones, in particular). Nonetheless, we have valuable examples of classical repertoire studies, the oldest probably being Sittl's (1898) on the gestures of the Greeks and Romans. Fornés and Puig (2008) have also examined the history of a number of classic emblematic gestures, and have connected them with contemporary gestures: among others, for example the finger kiss (<I, 71>), the impudent finger (<I, 55>, <II, 3>, <IV, 12>, <V, 33>), the arm jerk (<I, 56>, <II, 2>, <V, 31>), or the fig (<II, 4>, <V, 32>).

In addition to this historical variation, which is very difficult to document and analyze, we discuss in the following sub-sections, on the one hand, aspects and factors related to geographical and sociocultural variation of some Catalan and Spanish emblems and, on the other, aspects related to functional and stylistic variation. In the case of dialectal variation, different kinds of (geographical, historical, and social) varieties and subvarieties can be distinguished, but the precise delimitation of each modality is an extremely difficult task. Indeed, dialectal linguistic variation (and possibly non-verbal variation) appears to be a continuum or, more precisely, several continua depending on the variables considered: the geography, the history, or the social base (which may in turn be made more specific if we talk about more particular (sub)variables like social class, cultural level, sex, generation, ethnic group or other). Poggi's (1983) work on *la mano a borsa*, Müller's (2014) on the ring-gestures across cultures and time, and Sherzer's and Brookes' ethnographic works (see 4.4.1) are excellent examples that illustrate the kind of studies that are needed (cf. also Müller et al. (eds.) 2014 for an overall view).

4.2.1 Emblems, culture, and linguistic variety

Throughout the book, we have underscored that the association between emblems and cultural environments, or habitats, is unavoidable and at the same time very intimate. However, certain gestures cover large territorial areas, while others are absolutely local and are no longer linked to languages (understood as standard and supra-dialectal varieties), but rather to specific sociocultural linguistic varieties (for example, young people, argots, etc.). Payrató (2008) described the first as "culture dependent emblems" and the latter as "language dependent emblems" (in the sense of *"variety* dependent emblems").

Among the emblematic gestures that cover large areas there are several possibilities:

(a) Emblems with a common historical origin, which have been disseminated for hundreds of years, as the classics already mentioned: fig (<II, 4>, <V, 32>, impudent finger (<I, 55>, <II, 3>, <IV, 12>, <V, 33>), horns (<IV, 18>, <VII, 10>, finger kiss (<I, 71>, <VI, 2>), etc. (cf. Morris et al. 1979, Fornés and Puig 2006, Müller 2014).

(b) Relatively recent emblems (particularly originating during the second half of the 20th century) that have spread because of the great power of the mass media. Audiovisual power has spread, for example, the use of the thumb up (<I, 21>) or the ring (<I, 20>) as "positive" signs of evaluation; the thumb up is also used as a greeting.

(c) Emblems that originate from a relatively common physiological basis (for example, the actions of drinking, eating, or smoking) and with a high degree of iconicity. The morphological variants are quite similar (they do not need to be the same ones, though) and are often emblems that can be recognized inter-culturally, for instance, the "suicide" emblem (in Catalan or Spanish, cf. <I, 100> and <VIII, 80>).

In many other emblems the level of iconicity is lower or much lower, and the cultural base is so specific that they cannot be recognized inter-culturally. There are often emblems that are linked to a linguistic construction (such as some of those mentioned in 4.1.3), and they are often not linked to an entire language but only to a specific linguistic variety. This is often the case of languages with very large linguistic domains, such as English, Spanish, Arabic, etc. For example, it is clear that the gestures studied by Saitz and Cervenka (1972) in the United States and Colombia are not common to the entirety of the English-speaking world, nor are they known in all the Spanish-speaking areas, respectively.

However, even in languages with a much smaller territory, as is the case with Catalan, the situation is similar. Typical emblems used in association with peninsular Catalan language should be carefully tested in the Balearic Islands, where the native language is also Catalan but developed in insular contexts, favoring special cultural features. In the territory of the so-called Northern Catalonia (currently part of the state of France[5]), speakers of Catalan use emblems associated with the French language and culture. In Alghero, island of Sardinia, Martí (1992) collects at least three cases of emblems typically associated with Italian that are also found in the communicative expression of native Catalan speakers of the island: the ear touch ('homosexual'), the cheek stroke ('handsome'; see Flachskampf 1938/1941) and the cheek screw ('very good', see Morris et al. 1979). All these examples are clear instances of emblems that do not depend on the linguistic variety, since we find them associated with Catalan, French, and Italian. They are instead "culture dependent" emblems.[6]

4.2.2 Multilingualism and emblem borrowings

Although there are some earlier references about the relationships between co-speech gestures and the language of bilingual (or multilingual) speakers (see Gullberg 2012, 2013), the question of the relationship between emblematic

---

[5] Catalan has progressively been replaced by French in this zone, but it is still spoken by many people (circa 300,000 speakers). These people maintain a bilingualism and biculturalism that are in some respects similar to those of Catalan/Spanish people.

[6] In more general terms, Kita (2009) identifies four factors related to the cross-cultural variation of gestures: culture-specific convention for form-meaning associations (very evident in the case of emblems); culture-specific spatial cognition (for example in the case of the deictics); linguistic differences; and pragmatic gestural culture-specific (principles that would control the use of gestures in communication).

repertoires and multilingualism has been under-examined.[7] Efron (1941) discusses it for the first time in a study that demonstrates the culturality of gestures, based precisely on the differences among symbolic gestures, as well as the mixing, over the successive generations of immigrants, of features of the co-speech gestures of different peoples or groups (Italians and Jews in the city of New York). However, we do not have comparative studies of the use of emblematic repertoires of bilingual speakers.

We have examples of transference (or interference) of emblems that can shed some light on the topic,[8] as the processes of transference of emblems between cultures provide an interesting case of cultural borrowing. Several examples can be adduced in the context of contact between Catalan and Spanish languages and cultures. For example, the emblem described in (1) is the Hispanic correlate to the emblem *barrut*, the traditional or genuine Catalan emblem.[9] In this case, the borrowing of a language-dependent emblem has been possible because of the previous or contemporary transfer of the verbal item (Sp. *caradura* as a generalized borrowing in Catalan), usually used as an interjection or insult:

(1) Cat. *ser un caradura, tenir la cara dura* (from Sp. *ser un caradura, tener la cara dura*, 'to have a nerve', literally 'to have a hard face'; Eng. 'to be a rotter/cheeky'). Description: palm lightly slaps cheek (for video see <VIII, 13>; for illustrations see Meo-Zilio and Mejía 1980–1983, or Payrató 1989).

Inversely, a Catalan gesture or, rather, a Catalan use of a traditional, widespread gesture (Eng. the nose thumb, the Shanghai gesture, discussed above) seems to have been borrowed in Spanish by the Argentinean people, as shown in the following example:

(2) Argentinean Sp. *hacer un/el pito catalán* (literally 'to do a/the Catalan whistle'; from Cat. *pam i pipa*, literally 'span/inch and pipe'; the gesture

---

[7] See for instance, the oldest one by Raffler-Engel (1971, 1976) and Lacroix and Rioux (1978). For later ones, see Kita (1990), Santi and Ruiz (1998) and Ussa and Ussa (2001). In Catalan, Fitó (2009) examines the multimodal deixis of Catalan-speaking and Spanish speaking youth in the corpus CAP (Corpus Audiovisual Multilingüe), in Catalan and Spanish as first languages, and English as a second language; see also Gullberg (2012, 2013) and specially Newbury (2011) on the Uruguayan-Brazilian border).
[8] The following fragments in this section are reproduced from Payrató (2008).
[9] It involves an emblem that is no longer used, but documented in the Balearic Islands: open hand with the thumb to one side and the rest of the fingers caressing the sides of the face with downward movements.

has no name in Spanish). Description: thumb placed on nose, with remaining fingers vertically extended and often wagging (for illustrations see <III, 6>, <V, 28>, Morris et al. 1979, Meo-Zilio and Mejía 1980–1983).

In this case, an old, well-known culture-dependent emblem has been attributed to another geographical region (as with the Shanghai gesture denomination in English). More information is needed to describe the exact influence that the (hypothetically very frequent) usage of the emblem in one area (Catalonia) can have exerted in the naming and the using of the emblem in another one (Argentina), probably due to the influence of immigrants.

The Catalan situation is very interesting because it combines a language with a rather small regional variation (at least compared with other Romance languages, such as Italian) with the fact that it is in contact with many different languages: with Spanish (in the Iberian Peninsula), with French (in Roussillon or Northern Catalonia), with Italian and Sardinian (in Alghero, Sardinia). So we find interesting combinations of languages and emblematic gestures, which reflect numerous cases of gestural and cultural interference on the one hand and the contrast between emblems that are language-dependent and those that are language independent on the other. For example, the case of *caradura* mentioned above clearly comes from Spanish and is intimately linked with the language. Catalan shares other language-dependent emblems with Spanish: for instance, the Catalan expression *fer el pilota* ('to flatter', simulating the bouncing of a ball), is completely unknown in other linguistic and cultural domains due to its dependency on phraseology (see 5.5.5).

If we take into account the entirety of the Mediterranean region, the head toss, a gesture of negation surely originating in Greece, is another excellent case study for analyzing features of the origin and historical development of emblems in the region, and also for comparing what may very probably be seen as (morphological and functional) variants of the gesture or related cases of family gesture resemblance.[10]

---

10 In Catalan and (Peninsular) Spanish, for example, negation can be conveyed (particularly categorical negation) with a gesture of a backward head movement (and often, sticking out tongue simultaneously). For more references on this type of negation, see next section (4.3.1 and note 71), and specially Harrison (2014b) for a recent synthesis.

4.3 Geographic distribution of emblems

The examples discussed above raise a question that has been studied at length and has a long tradition in the field of dialectology and linguistic geography: the possibility of widening the methodology of these disciplines to the study of emblematic gestures, and therefore to analyze the distribution of emblems from a geographic and cultural perspective.

4.3.1 Precedents. Emblems and classical dialectology

The inclusion of the gestural phenomenon in studies carried out from the perspective of dialectology and linguistic geography does not occur until the 20th century. Specifically, Danguitsis (1943) includes for the first time a section dedicated to gesture within a dialectological study.[11] The work is a clear example of dialectal monograph, with the peculiarity that, from pages 167 to 171, it offers a classification and explanation of the types of gestures of the Greek community that the author studied. It is a classification in which the pragmatic dimension is very evident, and in this sense it is surprising for its modernity:
(1) Gestures that accompany speech.
(2) Gestures that do not accompany speech (it is not wanted or one cannot speak).
(3) Gestures that accompany verbal expression and reinforces it.
(4) Gestures that express an individual's internal states.
(5) Gestures that support speech.
(6) Gestures that constitute a secret code.

The inclusion of gestural elements in dialectological maps will be found a few years later in the Swiss folklore atlas by Geiger and Weiss (1950), with a map on the distribution of gestures that are used to close a commercial exchange in the market,[12] and the pioneering study by Rohlfs (1959), with a letter (24) on the

---

[11] Constantin Danguitsis: *Étude descriptive du dialecte de Démirdési (Brousse, Asie Mineure.* Paris, G.-P. Maisonneuve, 1943 (Doctoral thesis presented at the Faculty of Arts of the University of Paris).

[12] Map I 111 covers the "Bräuche beim Kaufabschluss. Kauf von Vieh: Formel, Handslag", and therefore, the formulas and gestures that seal a sell-purchase transaction in the market. Question 51 elicits this formula and gesture: "Welche Formeln oder sonstigen Gebrräuche sind üblich beim Abschluss von Kauf und Verkauf von a) Vieh, b) Grundstücken, c) Häusern?" (page 680), specifically the answers to the first part of the question.

gesture of Greek or Greco-Eastern origin for negation, which has been mentioned in the previous section and which is presented below:

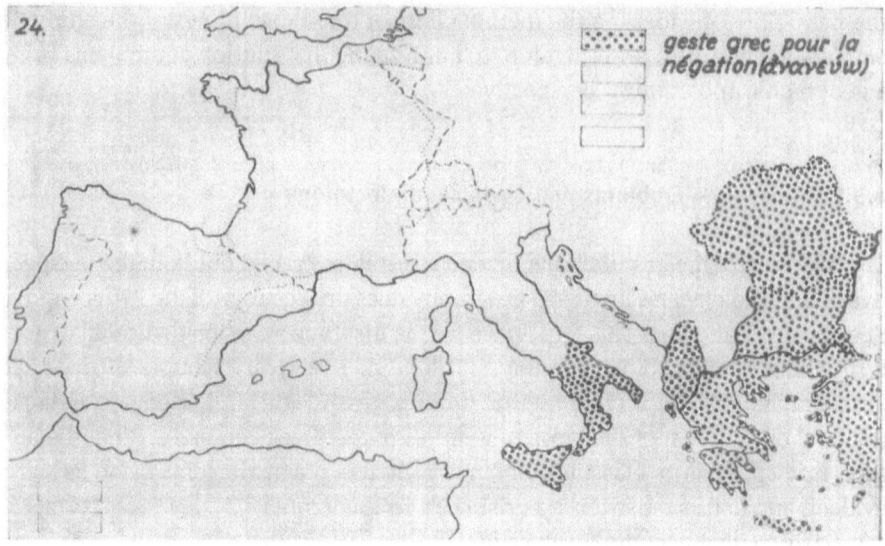

Figure 4.1: Spatial distribution of the Greek gesture for negation (Rohlfs 1959).

Rohlfs describes the map in the following terms:

> Pour terminer mon exposé, je vous présente un dernier tableau pris dans le domaine des gestes. On sait que chaque peuple dispose de certains mouvements du corps pour exprimer, sans mot dire, par un simple signe de la main, des doigts ou du visage une pensée ou une réponse. Or il y a des gestes de caractère international, et il y en a d'autres limités à un seul peuple ou à un groupe de peuples. Tout le monde [sic] connaît le geste, se manifestant par une secousse de la tête, avec lequel en Europe centrale et en Europe occidentale on exprime une négation. Or, tandis que ce mouvement de la tête est exécuté par un tournement circulaire en sens horizontal, dans toute l'Italie méridionale le geste de la négation s'exprime par un rejet de la tête vers l'arrière, en sens verticale. Ce geste est souvent accompagné d'un claquement de la langue. C'est le même signe qui, en fonction d'une négation, domine dans toute la Grèce, en Macédoine et en Albanie. Il est très fréquent parmi le bas peuple en Bulgarie et en Roumanie, et il représente l'unique geste employé pour la négation dans les terres du Proche Orient. Il n'y a pas de doute que ce geste très typique, qu'on a connu déjà dans l'antiquité sous la forme de l'ἀνανεύω, correspond à un usage grec ou grec-oriental. C'est peut-être l'expression la plus visible avec laquelle l'ancienne Hellade est toujours présente dans la mentalité de ces terres d'Italie qu'on a appelées autrefois la Grande Grèce. (Rohlfs (1959: 247)

To conclude my presentation, I would like to present to you a last map from the field of gestures. We know that each [folk] people has certain movements of the body to express a thought or give an answer, without saying a word, with a simple sign of the hand, fingers, or face. Nonetheless, there are gestures of an international character, and there are others that are limited to a single [folk] people or a group of peoples. Everyone [sic] is familiar with the gesture, consisting of a headshake, with which negation is expressed in Central Europe and Western Europe. Now, while this movement of the head is executed by a circular turn in a horizontal direction, the gesture of negation is expressed by throwing one's head back, in a vertical direction, in all southern Italy. This gesture is often accompanied by a clicking of the tongue. It is the same sign which, functioning as negation, dominates throughout Greece, Macedonia and Albania. It is very common among the low people in Bulgaria and Romania, and it represents the only gesture used for the negation in the lands of the Middle East. There is no doubt that this very typical gesture, already known in antiquity in the form of the ἀνανεύω, corresponds to a Greek or Eastern Greek usage. This is perhaps the most visible expression with which Ancient Hellas is still present in the mentality of these lands of Italy that which were once called Great Greece.

(Rohlfs (1959: 247))

The different gestural systems of affirmation and negation are the subject of additional studies from a dialectological or geographical perspective. Jakobson (1972) devoted a study to the "Motor Signs for 'Yes' and 'No'", published in the first issue of journal *Language in Society*. Vávra (1976) questions Jakobson's study, and in turn, Collet and Chilton (1981) questions Vávra's methodology. In the study by Morris et al. (1979), which will be discussed in the following subsection, the authors analyze this emblem (referred to as the head toss),[13] as well as a gestural boundary (a gesture isogloss, in this case) that the authors examine without reference to the one delineated by Rohlfs (1959) much earlier. The gestural boundary is located about twenty kilometers south of Rome and about fifty north of Naples, and runs through a strip of merely sixteen to twenty-one kilometers.

Following these studies, Kendon (2002) and Calbris (2011) have discussed the complexity of the negative (but also the positive, as a co-speech gesture) uses of the headshake. Furthermore, McClave (2000) and McClave et al. (2007) have analysed the linguistic functions of head movements in relation to speech and interculturally. More recently, Harrison (2014b) has made an excellent compendium, which takes into account the role of the headshake as a head movement related to "no", its variation in form and function, and its cultural distribution. In fact, the study of the emblems has frequently been carried out

---

13 Item number 13 of Morris et al.'s (1979) table is reproduced in Figure 4.3 of the following subsection. The name of the emblem is the head toss. Cf. also Flachskampf (1938/1941), Ferguson (1964), and Collet and Contarello (1987).

with similar or even analogous methods to those of linguistic fieldwork, and particularly dialectological. Cortelazzo (1969), in a classic dialectology handbook, probably the first one that includes a section on gesture, points out that:

> lo studio del gesto può correre parallelo a quello propiamente linguistico, gli stessi metodi, gli stessi richiami, le medesime partizioni. Se ne può studiare la propagazione, la semantica, l'etimologia secondo criteri del tutto analoghi. Il parallelismo è tale che l'applicazione de concetti (e termini) di una serie di fatti linguistici può essere senza difficoltà usata anche per i gesti. (Cortelazzo 1969: 268)

> the study of the gesture can run parallel to the strictly speaking linguistic one, the same methods, the same references, the same partitions. One can study the propagation, the semantics, the etymology according to completely analogous criteria. The parallelism is such that the application of concepts (and terms) of a series of linguistic facts can be easily used also for gestures. (Cortelazzo 1969: 268)

The *Atlas lingüístico-etnográfico de Colombia*, led by Luis Flórez, includes in volume III (1982) extensive information on greetings (welcome and farewell), address forms, gratitude formulas, and "gestures." Among these, the chapter on "Family – Life Cycle" includes maps and sheets for the following emblems:
– Gestures to indicate the height of a person (map 95 / sheet 102)
– Gestures to indicate the height of an animal
– Gestures to indicate stinginess (96/103)
– Gestures to indicate madness (97/104)
– Gestures to indicate money (98/105)
– Gestures to indicate a crowd of people (99/106)
– Gestures to indicate that someone is a thief (100/107)
– Gestures to indicate drunkenness (101/108)

Each sheet includes the drawings of the variants and the verbal description of the emblematic gestures, both the main ones and the less usual ones. The first two examples are especially interesting because of their deictic character (such as those described in section 2.3.3). In the case of indicating height of an animal, the hand is shaped flat and parallel to the ground, and to mark the height of a person, the hand is shaped perpendicular to the ground (cf. also Saitz and Cervenka 1972: 70 and Meo-Zilio and Mejía 1980–1983: II, 54–55). Meo-Zilio (1983: 305) also collects the case of the palm up, down, and to the side, to establish the human/non-human distinction, in countries such as Colombia and Ecuador. In other countries (Honduras, Mexico, Nicaragua) he describes a three-fold categorization: horizontally facing palm land (inanimate), horizontally lying palm on the ground (animate animal) and vertical corner palm (animate human).

Meo-Zilio and Mejía's (1980–3) study, published in the form of a Peninsular and American Spanish gesture dictionary, might be included in this line of work, since it provides information about the knowledge of the units throughout the countries in which the surveys were carried out, and by method similarities that are discussed in the introduction of the dictionary. However, the lack of mapping and comparative studies, as well as some methodological problems, such as the absence of information about informants, go against considering it as a geographic study of gesture or communication and anything more than a dictionary covering an extensive geographic area. We argue that for a study to be considered a geographic linguistic study of gesture, it should have the set of features that we discuss in the following section (cf. Payrató 2006 for the Catalan-speaking areas).

4.3.2 Gestural geography in Europe

To date, Morris et al.'s (1979) study comes closest to work what we would consider an accurate work of the linguistic geography of emblems. It is a very good example of the fact that, based on a study of a geographic area, valuable data can be obtained that clarifies not only the spatial distribution of a unit but also aspects related to its origin, its historical diffusion, and its gestural boundaries.

Morris et al. (1979) studied twenty emblems throughout forty European cities (including Tunisia, as the only exception). In each city, a random sample of thirty people (male adults) was selected in public places, and asked to answer a survey based on drawings of emblems (first, if the gesture is typical of the place and second, its meaning). The results obtained are quantified and shown in maps and tables. Figure 4.2 illustrates the forty locations, and Figure 4.3 illustrates the corresponding 20 gestures. Morris et al. prefer to use the denomination of *symbolic gestures*, rather than emblems, mainly because the sample selection eliminated emblems that represented actions that could easily be understood regardless of cultural factors (for example those corresponding to actions such as drinking, sleeping, eating, etc., in other words with a high degree of iconicity). In this fashion, the symbolic nature of the units was underscored.

The information collected by Morris et al. (1979) is of great value for its originality and novelty. The few works that preceded it, as discussed above, only examined highly partial aspects of gestural geography of a few emblems. The data collected by the authors make intercultural and contrasting studies possible, and, in turn, historical studies, in regards to the evolution of the units.

Figure 4.4 illustrates the case of the emblem 16 (the thump up), the use of which became widespread especially after the Second World War and

118 — 4 An ecological view on emblems

Figure 4.2: Locations sampled (Morris et al. 1979: xii).

Figure 4.3: Gestures and names (Morris et al. 1979: xxii–xxiii).

the second half of the 20th century. It is one of the emblems that has become more widespread and has achieved wider extension in the present day, but nevertheless the survey meanings associated with it vary greatly.

The lack of uniformity in the answers can be interpreted in some cases as a clue of some problems in Morris et al.'s work, which may have biased results. A first remark is whether European cultural diversity is adequately reflected. At least in the case of the Iberian Peninsula, the choice of only three points from north to south regardless of cultural and linguistic boundaries is very problematic. The same could be said about France and the former Yugoslavia (with only one city included). Italy receives comparatively excessive attention, becoming the most examined area with ten locations.

Along with these inaccuracies and shortcomings in the choice of locations, which causes the cultural and ethnographic base of the selection to fail, the

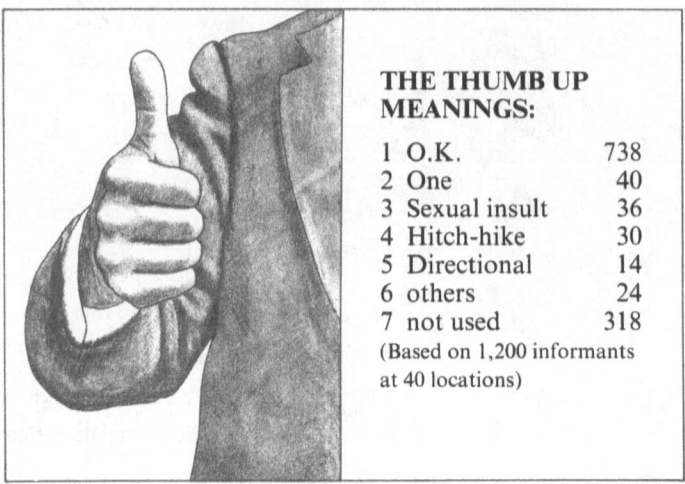

Figure 4.4: Results for the thumb up meanings (Morris et al. 1979: 186).

main problems are the methodological inaccuracies and the qualification of the results (in particular of frequencies) on one hand, and the confusion in the interpretation of some emblems on the other hand.

In regards to the first problem, the use of the labels "Relatively common," "Relatively rare" and "Absent" is very random. For example, a French location in the map of the hand purse (number 4) meaning 'fear' is included where the gesture is described as "relatively rare" (page 57) when, in fact, as shown in the table on page 59 (or in the final tables of the work, where numerical results are offered), only one person (among thirty) answered that he knew the gesture. If the map of the hand purse meaning 'lots' (page 58) is analyzed, the procedures used when mapping become even more surprising. In the Canary Islands and the city of Granada, the gesture is labeled as "Relatively common" with 6 and 8 productions, respectively, whereas it is described as "Relatively rare" with 4 responses in Lisbon (p. 59). The Canary Islands and Granada are equivalent, as such, to the city of Toledo (with 17 answers) and the city of Vitoria (with 16), which continue to be locations where the unit is labeled as "Relatively common" (p. 59).

The second problem is the confusion in the analysis of the meanings and the morphological aspects of the emblems. Although they are presented as a single unit, Morris et al. often mix different emblems, and the mixing in turn leads to the confusion of the informants. This seems the only plausible explanation of examples such as the following:

(1) On the map of the hand purse (number 4, page 56), the emblem appears with the meaning of 'good' in Spain, when it does not have it at all. The gesture was probably mixed up with number 1 (the fingertips kiss), with the meaning of 'excellent'.
(2) With the same configuration of the hand, and with the meaning of 'fear' (or exactly, in Catalan, of *culet*, literally in English 'little ass'), the emblem does not appear once in all Spain, when, although it is not a very common gesture, any speaker will recognize it without much difficulty if the context of elicitation is appropriate. The explanation of this confusion cannot be other than the fact that the gesture was not performed in an adequate way in front of the informants.
(3) The same explanation seems to apply to the low percentages obtained for the gesture with the meaning of 'many'. This gesture is a very frequent unit and recognized immediately by the informants, as long as it is done in the appropriate way (opening and closing the fingers of one hand and, often, of both hands).[14]

In conclusion, a detailed analysis of the tables raises serious questions about validity of some results, especially when it comes to different (semantically and functionally) gestures that are incorrectly included under one (single) similar morphology, or when an emblem is represented with an ambiguous drawing (for example the numbers 1, 6, 15 and 20).[15] Unfortunately, Morris et al. often leave out the fact the emblem is not constituted only by the final formal configuration

---

14 Cf. these two emblems in Appendix <VII>: 'fear' (<VII, 3>) and 'many' (<VII, 4>). A similar confusion can be found in the next citation, where the value of the hand purse is linked again to the meaning of 'a lot' in Spain, whereas the emblems are clearly different (cf. Morris et al. 1979: no. 4 for the hand purse and <VII, 3> for 'many'): "The meanings of emblems vary from place to place, even though the gesture form is the same. Each cultural region determines a meaning on its own. The Hand Purse is a clear case of such variation. There is no sensible connection among the 'query,' 'good,' or 'fear' meanings, and to these can be added 'slowly' (Tunisia), 'large quantity' (Spain), and 'emphasis' (Holland, Germany). This kind of wide variation among regions combined with stability of meaning in each region is possible only by conventions that are culturally reinforced." (McNeill 1992: 60). Throughout chapter 5 (cf. 5.1, 5.3 and 5.4), we argue that a principle of relevance should be taken into account to avoid all these possible confusions and misunderstandings in everyday interactions. In addition, the image schemas (see 4.1.1) which are found at the base of the origin of these emblems are different, they only coincide in the final phase of the stroke.
15 To avoid these errors, one can use a video recording. If it is not practical, the researcher can perform the emblem in front of the informant. Either option is better than showing a simple drawing. Other study errors could also have been avoided with a codification survey, which in addition always provides indirect data on the frequency of the units (information

of a movement (which is the one captured in drawings), but also by the previous and subsequent movements and the image schemas on which they are based. Such consideration would eliminate much confusion, for example, between the "food" emblems (shaking hands with the fingers in the form of a pear) and the one of "excellent" or "kissing the fingers" (number 1). The same can noted of the grouping under a single section (the last one, number 20) of two different gestural units – in terms of the movement, meaning, and use – such as the sign of victory (the "V") and the obscene sign of insult used only in Great Britain (equivalent to the impudent finger).

Regardless of inaccuracies and errors, Morris et al.'s work provides much valuable information as a whole, and of course, it invites a good number of questions about the emblematic repertoires that emerge from behind the maps, about their similarities and differences, and about the origin and dissemination of the units.

It is worth pointing out that only two of the twenty emblems studied (number 3, *pam i pipa* / Shanghai gesture, and number 9, the ring) were recognized by more than half of the informants throughout all locations. This corroborates the strongly cultural and local roots of these communicative forms, and also shows that the most widespread (in geography) units are those that present simultaneously fewer morphological and semantic variants.

The analysis of the areas with the most gestural affinities brings together – in broad strokes – the geographic areas that are closest to each other: Greece-Turkey, Spain-France-Italy, and Great Britain-Scandinavia. In this respect, the most serious problem in Morris et al.'s work is the highly reduced number of units that are examined. The consequence of this limitation is that the results must always be considered proportionally, and not, as it would be desired, as full repertoires of emblems of the respective locations or regions. The concept of gestural distance used by the authors (Morris et al. 1979: 260–262), and parallel to linguistic distance, presents, as in the so-called dialectometrics, multiple problems in terms of the selection criteria of elements to be contrasted.

In short, the work of Morris et al. (1979) is greatly innovative and without any subsequent study to date that has either followed or developed further the advances that their work represents.[16] Despite the abundance of inaccuracies, it constitutes an enormously stimulating step forward for research on emblematic units from a geographical and cultural perspective. This cross-linguistic

---

that is not found in a decodification survey). Kendon (1981a) discusses other limitations of Morris et al.'s study and raises interesting questions about its contents.

16 There are some studies that are worth being mentioned, such as Chauvin's (1999) analysis of children's games from a geo-linguistic perspective.

and cross-cultural comparative aspect becomes especially important in light of fruitful ethnographic and sociocultural studies of specific areas and communities that we discuss next.

4.4 Social distribution of emblems

The crucial complement of emblem studies from a geographical and regional perspective is an analysis that takes into account its sociocultural and pragmatic aspects observable in human interaction (see 5.6). However, there is not much in-depth research available in either case, whether interactional, sociocultural, or pragmatic.

As noted in the first chapter, there are precedents of ethnographic and cultural analysis, such as De Jorio's (1832) research on Italian emblems, and Mallery's (1881b) on the sign language of the American Indians, and especially, Efron's (1941) on Jews and Italians in the city of New York in the 20th century. Efron uses the methodological approach associated with modern ethnography, including filming, surveys, systematic observation, and a very high number of informants, as well as a rigorous and systematic contrastive data analysis. Efron robustly illustrates the main goal of his research, which is to demonstrate that gesture does not depend on genetic factors (as some anthropologists of Nazi affiliation had tried to prove) but rather on cultural roots.

Regarding strictly the social distribution in the knowledge and use of the emblems, we still have very little information, which often focuses on two aspects:
(a) The consideration of emblems in particular (and of gesture in general) as a practice to be discouraged (or at least its profusion), and
(b) The consideration of certain gestures as impolite or vulgar, which parallels the same "vulgarity" applied to the verbal elements that are associated with it.

In regards to the first aspect, we find a tendency of a general prejudice against gestures in many societies -or at least when used in excess- (see for instance Kendon 2004: 328). The prejudice is based on the (poor) argument that gesture harms the clarity of verbal expression. This consideration, however, is rather contradictory in the case of the emblems, since they can be envisaged as clearly and relevantly items in interaction (see 5.4 and 5.6). Nevertheless, the existence of social control over gestural use is undeniable, as Scheflen and Scheflen (1972) and Ellyson and Dovidio (eds.) (1985) have shown (cf. also Kendon 2004: 329). Social control is very visible and explicit when it comes to the control of the emotions, as it has been highlighted many times in the case – often too generalizing – of Asian societies.

In the second case it is also undeniable that people will refrain from gesturing for politeness reasons. For example, children are often advised or forbidden from pointing at people, because it is inappropriate to use deictic gestures to refer to other people, especially in formal contexts. Emblems with sexual content, on the other hand, whether insulting (exhortative) or assertive speech acts, are not considered "acceptable" in terms of politeness, because they are regarded as having an effect on the "face" or image of the other interlocutors. In her cross-cultural comparative synthesis, Brookes (2014b) illustrates in detail the complex and diverse relationships that are established between gesture and socially awkward, sensitive, and taboo topics.

With the exception of these general remarks, little is known about the social background of the emblems, which has been examined mostly as items of a strictly cultural origin. Social variation has been dismissed in benefit of cultural variation. However, we find some references to the social aspects of the gestures, particularly the classic works by Weiss (1943) and Barakat (1973). Specifically, Barakat (1973) discusses the social significance of emblems in his collection of Arab emblematic gestures. He also takes up emblem variation according to gender, which had been rarely studied explicitly in the context of non-verbal communication until the 1980s (see Vrugt and Kerksten 1984 and Vrugt 1987). For example, when studies contain remarks on the abundant use of emblems in Italy, it should be noted that such use is especially high among men (cf. the experimental and intercultural study of Scherer 1977). The same should be assumed in research on Catalan and Spanish, although we do not have gender studies that either confirm or challenge such assumption. The progressive diffusion and use of emblems of sexual content insult among women is also evident in Western societies, where it has ceased to be an exceptional practice.

On the other hand it seems quite obvious that there are also important generational changes, and that the loss of classic emblems, some with more than two thousand years of history and collected in dictionaries, such as the fig, is accompanied by the incorporation of new emblems under the influence of the mass media (i.e. the case of the thumb up, which has spread during the second half of the 20th century), or by the incorporation of gestural neologisms. For example, in the latter case, an emblem such as "I am breaking up (with laughter)", discussed in section 4.1.3, which is typical of Peninsular Spanish speakers, with the hand with the palm down hitting the chest, as if one "is splitting up", it is exclusively used by young generations at present, and it has not been extended among adults yet.

The concept of *habitus* (see Bourdieu 1977) seems to be appropriate to provide a first analysis of how emblems are used by different social groups, with internal influences such as sex, generation, social class, among other factors. To a large degree, it represents the resumption of classical conceptions such as Mauss' (1973) "body techniques" (he himself also speaks about social habits), and allows us to explain more accurately the diversity in the use of emblems, compared to analysis exclusivly based on cultural factors. Although he does not cite the concept of habitus, Meo-Zilio gives examples that illustrate this case in his collection of Latin America gestures, particularly in his assertion that hand configuration varies according to the status of the interlocutor:

> (a) [in Uruguay] el gesto correspondiente a *vení* (ven) se realiza con uno o más movimientos de los cuatro dedos apretados, *palma hacia abajo*; el que corresponde a *venga* (usted) se realiza, al contrario, con la *palma hacia arriba*. (Meo-Zilio 1983: 306)

> (b) Al dirigirse a un solo interlocutor, en Colombia, como en otros países, el gesto de *ven* o *venga* se realiza por el movimiento del solo índice (o también del índice y el medio simultáneamente) con punta hacia arriba y yema hacia el hablante (resto del puño cerrado), siempre que se trate de un superior dirigiéndose a un inferior. En la misma Colombia, cuando, en cambio, se trata de igual a igual este último gesto se realiza con la yema del índice hacia abajo. (Meo-Zilio 1983: 306)

> (a) [in Uruguay] the gesture corresponding to *come* [imperative, Latin American variant] (*come* [imperative, Peninsular variant]) is performed with one or more movements of the four fingers pressed, *palm downward*; the one corresponding to *come* (you [polite formal]) is produced, on the contrary, with the *palm upward*. (Meo-Zilio 1983: 306)

> (b) When addressing a single interlocutor, in Colombia, as in other countries, the gesture of *come* [neutral] or *come* [polite] is made by the movement of the single index [finger] (or also the index and the medium simultaneously) with the fingertip up and soft pad of the finger towards the speaker (rest in a closed fist), whenever it is a superior addressing to an inferior. In Colombia itself, when, on the other hand, when it involves from an equal to an equal, this last gesture is carried out with the index fingertip soft pad pointing downward. (Meo-Zilio 1983: 306)

There seems not to be similar distinctions associated with Peninsular Spanish. If there were, we would argue that these distinctions would be more closely associated with issues related to modality (ironical for example in the case of making the call gesture by only moving the index with the palm up). Meo-Zilio associates this gesture with attitudes of superiority (Colombia) and even of provocation (Mexico) in other cases and in some countries. He also associates hand configuration to internal states of the speaker, and consequently, he suggests these emblems can be used as pragmatic markers of (im)politeness (see 5.6).

4.4.1 Ethnographic analysis of emblems: A sample

Qualitative ethnographic research has made possible the study of emblems in their actual contexts, highlighting very accurately their semantic and pragmatic peculiarities (Sherzer 1973, 1991, 1993) and their processes of birth and spread (Brookes 2001, 2004, 2011).

Sherzer's work is an example of how ethnographic analysis captures the appropriate contextualization of the precise conditions of production and reception of an emblem, so that it can be analyzed with all the complexity required by its different meanings in different situational contexts. If we focus on the work of 1973, we will see how Sherzer analyzes the gesture reproduced in Figure 4.5, which is typical of the speakers Cuna de San Blas (Panama). Although at first it may be considered a deictic emblem (such as those treated in 2.3.3), in reality the description of the contexts of use shows that it is able to display up to nine different meanings (Table 4.1).

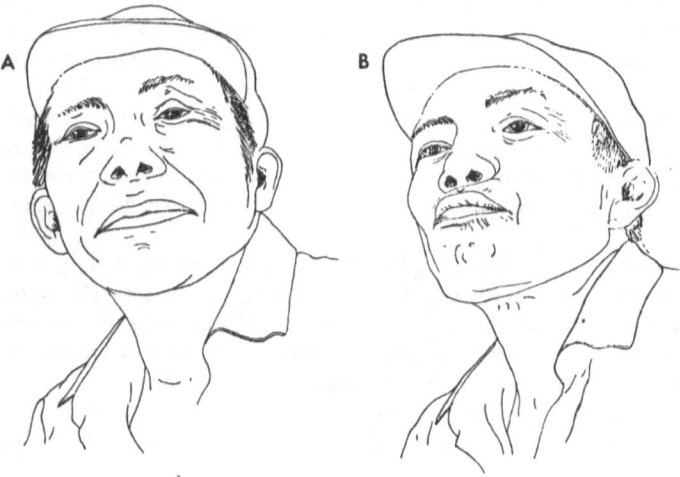

Figure 4.5: Illustration of the pointed-lip gesture (Sherzer 1973: 117).

Sherzer organizes these meanings in the form of a tree according to dichotomous criteria, as can be seen in Figure 4.6, and classifies the meanings of the gesture in Table 4.2.

Sherzer (1993) carries out a similar study in the case of Brazilian thumbs-up gesture (no. 16 in the work of Morris et al., 1979, cf. Figures 4.3 and 4.4). Brookes (2001, 2005, 2011, 2014a) has also offered excellent samples of how a rigorous ethnographic work provides important information to understand semantic and

Table 4.1: Meanings and contexts of the pointed-lip gesture (Sherzer 1973: 120–128).

(1) As part of a question involving direction or location, with or without verbal accompaniment.
(2) As part of an answer to a question involving direction or location, with or without verbal accompaniment.
(3) As a demonstrative element in a statement on information, a direction, or a command.
(4) During an event of any kind involving two individuals, one individual makes the pointed lip gesture toward the other. It seems as though the second individual is being made fun of or mocked by the first.
(5) During an event of any kind involving more than two individuals, one individual makes the pointed lip gesture towards a second, who may or may not be aware of its being made, for the benefit of a third or more. It seems as though the second individual is being made fun of or mocked.
(6) During an event of any kind involving more than two individuals, one individual makes the pointed lip gesture toward a second, who is not be aware of its being made, for the benefit of a third or more. It seems as though the unknowing individual is being made fun of or mocked.
(7) The pointed-lip gesture is used as a greeting between two individuals.
(8) Two individuals make the pointed-lip gesture to one another as a greeting. This reciprocal greeting takes on a jokingly insulting or mocking aspect.
(9) Two individuals in passing exchange a series of pointed-lip gestures as mocking greetings.

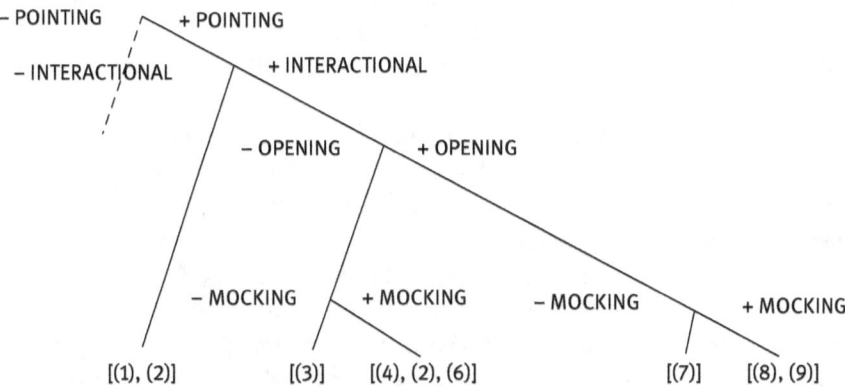

Figure 4.6: Relationship between the meanings of the pointed-lip gesture (Sherzer 1973: 130).

Table 4.2: Classification of the meanings of the pointed-lip gesture according to dichotomous criteria (Sherzer 1973: 130).

	I	IIA			IIB		IIIA		IIIB
	(1)	(2)	(3)	(4)	(5)	(6)	(7)	(8)	(9)
Pointing	+	+	+	+	+	+	+	+	+
Interactional		+	+	+	+	+	+	+	+
Opening		−	−	−	−		+	+	+
Mocking		−	+	+	+	−		+	+

pragmatic details of the use of emblems or quotable gestures. In Brookes (2001), the author relies on Sherzer's analysis of the thumbs-up gesture and applies it to examine the multiples uses and meanings of the Clever gesture among urban young black (mostly men) dwellers of townships surrounding central Johannesburg in South Africa. Brookes' video recordings of everyday emblems *in situ* are innovative in that the emblems she micro-analyzes are not found in retrospective descriptive/narrative recalls elicited through interviews, but instead they are emblems produced by one participant for another participant with a specific communicative goal and to get something done. Furthermore, Brookes (2005) also innovates methodologically by handing over the video-recorder to one participant so he can record his own everyday conversations, and by providing detailed transcripts of the simultaneous and coordinated production of emblems and talk, a recurrent method in co-speech gesture analysis, but fairly new when it comes to emblem research. Brookes uncovers the polysemy of the Clever gesture that is usually glossed as 'streetwise' and 'city' slick but a meaning ranging from 'he's streetwise', 'I want to see you', 'Be alert', 'Watch out', and to 'You are being watched', and 'I see you'. Although even more variation occurs because of changes in the shape/performance and of the position of the emblem vis-à-vis talk and other gestures, Brookes argues there is a semantic-pragmatic commonality around the action of "seeing."

As she develops her argument here and in other articles, Brookes connects the emergence and use of emblems such as the Clever gesture to identity, in particular to the modern urban African identity of young black township dwellers who construct themselves as taking on a progressive and integrative identity not associated with rural, ethnic, and tribal-based identities. In Brookes (2004), she illustrates how the production of emblems is tied to social signification, as emblems are part of bodily management within the articulation of a

male identity and of subcultural styles. Her detailed ethnographic study of quotable gestures in everyday interactions leads her to argue the following:
(1) the situated function of an emblem is key to its classification over semantic-lexical and form criteria;
(2) categorical classifications that sharply distinguish different types of gestures hide many continuities among gestures, as well as the birth, development, widening or narrowing shifts of meaning and function; see for instance, her examination of taboo, cf. Brookes (2014b) and of the quotable gesture *Amangama amathathu*, 'the three letters' in the context of a tremendously high rate of HIV/AIDS-related mortality (Brookes 2011); and
(3) beyond a narrow communicative purpose perspective, emblems constitute also a visual medium of self-expression, creativity, stylization, and aesthetics.

4.4.2 A background for the ethnographic research on emblems

The analysis of emblems and the study of their interpretation and their organization are never built on a vacuum. Any study is based on a set of assumptions which outline the communicative model and the sociocultural frames that serves as a reference points. The following are the assumptions and the background of this kind which we propose as the starting point for the research on emblems:[17]
(1) From a sociolinguistic point of view, as usually represented in the ethnography of communication, *speakers* are members of a *speech community*. From a sociopragmatic, holistic perspective, we can stipulate that *communicators* (including gesture producers) are members of a (particular, non exclusive)[18] *communicative* community.
(2) A communicative community is conceivable as a social space of communication (or *habitat*) based on the establishment and maintenance of social networks and identities (a *communicative ecosystem*). Specific interactions are culturally and socially bound within this kind of *habitat* and *ecosystem*, which we can interpret in the usual, biological sense of the terms.
(3) Emblem repertoires are subject to dialectal variation (geographical, historical, and social) and to functional variation (situational, stylistic). Consequently,

---

[17] This section builds on and expands Payrató (2003).
[18] The term "non-exclusive" refers to the fact that a speaker may belong to multiple speech communities simultanously.

repertoires of emblems must be conceived and described paying attention to both their sociocultural and functional/stylistic frames of usage.

4.4.3 Everyday emblems in Catalonia: An example

Ethnographic research involving participant observation and video-recording of interactions makes it possible to study the semantic and pragmatic properties of emblems, as well as to study gestures more generally as part of multimodal embodied assemblages, which participants construct meaning and carry out actions in situated, moment-by-moment interactions (Mondada 2016). In an ethnographic study of the communicative practices of a group of pediatric cancer patients, their parents, and healthcare professionals at a hospital in Catalonia (Spain), Clemente (2015) identified children's and adults' gestures within multimodal courses of action during routine medical interactions. Two of these gestures constitute well-known and documented emblems: vertical nodding to assent (see Appendix <I, 4>, <VI, 1>, and Figure 4.7) and the hitting of a vertical hand against the bottom a horizontal hand to indicate the action of leaving hastily, escaping, or fledging (see <I, 59>, and Figures 4.8 and 4.9). The vertical head nod affirmation gesture is well documented also across many languages and cultures (see Morris et al. 1979 and section 4.3.1) while the gesture for 'leaving hastily' has been documented in Catalan and Spanish (see for instance the Spanish emblem *nos vamos / me piro* ('Let's go/I'm off') in the newspaper the Guardian's collection of Spanish gestures).[19]

If we look at the situated interactive organization within which these two Catalan emblems occur, a pediatric oncologist is finishing her daily hospital round visit with Gemma, a 15-year old girl with metastatic bone cancer. Gemma is lying in her hospital bed with her father, a second doctor, and a nurse who stands right below the camera (see Figure 4.7). The positioning of the camera only makes visible the back of the pediatric oncologist, who stands near the foot of Gemma's bed; Gemma's father is partially visible; and the nurse who stands right below the camera is out of frame. All participants are looking at Gemma, while Gemma faces the pediatric oncologist and only looks at her.

Gemma has been hospitalized for about three weeks. A recent surgery had weakened her already chemotherapy-compromised immune system. But she has not had a fever over the last few days and, finally, going home is on the horizon. As the pediatric oncologist closes the visit, she proposes that if the

---

19 See https://www.theguardian.com/travel/series/learn-spanish.

4.4 Social distribution of emblems — 131

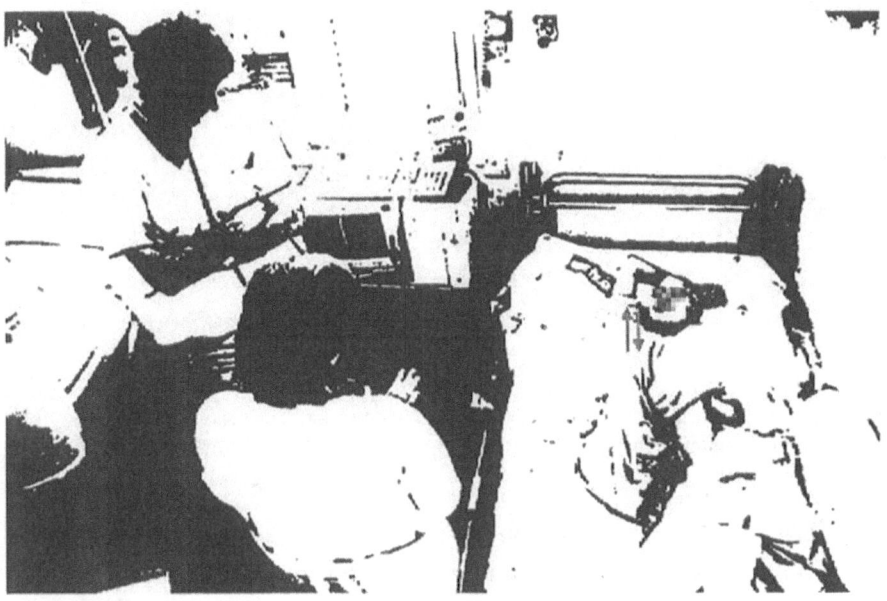

Figure 4.7: Gemma, a 15-year old girl with cancer, tilts her head back while lying in bed.

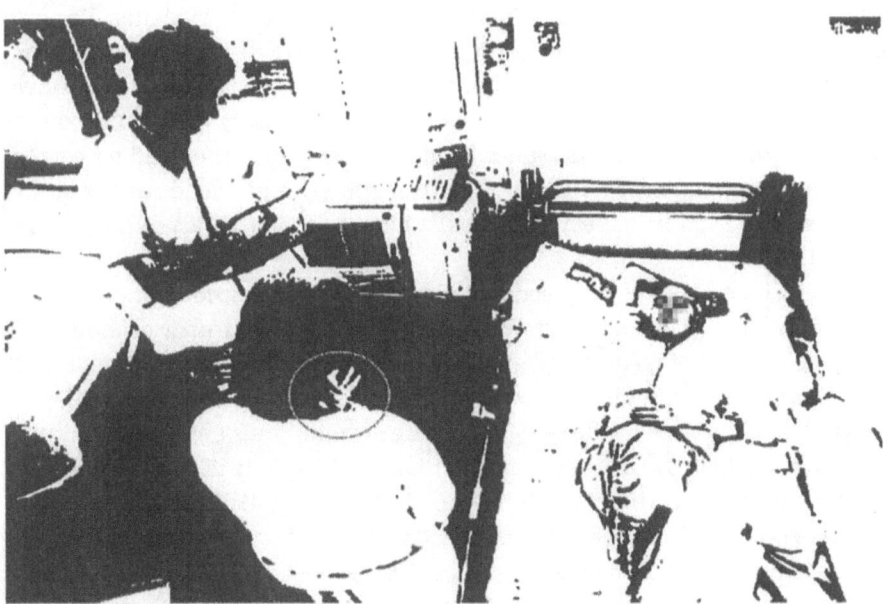

Figure 4.8: A pediatric oncologist produces the emblem 'leaving/escaping/fledging' as she says *i cap a casa* (lit. 'and to home').

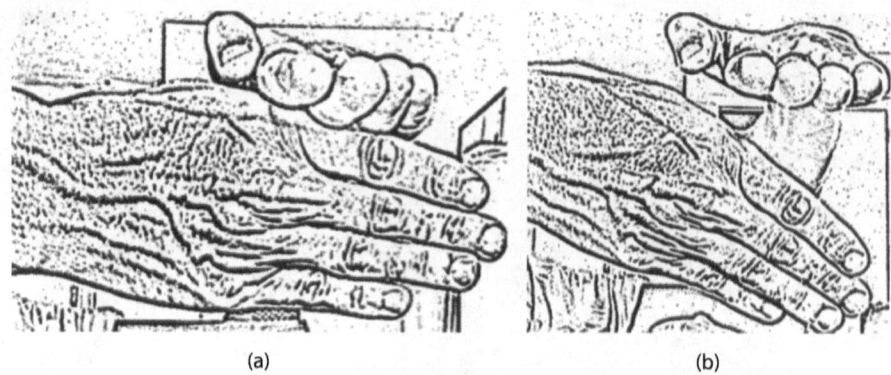

Figure 4.9: Hand configurations in the Catalan and Spanish emblem for leaving hastily/ escaping /fledging (cf. also <II, 1>, Morris et al. 1979: 94, and Payrató 1989/1991: 339).

blood test results confirm that the fever has indeed stopped, they will finish the antibiotic treatment, which is the first step towards Gemma's hospital discharge to go home. The doctor seeks Gemma's agreement with the proposed course of events by asking in Catalan *d'acord, senyoreta?* ('okay, young lady?'). Gemma responds non-verbally by producing an affirmation head emblem: she nods three times with small head movements. Because she is lying in a horizontal position with her head resting over her arm, Gemma's head nod is slightly different when compared to the head movement that an individual standing up would produce (<I, 4>, <VI, 1>). Rather than lowering and then raising her head, Gemma begins the head movement by tilting her head backward and then forward. With her head resting on her arm, the most visible aspect of Gemma's head nods is the raising and lowering of the chin.

This first emblem is followed quite immediately by a second one. The doctor produces an utterance that combines an emblem with talk, each of them carrying a different meaning (Figure 4.8). She says *i cap a casa* (literal 'and to home,' non-literal 'and home') while producing simultaneously the emblem of leaving hastily/escaping/fledging by hitting several times her right hand held vertically against the bottom of her left hand which is held horizontally (see Figure 4.9; cf. <II, 1>, Morris et al. 1979: 94, and Payrató 1989/1991: 339).

This is a mixed syntactic and multimodal construction, with clear resonances with concepts such as Slama-Cazacu's (1976) "mixed syntax," Janney's (1987) "intergrammar," and Enfield (2009) "composite utterances." Specifically, the gestural action of the leaving hastily/escaping/fledging is accompanied by a verbal locative indicating the place for which the patient will be leaving as soon as she can. The gestural and verbal components together produce the overall meaning of "(you) leave quickly to go home." Furthermore, the situated combination of talk and emblem reduces the overall polysemy and multi-functionality of the emblem, which could also be interpreted as "being ready" in addition to the meanings of leaving hastily, escaping, or fledging (Payrató 1989/1991: 339) and also different types of action, as we have seen in Sherzer's analysis of the pointed lip and the thumb up gestures, and Brookes' analysis of 'clever.'

The example also illustrates how without a theory like relevance, it is difficult to explain the assignment of referents to a gesture. Let us note, for instance, that without knowing what is happening and of the previous context, the subject of the gesture could be the doctor (who goes home once the patient is well). However, the most relevant interpretation – more enriching and clearly the one that demands less processing effort – is that it will be the patient who can leave.

In the same line of argument, we could also state that the affirmation head nod is performative, since the emblem is the action in itself, as we would find in the equivalent verbal of saying "yes." However, this is not the case for the emblem of leaving hastily: the patient is the one who will leave hastily after being discharged. We could also consider that the doctor adopts the point of view of the patient (Character View Point or C-VPT, McNeill 1992) with the meaning of 'I leave hastily' or adopts an observer view point (O-VPT) with the meaning 'you leave hastily.' In the latter interpretation, the emblem has clearly an exhortative component, but it could also be considered as simply assertive or representative.

In addition to illustrating the integration of emblems as part of the overall construction of meaning and action in multimodal turns, these emblems also illustrate the types of action for which emblems are recurrently used to carry out. As we describe in more detail the examination of the meaning and functional distribution of emblems in section 5.6, the (mostly) exhortative emblem of "leaving hastily" is used to change the recipient's behavior and the emblem of affirmation head nod is a gesture used to express one's physical or mental state. As such, they represent two of the three most common categories of emblems found in repertoires (Kendon 1981a, Payrató 1993): interpersonal control and expressions of one's condition.

Throughout chapter 4, we have examined different forms of variation associated with emblems from an ecological perspective that complement the theoretical efforts to categorize them in chapter 2 and the taxonomical methodologies to catalog them in gesture dictionaries and repertoires (chapter 3). In addition to a discussion of their origins and historical evolution, this chapter has focused on the cultural, linguistic, and geographic distribution of emblems. The last part of the chapter has explored the social distribution of emblems, with particular attention to the semantic and pragmatic variation of emblems when analyzed within the situated context of production and interpretation. To complete a "holistic" multidisciplinary perspective on the study of emblematic gestures, we turn to analyze their cognitive and interactive aspects in the next chapter.

5 The cognitive and interactive dimensions of emblems

5.1 Variants and repertoires: What does "the same emblem" (exactly) mean?

The determination of gestural variants is one of the problems that commonly arise in the process of establishing the repertoire of emblematic gestures that can be associated with a sociocultural group.[1] Sometimes even to stipulate what we conceive as two (or more) variants of the same emblem or as two (or more) different emblems are no easy tasks. In other words, and to put it simply: what does 'the same emblem' mean?

This well-known fact reproduces in the non-verbal dimension the old lexical, semantic question of synonymy, polysemy, and homonymy in the verbal codes. For a few years now, this problem has been reanalyzed in the light of new cognitive theories applied to language, and the new approach brings some interesting cues to solve – or at least to revisit – the problem.

The application of cognitive linguistic theories to the analysis of emblems allows us to re-assess certain phenomena and to try to explain some of their paradoxes and obscure points:
(a) the conception and delimitation of emblematic units (and morphological variation),
(b) the coordinated production of speech and emblems,
(c) their interpretation (as a matter of relevance),
(d) their direct or indirect (non-literal) or their natural/non-natural meaning (and multimodal tropes),
(e) and more generally, the overall processes of emblematization and conventionalization of these units that parallel the similar processes of lexicalization and grammaticalization of linguistic units.

Moreover, a cognitive approach makes possible a global explanation of many aspects of verbal and non-verbal communication together. In this way, it breaks the verbal/nonverbal dichotomy, which can be handy shortcut for analysts but it is sometimes artificial and not well founded in empirical facts.

---

[1] A part of this section and the following one are updated versions of work included in Payrató (2003), which has been reviewed and modified (summarized in some cases and expanded in others).

5.1.1 Introduction: Assumptions and basic questions for the research

We argue that emblematic gesture research greatly benefits from widening its perspective to include cognitive and interactional approaches, in addition to the sociocultural and ethnographic approaches that we have discussed in the previous chapter (see 4.4). Consequently, some assumptions must be added to the ones formulated in chapter 4, a first that is specifically pragmatic, a second that is pragmatic and structural, and a third and fourth that have a cognitive basis:

(a) Communicators have at their disposal common multimodal repertoires of units (emblems), which they perform in a contextualized way according to their needs, intentions, and communicative goals (this assumption is developed in sections 5.2 and 5.6).
(b) The organization of units within the repertoires reflects the functional nature of the units (as seen in detail in the Sherzer's example in 4.4.1; cf. also next section, 5.2).
(c) The establishment of repertoires (5.1.2) and the contextual interpretation of emblems (5.3) depend on the same cognitive principles that govern the overall cognitive and communicative activity, for which a principle of relevance is needed (5.4).
(d) As verbal units (words and utterances) are (cognitive) *constructions* where a phonological form is associated with a semantic form (merging sound and meaning), emblematic gestures are also constructions in which a gestural form is associated with a (recurrent, systematic) meaning. Operations and tropes involved in the formation of these associations are the same as those involved in verbal constructions (5.5).

From these assumptions, at least two basic, initial questions can be asked about how emblems have to be selected and categorized in repertoires. The first one is related to units and repertories, and it can be put in a very simple way: (i) *how are emblematic units organized?* The second one is from the perspective of speakers or communicators, and it can also be posed simply: (ii) *how are emblematic units interpreted?* All the possible answers to the (i) and (ii) questions rely on the answer to a still more basic, previous question, the issue of classification of gestures. Also to put it simply: (iii) *what does "the same emblem" mean?*

An obvious remark is that here we must revisit the *taxonomical* problem that arises in the elaboration of any repertoire of gestures or emblems (see chapter 3). Question (iii), the most fundamental one, could be reformulated in a different number of alternative questions, all linked to the same central point,

5.1 Variants and repertoires: What does "the same emblem" (exactly) mean? — 137

the relation between two or more instances (gestural utterances, tokens or performances) and the concept of *category* (or *class*), and possibly *subcategories* (or *subclasses*): (iv) *when can two or more instances be considered as different units?* And the complementary question is: (v) *when can two or more instances be considered as variants of the same unit?*

In the following section, different and similar emblems from the repertoire established for the contemporary Catalan of Barcelona (cf. 3.5. and Appendix I) are considered to exemplify and answer these questions.

5.1.2 Filtering samples: Interpreting items to elaborate repertoires

The traditional answer to the taxonomical problem in research on emblems and repertoires has been to choose the semantic contents of the gestures and their formal performance as the criteria for separating variants of what was considered "the same" unit. This procedure is founded on the well-known, structuralist distinction between meaning and form (or *signified* and *signifier*). If we take these criteria into account, we can show some examples of (more or less related) emblems according to their semantic and/or formal resemblance. Prime examples (in brackets) were not included as emblems (or different emblems) in the original repertoire, and are added now to illustrate the discussion:[2]

(A1) *Very similar meaning/usage and very similar shape*
    (1) Apropar-se ("Vine!"). **To approach ("Come here!")**. Extended fingers fold to downturned palm (<I, 14>, <VII, 2>).
    (2) Apropar-se ("Vine!"). **To approach ("Come here!")**. Extended fingers fold to upturned palm (<I, 15>, VII, 1>).

(A2) *Similar meaning/usage and very similar shape*
    (3) Llegir. **To read**. Open hands together before body (<I, 69>, <II, 9>).
    (4) Llegir (Mirar). **To read (To look at)**. Open hand held before body (<I, 70>, <VII, 11>).

---

2 These examples also come from the repertoires established in Payrató (1989/1991), which were discussed in chapter 3 and in previous sections of chapter 4. The full basic repertoire of Payrató (1989/1991) is included in Appendix I. Similar cases are reported in the discussion of Morris et al.'s (1979) confusions in section 4.3.2 of the present book. Examples (1)/(2), (15)/(16), (17)/(18), (19)/(20) and (22) can also be checked in Morris et al. (1979). Example (7) was considered as a secondary variant of <I, 77> in Payrató (1989/1991). Examples (10) and (10′) were considered as the same item for the sake of clarity, although the metaphor involved is different (see 5.5.2).

(5) Prou (Final). **Enough (End)**. Palm down, hands held side by side separate laterally (<I, 88>, <VI, 10>, <VII, 12>, Payrató 1989/1991: 289).
(6) Prou (Final, Res). **Enough (End, Nothing)**. Upheld hands side by side separate laterally (<I, 89>, Payrató 1989/1991: 290).

(A3) *No similar meaning/usage and very similar shape*
  (7) Negativa. **Negative**. Open hand moves from side to side (cf. Meo-Zilio and Mejía 1980–1983: no. 24.4, and moving to side to side).
  (8) Salutació/comiat. **Greeting**. Open hand moves from side to side (<VII, 14>).
  (9) Cardar (Fotre). **To fuck (To fuck up)**. Arms in skiing position in pulling motion (<I, 34>, <V, 41>).
  [(9') Esquiar. **To ski**. Pantomime of skiing.]

(B1) *Very similar meaning/usage and similar shape*
  (10) Boig (Bogeria). **Mad (Madness)**. Index finger rotates at temple (<I, 23>, <III, 3>, <VI, 8>).
  [(10') Boig (Bogeria). **Mad (Madness)**. Index finger taps temple (<I, 23>, <III, 4>, <VI, 9>)].

(B2) *Similar meaning/usage and similar shape*
  (11) Aproximadament (Dubte, Desconeixement). **Approximately (Doubt, Ignorance)**. Side to side motion with head (<I, 16>, <VI, 7>).
  (12) Aproximadament (Regular). **Approximately (Regular)**. Flat hand undulates side to side (<I, 17>, <VI, 6>).

(B3) *No similar meaning/usage and similar shape*
  (13) Adulador. **Toady**. Flat hand moves up and down (<I, 2>, <VII, 9>).
  (14) Calma. **Calm**. Open hands, palms down, move up and down (<I, 28>, Meo-Zilio and Mejía 1980–1983: no. 34).
  (15) Cabró. **Cuckold**. Index and small finger extended upwards (<I, 27>, <V, 42>).
  (16) Conjur. **Conjuration**. Index and small finger extended horizontally (<V, 1>, <VII, 10>).

(C1) *Very similar meaning/usage and no similar shape*
  (17) Bé (Perfecte, "D'acord!"). **All right (perfect, "O.K.!")**. Index finger and thumb form circle (<I, 20>, Morris et al. 1979: 100).
  (18) Bé (Perfecte, "D'acord!"). **All right (perfect, "O.K.!")**. Thumb extended upwards from fist (<I, 21>, Morris et al. 1979: 186).

5.1 Variants and repertoires: What does "the same emblem" (exactly) mean? —— 139

(C2) *Similar meaning/usage and no similar shape*
(19) Fot-et (Dit impúdic). **Fuck you (Raised finger)**. Extend middle finger from fist (<I, 55>, <II, 3>).
(20) Fot-et (Botifarra). **Fuck you (Forearm jerk)**. Bend one arm while slapping its biceps with the other hand (<I, 56>, <II, 2>).

(C3) *No similar meaning/usage and no similar shape*
(21) Robar. **To steal**. Fingers rotate and fold (<I, 93>, <V, 23>, <VII, 13>).
(22) Victòria. **Victory**. Index and middle finger form a V (<I, 103>, cf. Morris et al. 1979: 234).

The combination of semantic and formal criteria succeeds easily in separating cases like those of C3 (21 and 22), where we have two emblems without any relation, and also in the case of what are often called morphological variants: examples (1) and (2), from (A1), or the two variants, (10) and (10′), in (B1). These are the two extremes of the continuum (A1/B1 – C3) that the previous list of emblems represents.

However, problems arise in many other cases, very similar to those which have been studied in traditional linguistics as synonymy (cf. pairs of (A2), (B2) and (C2)) or homonymy (cf. pairs of (A3) and (B3)). In fact, it is very difficult to say if pairs of examples like those included in (A2), (B2) and (C2) should be considered as the same unit. The semantics and the formal appearance are only "similar" in a non-defined way, so we do not have a good criterion for making the classification, and it is somewhat arbitrary to decide if there is a simple unit (with subclasses) or different classes. In cases like those of (A3) and (B3) another problem arises, which is the (very different) interpretation of very similar gestures in shape. We highlight the significance of this problem in the previous review of Morris et al.'s work (1979) in section 4.3.2.

To configure a repertoire, problems of this type that derive from emblem (sub) categorization can be resolved only if we analyze more accurately how emblems are interpreted, with a procedure such as Sherzer's (1977) (or the "anatomy of meaning" proposed by Enfield 2009). As illustrated in section 4.4.1, following Sherzer's procedure, each possible variant of the emblem is made to correspond to a precise and differentiated meaning. The process of emblem interpretation (cf. 5.3 and 5.4) shows the following characteristics:

(a) It is based first and foremost on the identification of a symbolic association between a form and a meaning (as in the case of linguistic items), and this association constitutes a special type of *construction*, where the two parts are inseparable. The identification relies on a categorization of the emblems as prototypes (and not as traditional categories), and on entities that are

connected through the concept of family resemblance. Therefore the variants can only be reduced when taking into account whether they are more or less prototypical (more or less frequent, known and accessible).
(b) The actual process of interpretation depends on the situational context of the interaction: it is pragmatic in the most consistent sense of the term. The interpretation of an emblem in terms of its inclusion in a repertoire requires a process of abstraction, and this abstracted interpretation can only be established because a (prototypical) emblem has undergone a process of conventionalization and social diffusion, has become an idealized exemplar, and has been associated to specific situational contexts of production/reception.
(c) The interpretation process is only supported and understandable if we conceive that it is guided by a principle of relevance (in communicative and cognitive terms), based on attributing communicative value to a gesture (as an interactive act, with a high degree of salience) as well as illocutionary value (as a speech act, with an optimal degree of relevance).

The first characteristic (a) is the most basic. As is the case of a linguistic sign, the emblem functions as an entity with two aspects: it is a symbolic association between a meaning and a movement of the body. The clarification of its variants and of inter-emblematic differences can be carried out based on the concepts of prototype/exemplar and family resemblance (see 5.2.2). The more conventional the association has been made, and the more frequent use the sign has, the easier it will be recognized. In other words, the more progress or advance along an emblematization spectrum, the more prototypical the emblem is (see 5.2.1). Such emblem will be produced and recognized more quickly, will be the first to be acquired, and so forth and so on.

The second characteristic (b) explicates how the same form – the same signifier, in structuralist terms – can mean different things in different contexts, in other words, the polisemy of emblems (cf. Figure 4.4 in section 4.3.2 and section 5.3). For instance, the raised-up thumb emblem (see Morris et al. 1979) can acquire different concrete meanings according to the specific situational context as a greeting or an approval sign. In a similar fashion, some insult emblems can also be used as conjuration gestures (see 2.3.4), just as different metaphors can have the same gesture configuration, as is the case in the emblem for "scissors," understood as 'cutting' or 'criticizing' (see 5.5.2).

The third characteristic (c) contends that the overall meaning of the emblematic gesture cannot be understood and interpreted appropriately without a principle of relevance (Sperber and Wilson 1986 [1995], see 5.4). This principle controls operations such as the reference assignments, the concretion of semantic core, and the literal or non-literal interpretation of the gesture. In brief, the principle guides all the inferential stages that are needed in the global process of the interpretation of the emblem. In this process it is fundamental that the communicative character of the gesture (which is assured by its salience or prominence) is recognized and that an illocutionary force is given to the action (which will be interpreted as a demand, an assertion, a jury, etc.).

All these characteristics are analyzed in more detail in the following sections, and also exemplified in other specific contexts (see 5.2–5.6).

5.2 The emblematic web: Organization of emblems within a repertoire

We assume that emblems as units and their overall repertoire reflect the functional nature of these kinds of communicative signs. Emblems are here understood as a category of gestures similar to that of verbal interjections, designed to encapsulate different messages in a very autonomous way (cf. 2.4.3). Assuming also that most emblems proceed from another gestural category, that of *illustrators* in Ekman and Friesen's (1969) taxonomy or *co-speech gestures* in other classifications (cf. McNeill 1992, Müller at al. (eds.) 2013, 2014), and in general from purpose-built body movements (see Posner 2003, cf. 4.1.1), what is most important in the holistic, communicative interaction is not the precise shape of the emblem (its standard of form), but the process of local emblematization that takes place in the situational context. This semiotic process is re-created every time and always regulated by relevance (see 5.3 below for a detailed explanation). The process also represents the (very narrow) separation line between pantomime and emblems, and when it is linked to a process of (social) conventionalization, it can be conceived as the genesis of a social, well-established emblem in a community. As in the case of verbal utterances, the process of conventionalization also involves the acquisition of illocutionary force, so the emblem can be used in a way that is totally equivalent to a speech (verbal) act.

The diversity of this kind of process and the inherent diversity of communities lead to diffused and blurred repertoires of emblems. Their contours are not precisely defined, nor are the relations between the units. Two related models can represent these relations: the prototypical model and the family resemblance model.[3]

---

[3] The prototype theory and the theory of family resemblance are well known inside the cognitive approach to categorization. The former is based on the seminal works of Eleanor Rosch, and the latter on the works of Wittgenstein; cf. Kleiber (1990), Croft and Cruse (2004), and Geeraerts and Cuykens (eds.) (2007), inter alia, and what has been discussed in section 2.1.1.

5.2.1 The prototypical model: Emblems as symbolic associations

The prototypical model is useful to describe and explain many instances such as clear morphological variants: the prototypical emblem brings together the most representative features of all the related signs, and as exemplar is the most widespread, usual and well-recognized item among all the partners. An actual emblem is the prototype (or is *more* prototypical than any other) in the same sense that a cow is a prototypical mammal (much more than a whale or a platypus). Prototypical emblematic gestures are autonomous and quotable (in the sense of Kendon's works), sometimes have names, and correspond to what is usually called the *basic level* of categorization of beings, objects or events: an intermediate level (i.e. *dog*) between a higher one (i.e. *animal*), the supraordinate level, and the more specific one (i.e. *bobtail*), the subordinate level.

For instance, in the case of insult gestures like those of (C2), the prototypical raised finger or the prototypical forearm jerk is (morphologically) different in each community. This kind of prototypicity can be shown through one of the two ways that are presented in Figure 5.1.

In the diagrams in Figure 5.1, *P* represents the exemplar of a prototypical emblem (such as the forearm jerk or the raised finger) and *a*, *b*, *c*, and *d* its morphological variants. For instance, the prototypical forearm jerk in Catalonia, briefly described, is made with the left hand on the right biceps, frontally and with the fingers closed on the right fist. However, a large number of variants are also performed in this community, the majority of them recorded and described by Morris et al. (1979: 87–88): upward jerk, multiple upward jerk, forward jerk, diagonal jerk, cryptic forearm jerk, miniature forearm jerk, abbreviated forearm jerk, and simplified forearm jerk. The prototypical raised finger emblem is made with the middle finger, but there are other variants: bent middle finger, raised index finger, or bent index finger. As it has been noted above, the emblematic gesture consists of a symbolic association between a (gestural) form and a meaning, and this association must be conventional. If this conventionalization is achieved, the original association (form-meaning) will become an emblem proper, and there will be more or less prototypical morphological variants, that will have more – or less – characteristic features from a set of possibilities.

What the classical prototypical model does not seem to explain or clarify is the connection between morphologically distinct units (or "sufficiently different" to not be considered as merely variants) but which nonetheless present a clear connection in terms of the meaning and functions they carry out, for instance the kind of relation between the forearm jerk and the raised finger. The two gestures have sometimes been considered as the same unit, i.e. as two subclasses of the same category (for instance, Amades 1953 for Catalan; see

5.2 The emblematic web: Organization of emblems within a repertoire — 143

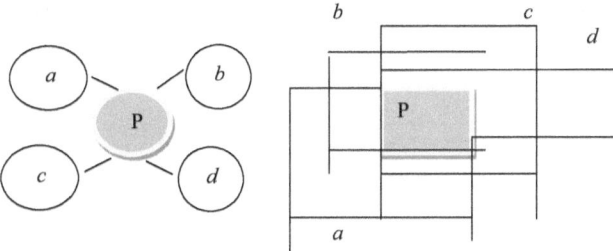

Figure 5.1: Diagrams or graphs of prototypical emblems and morphological variants (Payrató 2003).

also the discussion in Morris et al. 1979). However, there are no clear reasons for accepting or rejecting this (intriguing) supposition. In fact, although we might admit that the meaning and the usage of the two items is "very similar" (a supposition that merits further discussion), the formal similarity between the two gestures seems limited. We may well be on the threshold of what is usually regarded as *sufficient* formal dissimilarity for postulating two different units or categories (with a parallel meaning and usage, i.e. a kind of gestural synonymy).

The case presented is very similar to that of other pairs of emblems, for which probably nobody would defend a background unity. For instance, widespread appraisal gestures like (17) and (18), the "O.K." gesture and the thumb up or the emblems for demanding silence or for rejection (see next section). The relations between these emblems, like those between many others, are not well accounted for in terms of prototypicity, as a kind of mathematical function depending on sharing more or less typical features. Instead, this relation seems very close to what in some cognitive models is presented as the concept of family resemblance.

5.2.2 The family resemblance model

The family resemblance model differs from the classical prototype/exemplar model in not presupposing that there is a unique, prototypical, most representative unit or exemplar on the top or at the center of the variants. From this viewpoint, any item can be considered as a particular (sub)class, and the category has to be conceived at a higher level. The criterion of family resemblance is precisely what allows, in turn, putting forward the concept of a gesture family.[4]

---

[4] The gesture family concept, outlined for emblems in Payrató (2003), can be (re)found in Kendon (2004) and especially in Müller et al. (eds.) (2013, 2014). As discussed in section 2.4.2,

The model can be presented in a simple and linear diagrammatical way as in Figure 5.2.

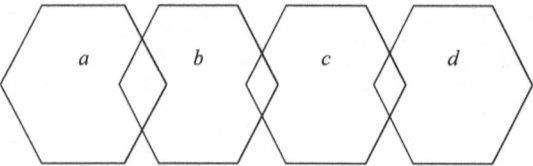

Figure 5.2: Linear diagram of a family resemblance model for related emblems (Payrató 2003).

The space of intersection between the links of the chain represents both the formal and the semantic similarity of the items, in other words, their shared features. Different chains could be depicted to match units with their pragmatic function, as more or less conventional, as sociocultural communicative tools at the service of communicators in communicative ecosystems (see 4.4.2). Some examples of emblems discussed before can now be presented as family resemblance models. They are presented in Figures 5.3, 5.4, and 5.5 going from the simplest to the most complex.[5]

The model of family resemblance applied to emblematic repertoires allows for a description of links between many connected emblems that cannot be reduced to a simple prototypical relation. We should note that historical, chronological or genetic (i.e. one gesture derived from another one) relationships between emblems are not taken into account in this approach. The relation between the items is formulated according to a synchronic, current view that communicators have with regard to the meaning, usage and shape of the emblems,

---

Kendon (2004: 227) refers to families of gestures as "groupings of gestural expressions that have in common one or more kinesic of formational characteristics."

5 The space of intersection between the units is represented now by lines in the diagrams for reasons of simplicity and clarity. If the diagrams could be depicted in a three dimensional way, they would offer a more precise image of the many-sided bonds suggested among the emblematic items. The thickness of the connection lines is proportional to the semantic and formal similarity between the items, where two degrees are distinguished. Dashed lines indicate few formal or semantic similarities. The central and upper hexagons represent the most prototypical examples of the entire diagram, and in turn each hexagon represents the most prototypical exemplar of each group of variants (formal, emphatic, iterative, intensive, combining items, etc.). The furthest and weakest connections have not been indicated so as not to complicate excessively the diagram. The more variants we introduce the more complex the diagram becomes (see for this particular case Meo-Zilio and Mejía 1980–1983: no. 36).

5.2 The emblematic web: Organization of emblems within a repertoire — 145

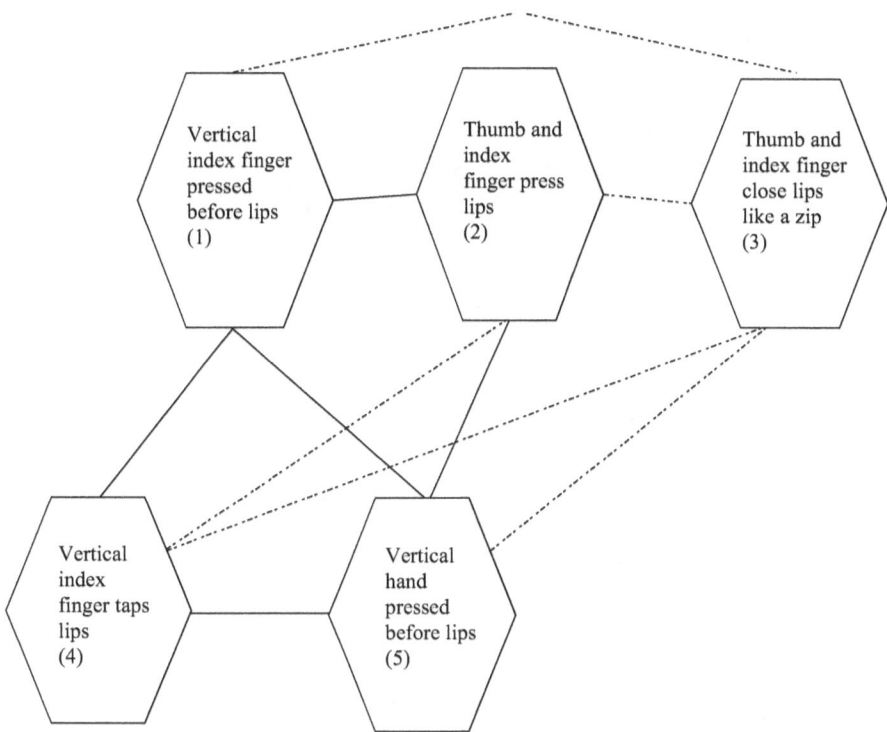

Figure 5.3: The family resemblance model and the categorization of emblems in the repertoire: the case of the request for silence (one person asks another to be quiet). Emblems: (1) ‹1, 96›. (2) ‹II, 72›, Payrató (1989/1991: 364). (3) Payrató (1989/1991: 363), Meo-Zilio and Mejía (1980–1983: no. 36.7). (4) ‹I, 96› (intensive variant). (5) Payrató (1989/1991: 417), Meo-Zilio and Mejía (1980–1983: no. 36.1).

which can be analyzed with precision following the model of Sherzer's and Brookes' ethnographic works, as seen in section 4.4.1. Genetic relations, for instance the possibility that the forearm jerk might be, chronologically, an enhanced version of the raised finger, as suggested by Morris et al. (1979) are irrelevant from a synchronic perspective, as the fact that Catalan *càtedra* ('chair', 'professorship') or *cadira* ('chair', 'seat') are relative words, from the same original lexical item in Latin (and Greek). The family resemblance model explains more accurately the multiple variants and differing standard, so as to present the emblems as pragmatic resources at the service of members of a community. These resources are deployed in communicative interaction with many different nuances that depend on each one particular context (see also more generally Enfield 2009 and the case of "composite utterances").

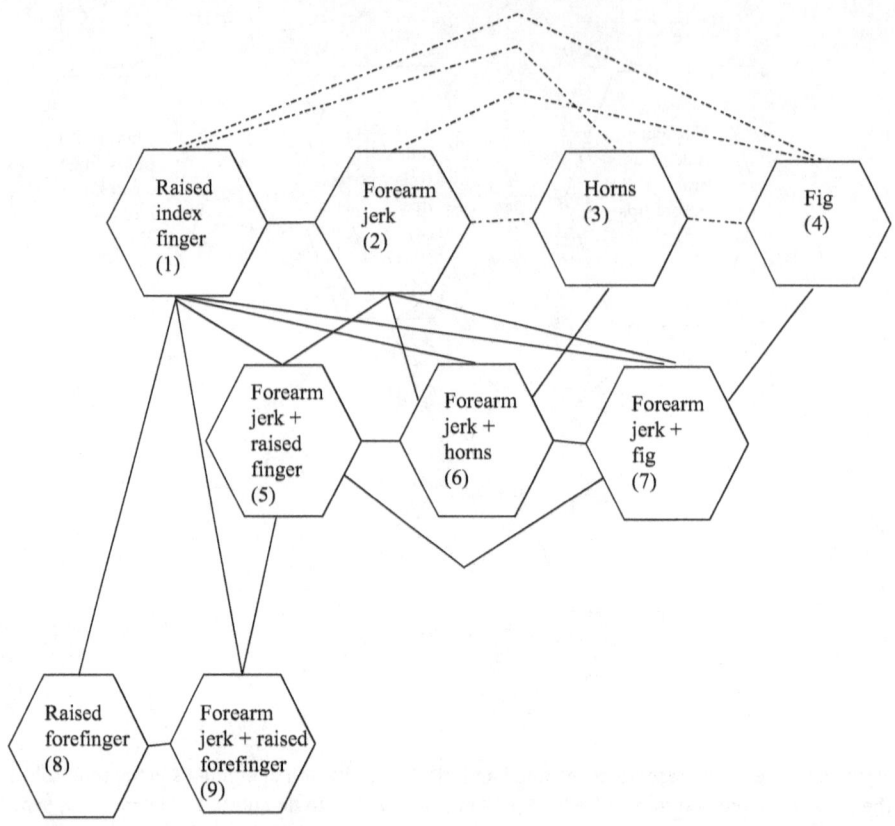

Figure 5.4: The family resemblance model and the organization of emblems in the repertoire: the case of aggressive behaviour or insult (one person insults another) (Payrató 2003). Emblems: (1) <I, 55>. (2) <I, 56>. (3) <I, 27>. (4) Morris et al. (1979: 148). (5) Morris et al. (1979: 88). (6) Morris et al. (1979: 88). (7) Morris et al. (1979: 88). (8) Amades (1959: 118, 1). (9) Morris et al. (1979: 88).

Prototypical and family resemblance models do not solve all the questions related to the taxonomical trouble of gestures and emblems in particular, and many issues should still be posed – for instance the precise complementary or supplementary criteria for separating some morphological variants (subject to prototypical relations) and different members of the same emblematic family. However, at least they offer a new, potentially useful perspective on the traditional, and lexicographic procedures of classifying emblematic units. Now, these perspectives should be completed with some remarks on the process of interpretation of emblems by communicators in specific situational contexts.

5.3 The interpretation of emblems: From context through relevance — 147

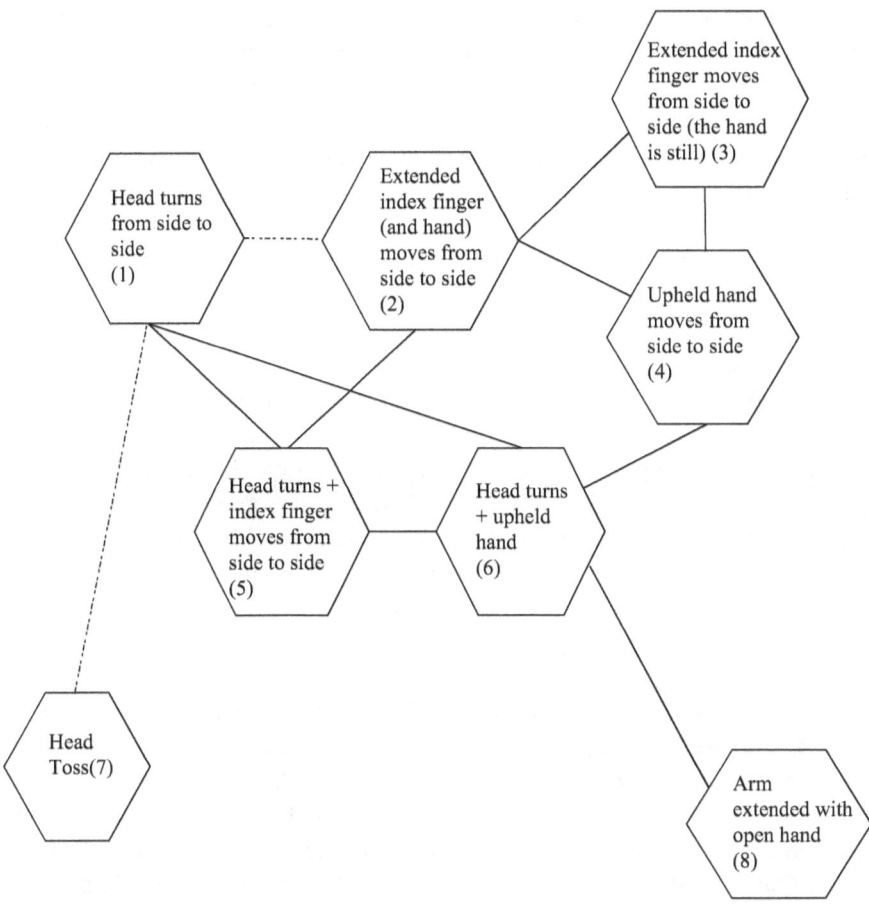

Figure 5.5: The family resemblance model and the categorization of emblems in the repertoire; the case of refusal/rejection (one person refuses another's demand). Emblems: <I, 76>; (2) <I, 77>; (3) Meo-Zilio and Mejía (1980–1983: no. 159.3); (4) See Meo-Zilio and Mejía (1980–1983: no. 24.4), and the hand moves from side to side. (5) Meo-Zilio and Mejía (1989–1983: no. 159.4). (6) Combination of <I, 76> and Meo-Zilio and Mejía (1980–1983: no. 24.4). (7) Morris et al. (1979: 162). (8) Meo-Zilio and Mejía (1980–1983: no. 24.4).

5.3 The interpretation of emblems: From context through relevance

In this section, we propose specific pragmatic principles that explicate the processes of emblematic gesture interpretation. Our proposed principles have been developed from the general traits that must be present for the process of emblem interpretation to take place –and which we have discussed relying on a small sample in section 5.1.2– as well as from our preceding discussion of the ways in which relations may be established among emblematic repertoire units.

The process of interpretation of an emblem can be conceived as the same interpretative process that takes place when people interpret other typical signs embedded in casual communicative activity. In particular, and resting on economic and common sense reasons applied to cognitive processes, we propose that the interpretation of emblems should follow at least the following four principles, ordered from the most specific to the most general:

(i) Holistic principle: emblems are interpreted as a whole, different from the simple additions of their parts.
(ii) Contextual principle: emblems are interpreted contextually, as units embedded in situational, interactional sequences.
(iii) Communicative principle: emblems are interpreted as communicative (intentional and deliberate) acts provided with illocutionary force.
(iv) Relevance principle: emblems are interpreted according to principles of relevance (Sperber and Wilson 1986 [1995]), as a combination of two factors:
   (a) Maximization of the effect on the mental environment.
   (b) Minimization of the processing cost.

Emblems are commonly recognized as verbal or quasi-verbal items. As we have seen, the terminology that we find in the literature testifies to this qualification (*autonomous gestures, quotable gestures, semiotic gestures, folkloric* or *symbolic gestures, conventional gestures, quasiverbales* ...). The definition of emblems also constantly refers to their capacity to emulate or substitute words and utterances. Consequently, it is not unreasonable to suppose that economic processing reasons imply that the interpretation of emblems is (very) similar to the interpretation of words and utterances. In the process of interpretation, at least one common phase should be proposed to permit a joint analysis of verbal and nonverbal meaning, and some kind of central processor must coordinate the process, independently of the obvious fact that the informational input is gathered and transmitted by different channels.

From this view, there seems to be no point in proposing different mechanisms in the interpretation of verbal and nonverbal utterances, so the process must be guided by some common principles, such as the ones adduced above. Let's see how they can be applied to specific case of examples (a), (b) and (c)/(d) in Figure 5.6, which are related to the well-known insult of the impudent finger (see <I, 55>, <II, 3>, <IV, 12>). Example (a) comes from a printed sign poster advertising of a Spanish movie, whereas (b) is an ambiguous example of a photograph of featuring a wedding ring that an artist uploaded to Instagram; we will see that

5.3 The interpretation of emblems: From context through relevance —— 149

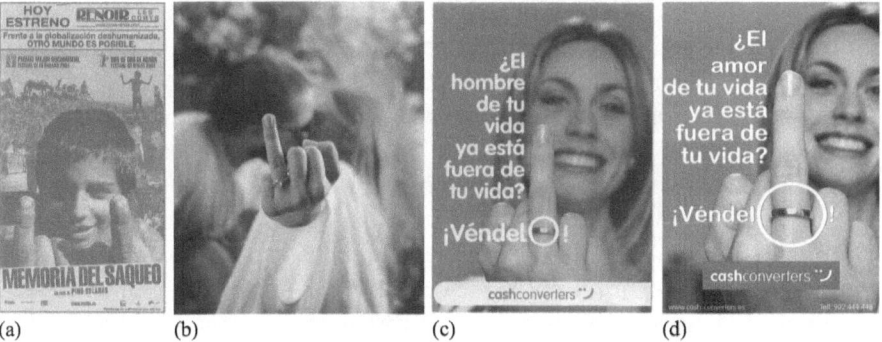

(a) (b) (c) (d)

Figure 5.6: Film advertisement (a), ambiguous photograph (b), and buy and sell store advertisements (c) and (d), which are related to the impudent finger emblem (cf. <I, 55>, <II, 3> and <IV, 12> in Appendices). Illustration (a) is from Payrató (2013a), and illustrations (c) and (d) are from Payrató (2013b). Illustration (b) is from actress Margot Robbie's Instagram account.

all of the previous principles cannot be applied to it. Examples (c) and (d) are two versions of a complex case that clearly illustrate how one cannot understand them without resorting to principles such as relevance. In these latter examples, a woman shows a wedding ring while simultaneously making the impudent finger emblem, and which is accompanied with a written text suggesting that she is selling the ring: if the man of her life (or the love of her life, in a second more politically correct version) is no longer in her life, the best she can do is to sell the ring (and with it, it is implied, to get rid altogether of the man or person who gave it her and the bad memories associated with the ring and the person).

The four principles apply to the interpretation of these examples:
(i) The holistic principle recognizes that emblems are multimodal signs, symbolic clusters or gestalts of different features performed at the same time: manual, facial, vocal, and verbal traits. Specifically in the case of (a) and (c)/(d) these are manual and facial. There is apparently no reason to limit emblems to manual gestures: some facial expressions present the same characteristics as manual emblems. Besides, facial expression does not act as the nonverbal context (or *cotext*) of the emblem, but as a component of the emblem, in the same sense that intonation (or vocal, nonverbal features) is a component of a verbal utterance. In the case of (a) and (c)/(d), facial expression is clearly key: a rather threatening one in (a) and a big smile in (c)/(d). In case (b) facial expression is not available because the photograph only presents the manual component, and it is one of the reasons that makes the case ambiguous or difficult to be interpreted. All the components

of the communicative act are cues to guide the interpretation of the sign, for instance as irony, sarcasm, or in general as an item with a non-natural, non-literal meaning, as illustrated by (c)/(d).

(ii) The contextual principle states that emblems can only be interpreted as embedded or inserted signals in actual interactional sequences, in which different kinds of emblematization processes (similar to those of pantomime) are possible. An emblem is the result of an emblematization process that initially takes place in specific situational contexts, and which can reach the final phase of a process of sociocultural conventionalization (following dissemination channels like those of verbal neologisms). Obviously, what we have in the examples above are not cases of interaction but images that capture the emblem (or its stroke or central phase, to be precise). While in (a) and (c)/(d) this context is sufficient – at least if we participate in the same cultural background – in (b) the contextual principle fails: we do not have enough information to interpret the gesture, although we know – as a minimal contextualization – that it is an actress who displays (we do not know if in a derogatory way) her wedding ring.

(iii) The communicative principle holds that emblems are produced and interpreted as ostensive stimuli in the context of interaction. As the literature on emblems has stressed since its beginnings, the emblem is a deliberate sign. Consequently, an informative goal must underlie this kind of *display* (understood in the ethological sense, see 4). Through the emblem, a person encapsulates some information for another person, and displays an illocutionary force analogous to that of the speech acts performed by verbal utterances. This is clearly seen in all four cases, in which we can assume that there is a very clear attempt to communicate something, but in (b) we do not know if it is a purely descriptive or deictic use ("show") or if something else is being suggested.

(iv) Finally, the relevance principle states that emblems must properly be accounted for on the basis of an inferential theory of communication. Emblems cannot be accounted for only on the basis of a communicative model centered on the codes, which fails to explain the relation between the formal mechanisms and their interpretation (high number of variants, synonymy, polysemy, loose standards of form, metaphorical uses, irony, sarcasm ...). Assuming that relevance is the main property of the inferential processes involved in the communicative activity, and as will be developed in more detail in the next section, emblems can be considered as gestural items of optimal relevance: they synthesize through a minimum cost-effective non-verbal mechanism, a maximum of propositional and interactional information (their 'meaning', their illocutionary force) in communicative processes.

This is again evident in (a), and in a literal way, not figurative: it is an emblem of an obscene nature that acts as a directive speech act, with a perlocutory effect of insult, as an insult directly addressed to the receiver. Instead, the failure of the contextual principle (2) does not allow us to interpret the photography of (b) with full guarantees. There are two potential interpretations that the image of a ring worn in the middle finger does not disambiguate. Whereas the impudent finger is performed with the middle finger, the wedding ring is usually worn in the ring finger. If we interpret that there is an insult gesture, it is because we associate the (middle) finger in which the ring is worn here with the exemplar or prototype of the impudent finger emblem. We can even find relevance that justifies the interpretation and the unusual use of the finger to wear the ring: maybe the actress is tired of photos and questions about her wedding. However, if we interpret that it is simply a finger showing a ring, there is no more to say: it is a descriptive use, as if it were a citation, no more and no less. Finally, in (c) / (d) the relevance becomes indispensable. First, it is necessary to identify the referents and understand the message or "enriched" propositional content that is conveyed here (the pragmatic technical term used by relevance theory would be *explicature*). Second, there is an inference that completes the interpretation of the message in a relevant way: amplifying our cognitive context as much as possible, and as well as requiring simultaneously the lowest possible processing cost. In this case, the most relevant interpretation is that the lady is happy (smiling) to make a profit (to sell a ring) that symbolizes a relationship with a person that is no longer "the love of her life", that of the woman in the advertising or, by analogy the person who is reading the advertisement.

To summarize, from this perspective and with a cognitive conceptualization, emblems (also known as autonomous, quotable, or emblematic gestures) can be considered (a) as members of categories defined by prototypical relations and family resemblance, (b) which are holistically, contextually interpreted, (c) as communicative acts (d) according to principles of relevance. Obviously, further research on emblems and their repertoires should revisit this *re-visitation* in order to broaden our still limited knowledge of the organization, categorization and interpretation of this kind of communicative act. Next, we will take a closer look at the last point, specifying aspects related to relevance in more detail.

5.4 Relevance: Common principles and processes in verbal / non-verbal communication

The conception we propose rests on the idea that a notion of relevance is indispensable to deal with the avalanche of verbal and non-verbal information that we receive constantly and is presented in an interrelated way. There is a need for a clear criterion that separates the elements that constitute communicative acts from all the other dismissible information (mainly non-verbal) that is not pertinent. Indeed, the idea of relevance is not new in relation to gesture studies. Sanders (1980, 1985) writes about principles of relevance in the relationship between language and communication, in the meaning of non-verbal elements, and in the link between verbal and non-verbal elements. Another one of the clearest references is that of McNeill (1992), when he pointed out the following:

> Precisely because gestures are *not* obliged to meet standard of form, they are free to present just those aspects of meaning that are relevant and salient to the speaker and leave out aspects that language may require but are not relevant to the situation (linguists have discussed the problem of defining relevance, but have not availed themselves of the gesture channel as a source of evidence (22) [...] Precisely because gestures are not constrained by the requirements of a code or language, they are free to incorporate only the salient and relevant aspects of the context. Each gesture is created at the moment of speaking and highlights what is relevant, and the same entity can be referred to be by gestures that have changed their form. (McNeill 1992: 41)

Although McNeill is talking about co-speech gestures (or gesticulation), the remark is perfectly applicable to the emblems. Given that most emblems originate from other gestures, it involves having undergone a process of conventionalization and dissemination in a particular community or social group. An emblem is a gesture with clear properties of salience and relevance that has succeeded socially, and that therefore has become peculiar and specific of a group, as it may also be the case for some lexicon or phraseology, or even the case for clothing or a hairstyle. All these signs may become identifiable aspects of a group and stylistic identity markers. At the same time, they are elements with a clear *salience* in the context in which they are used, and also in this sense they are relevant. This is the same meaning in which later will use the concept Tomasello (2008), very related to social interaction:

> For humans the communicative context is not simply everything in the immediate environment, from the temperature of the room to the sounds of the birds in the background, but rather the communicative context is what is "relevant" to the social interaction, that is, what each participant sees as relevant and knows that the other sees as relevant as well – and knows that the other knows this as well, and so on, potentially ad infinitum. (Tomasello 2008: 74)

The publication of *Relevance* by Dan Sperber and Deirdre Wilson (1986, and the second edition in 1995) represents the most explicit formulation of a theory that is at the same time a communicative and a cognitive theory. Because of

that, the principles of relevance are formulated (in the second edition of the book) in a double way (Sperber and Wilson 1986 [1995]):
(I) First (or cognitive) principle of relevance: human cognition tends to be geared to the maximization of relevance.
(II) Second (or communicative) principle of relevance: every act of ostensive communication communicates a presumption of its own optimal relevance.

Relevance theory was elaborated for verbal language and applied to many verbal aspects, such as markers and discursive connectors, implicatures, grammaticalization, and politeness. However, the theoretical scope is wider, as the first cognitive principle illustrates: cognition is managed in order to maximize relevance. This first principle is perfectly applicable to the case of gestures (as McNeill 1992 suggested, mentioning Sperber and Wilson), and in particular to the case of emblems. The second principle also in also applicable, since it reflects a characteristic (prototype) of the emblems: their deliberate and intentional nature (*ostensive*, using relevance theory terminology). An emblem is a conscious gesture, aimed at interlocutors or recipients with the clear intention of encapsulating information that is propositional (with semantic content) and pragmatic (as a speech act, with an illocutionary value).

In the same manner that it has been applied to other interdisciplinary issues that extend across pragmatics and other disciplines (the analysis of politeness, literature, and cognitive procedures such as metaphor and metonymy), relevance theory has been used in the analysis of non-verbal field as an explanatory criterion. Wharton has probably been the most explicit author in this regard, especially with his work in 2009, in which he analyzes Grice's distinction between natural and non-natural meaning applied to non-verbal communication (for what concerns the theoretical assumptions, see the debate in Wharton 2011). Other explanations based on the theory of relevance have also been given to more specific aspects, such as greetings (Padilla 2003).

The degree of relevance of an element is measured in the theory as a quotient between the widening of the cognitive environment (understood as a set of propositions) and the ease of processing. The larger the widening of an element, the higher the relevance is; at the same time, the smaller the difficulty of processing, the higher relevance. When a stage of balance between the two factors is reached and is considered satisfactory, the interpretation becomes the most possible appropriate/relevant one. Then the interpretative process stops, and no more alternatives are sought (this can be applied to the case of the advertisement discussed in the preceding section, see 5.3, Figure 5.6).

At this point a question arises: what does it mean exactly that emblems are *relevant*? More specifically, what does it mean to propose that the emblems are marks of *optimum relevance*? On the one hand, the informative content of the emblems (always understood in a dual, propositional and simultaneously interactive or pragmatic way) manages to change the cognitive environment of the receptor or receptors. On the other hand, an emblem does so with a very low processing cost. In a non-technical way, the emblem gives a lot of information – it is synthesized or agglutinated easily –, and transmits it in such a manner that the cost of processing it by the receiver is low. Therefore, the combination of the two factors makes the degree of relevance achieved with an emblem very high, higher than with other types of gestures (and independent from speech). It seems logical to think that the fact that the emblems occur with clear borders and have a very obvious salience contributes to these circumstances.

Without using the theoretical concept of relevance, Kendon (1981a: 142–143) had already given several reasons for why emblems are very effective communicatively. From a relevance theory perspective, we could also understand Kendon's reasons as explanations of the relevance of emblems:
(1) They are faster than talking.
(2) They are silent (and can therefore be used in contexts where speech becomes ineffective).
(3) They resemble more (than speech) certain physical actions (to which they refer more or less directly).
(4) They do not require as much attention (as speech) on the part of the receiver.
(5) They can be used from a distance.

We could add to these factors that emblems provide clear information (in general they are not ambiguous at all), and that they are easy to understand. All these factors together are fundamental for instance in the cases already mentioned of greetings or insults (see 2.3.2 and 2.3.4, 5.3). Furthermore, they explain why speakers seem to prefer the use of emblems – instead of equivalent verbal items – in some everyday communicative situations. In addition to the fact that emblems can substitute speech in many contexts, a review of these factors illustrates that verbal and gestural elements can also be found together in a complementary distribution. Because emblems can be found with and without talk, it is important to underscore that emblems are autonomous communication devices with peculiar characteristics, which are not always coincident or interchangeable with those of verbal elements. In this sense, the research to be strengthened is twofold. On the one hand, the ethnographic and the interaction analyses (cf. 4.4.1 and 5.6) are fundamental to characterize the emblem in their contexts of use. On the other hand, the analysis of the coordinated gestural-speech production that has been carried out in the last few years, particularly of co-speech and pragmatic gestures (cf. 2.4.1 and 2.4.2), should also be included in emblem analysis.

Indeed, Slama-Cazacu (1976) had already proposed the concept of mixed syntax, and Poyatos (1976, 1983, 2013, inter alia) has always defended a tripartite structure coordinated between verbal, prosody and gestuality throughout his work. Following similar lines, Arndt and Janney (1987) has proposed an "intergrammar" model that is a tripartite between verbal, prosody, and kinetic that is reflected in the units of analysis, and Enfield (2009) has proposed what he calls "composite utterances." In recent models, the possibility of a very close coordination between gesture and speech has been raised, to the extent that gesture can be seen as part of a link in the grammatical chain. In particular, Fricke (2013) notes the possibility that gesture occupies the place, for example, of an attribute. On the other hand, while Fricke's grammatical models have generative roots, Alturo et al. (2016) propose this symbiosis in a similar way but from a functional model perspective (that of Functional Discourse Grammar, FDG), which considers the speech act as the minimum unit of the model. The FDG model has the advantage that it allows to include the emblem as an act with an illocutionary value (see the criteria discussed in 2.2.3 and in 5.6).

Cases, in which an emblem is the main focus of a speech act and is interpreted as a fully relevant gesture, can be supplemented by other alternatives. In these we find, for example, only verbal items (23), in the second (24) verbal and non-verbal (already emblematic) sequenced, and in the third (25) only non-verbal items in process of emblematization:[6]

(23) ((In a restaurant, the waiter asks what two people wish to order for lunch))
A: Have you chosen?
B: Beef.
C: Beef.
A: Beef, as well.

(24) ((At a bakery, a woman refers to the nougat she has at home, from the previous Christmas))
A: It's like...
(.)
(The hand, with the palm inwards, opens and closes in front of the nose, as if clearing the air to get rid of the bad smell)
(.)...
Rancid.

---

[6] The three examples are selected from Payrató (2003).

(25) ((Walking along the street in the same direction, a man addresses a woman, asking a question))
A: Do you still live round here?
B: No.
(..)
Now we're in El Remei [neighborhood].
A: (moves his head backwards, raises his eyebrows, opening his eyes very wide and sticking out his tongue)

Example (23) show connections, seldom observed, between politeness, grammar, the construction of conversation turns and text cohesion: the waiter (interlocutor A), in the fourth turn "repairs," by adding a polite *as well*, the apparent "impolite" turn from interlocutor C, who fails to use any marker of cohesion linking with B's utterance. Courtesy would require this linkage since the same dish is mentioned a second time (the unmarked form here would be something like *Me too, I'll have the same*, etc.).

Examples (24) and (25) exhibit multiple connections between verbal and nonverbal elements. In (24), a gesture with the basic meaning of 'bad smell' (see Meo-Zilio and Mejía 1980–1983: no. 163.14), precedes the verbal information on the state of the nougat. In (25), the complex gesture[7] of the interlocutor A denotes surprise, astonishment, but it is not accompanied by any verbal elements; nonetheless, the exchange would be impossible to analyze without this fragment, forming the whole, with the multiple non-verbal markers also showing who asked the question, or how the exchange ends (greetings are also exclusively non verbal). The relevance of verbal and non-verbal elements (or their combination, in (24)), is the guide that allows explaining the interpretation of the sequences.

As a final reflection, we should point out that the advantages of the inclusion of the production and interpretation of the emblems along with co-speech gestures are underscored in more classic models, such as Levelt's (see Leevelt 1989), and in more recent models as those by McNeill (2013), Kita and Ozyurek (2003), and Feyereisen (2013), just to mention some of the best-known ones.

From a holistic and multimodal perspective, it is evident that a psycholinguistic or neuro-linguistic model designed for the production and interpretation of verbal language should also include a design to explain its coordination with the gesture in general and in particular with emblematic gestures, which can accompany speech or replace it altogether.

---

[7] The corresponding illustration can be found in example <17> in Appendix IV (collected by Cardona and qualified as an emblem found both in Venezuela and Spain).

Other strong evidence regarding the proposal of a general principle of relevance as a guide to verbal and non-verbal communication may come from the fields of developmental acquisition and neurology-related pathology of communication. In the first, unfortunately we have very few studies on children's acquisition of emblems (cf. those of Guidetti 2003a, 2003b). They do not allow constructing an argumentation around relevance as principle criterion, although the topic is very appealing. In the area of pathology and neurology, the cerebral location of the centers of control of gestuality may depend on the specific types of gestures in question, but we also find that there are hardly any studies written specifically on emblems.[8] In any case, some of these studies place emblems as items that are closer to verbal rather than non-verbal items, which would reinforce what McNeill (1985, 1992) already proposed in the sense of reformulating the "verbal" / "non-verbal" categories and avoiding the simplification of classifying gestures as simply "non-verbal" items.

5.5 Multimodal tropes in emblematization processes

Principles of relevance seem to be applicable also to cognitive operations that have to do with rhetorical tropes or figures, be verbal, non-verbal, or combined, i. e. multimodal (see Yus 2009 in particular). Emblematic gestures resort to several fundamental tropes (for example metonymy/synecdoche, metaphor and irony/sarcasm; cf. 5.5.1 and 5.5.2) and displays interesting and complex interrelations between the verbal and non-verbal channels (5.5.3). In the case of the verbal metaphor, many theories have been proposed for their analysis, especially from new cognitive models, and can provide pertinent information for some non-verbal metaphors. Metonymy and synecdoche is also another basic field, to which emblematic gestures often resort, often as a first step towards metaphorization. Irony and sarcasm in the communicative and interactive processes show how different interrelations can occur between the verbal channel and the emblems, in the sense of literal/non-literal meanings and cross references (5.5.4). Finally, the relationships between verbal phraseology and emblematic gestures also show the variety and complexity that communicative multimodality can achieve (cf. 5.5.3 and 5.5.5). The aim of this section is to provide a panoramic view of the great possibilities of applying

---

[8] A central neurolinguistic finding would be to examine how emblems are affected, in relation to other gesture types and speech, when a person suffers with aphasia, but we do not have studies in this regard. It would also be very interesting to compare verbal and nonverbal pragmatic deficits (see Perkins 2007: 58–60).

theories of metaphor and metonymy to the field of emblematic gestures, a subject on which the whole book could have focused.

5.5.1 Around metonymy

In the case of metonymy (including synecdoche for the sake of simplicity) we find a change or semantic displacement that occurs within the same cognitive or experiential domain, and not in two (different) domains, such as in the metaphor. In traditional terms, metonymy implies a relation of (indexical) contiguity, while metaphor is a matter of (symbolic) substitution and similarity. However, delimiting boundaries can be difficult, as we shall see below; and we often find several types of combinations and gradations rather than dichotomies in the gestural and multimodal fields (cf. Mittelberg and Waugh 2009, 2014; Urios-Aparisi 2009).

A typical case of metonymy, for example, is found in the *hora*/hour (<I, 63>) emblem, in which the index finger taps the wrist. The gesture is used as a warning to indicate to someone that it is late (or to ask for the time, if the modality is interrogative, usually by raising the head (cf. Meo-Zilio and Mejía 1980–1983: no 120/121). In this emblem one can say that there is a double metonymy (Poggi 2014: 1490): on the one hand, the place for the object (the wrist where the watch is worn), and on the other hand, the object for the function (the watch for the indication of time). Similarly, the index finger touches the tip of the tongue in the emblem *xerraire (bocamoll)* / chatty (gossip) (<I, 106>), the object standing for the function (talk).

We can also consider as metonymies the semantic displacements that we find in some emblems of request, for instance, asking something to be opened by gesturing the action of opening or shaking keys (the movement for the object, see <I, 35>); asking for the bill or for a pen in a restaurant by gesturing the movement of signing a piece of paper (see Meo-Zilio & Mejía 1980–1983: no. 59); or the movement of counting money to ask for it (illustration 7 (a) in Figure 5.7). In the last case, the movement of counting money is contiguous to the global concept of 'money.'

Instances of mockery emblems, in which a body part becomes the highlighted focus and is extended toward the interlocutor, may also be considered partially metonymic, for example, sticking one's tongue out (*llengotes*, <I, 25>, <III, 5>, illustration 7(b) in Figure 5.7) or extending one's nose in the nose thumb or Shanghai gesture (*pam i pipa*, <I, 26>, illustration 7(c) in Figure 5.7). Such instances are more debatable, and can be interpreted simply as a pantomime (at least initially) that become emblems through conventionalization processes.

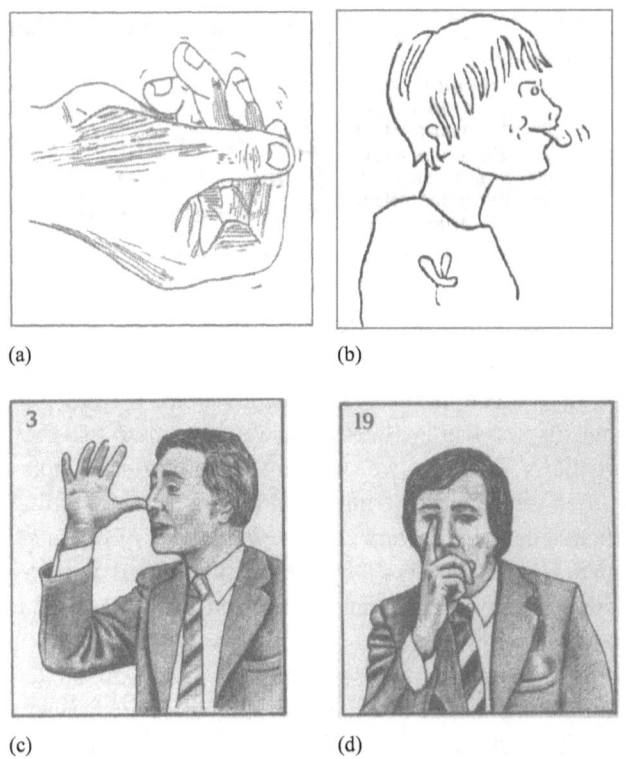

Figure 5.7: Examples of emblems based on metonymy. Illustration (a) is from Payrató (1989/1991), (b) from Mascaró (1981) and (c) and (d) from Morris et al. (1979).

In these cases, as in cases of the hyperbolical enlargement and imitation of animal body parts, such as ears and horns, which stand for the whole animal, the emblematic gestures represent metonymically the referent via a synecdoche in which the part stands for the whole. However, mockery, more generally, also implies a metaphor (after the metonymy). When we mock someone, this person is characterized as an animal because we see similarities between the person and the animal, and we project visually one domain over the other (cf. the combined cases illustrated in Figure 5.5.3), even sometimes with sounds (as for example in racist insults), in which metonymic and metaphorical processes are also combined.

Furthermore, there are other cases of great interest because metonymy may constitute the preceding (or the last) step of displacements that already are most likely metaphorical, as they constitute displacements that go beyond the contiguity of domains. In varying degrees, from lesser to greater, this is the case of emblems referring to the senses, specially the senses of hearing, sight, and smell. For instance, first, bringing the focus to one's ear (<I, 95>) is often used to indicate that a sound cannot be heard clearly. But the message can be displaced from 'Do you hear it?' to 'Do you understand it?' This phenomenon occurs with great frequency in emblems that mean literally 'I have seen it' (<I, 104>) and 'I have smelled it,' (illustration 7(d) in figure 5.7), as metonymies of the organ standing for the function and the result: from 'eye' or 'nose' to 'I see' or 'I smell (something)', that is, from the organ or instrument to the action that the organ makes (to see or to smell).

From these meanings, in turn, subsequent displacements may take place toward the meaning of 'I understood it' and 'something does not work well'. If we consider these semantic domains as adjacent or contiguous areas, we can continue to speak of metonymic displacements. However, if we understand that they already constituted differentiated domains, we can understand these examples as metaphors, which are often reinforced by a non-verbal meaning of the verbal channel (i.e. "I see" interpreted as 'I understand', or Cat. *fa pudor* 'it stinks' interpreted as 'something strange is going on here'). In these cases we find a combination of processes (the metaphor after metonymy, with the verbal support) that are also present in the examples below in 5.5.3.

The previous situation is repeated in the case of the 'convicted' emblem (cf. Payrató 1989/1991: 371 and Poggi 2014: 1490), in which the hand draws a Christian cross in the air, with a vertical first movement of up and down followed by a horizontal movement from left to right. This gesture is used as a technical ritual emblem (see 2.3.6) by Catholic priests to give blessings. In everyday language, however, a semantic shift has occurred whereas the emblem is used to refer to those convicted of a crime, as it used to be the case that convicted criminals who are about to die were blessed with this gesture before being executed. Since this semantic domain is contained in the term "very end", the meaning of the emblem can be generalized and the gesture can simply refer to a completely finished thing or relationship. Again, if we consider that the domains "to bless – to convict / to sentence – to finish" are contiguous, these constitute metonymic moves. But if we consider – in fact it seems more reasonable – that they are different, we find ourselves again in the kingdom of metaphor.

5.5.2 Around metaphors

The concept of metaphor has been applied to the study of gestures in multiple ways (see Cienki and Müller 2014), but it has been hardly used in the study of emblems. In metaphors we find shifts between two different cognitive domains

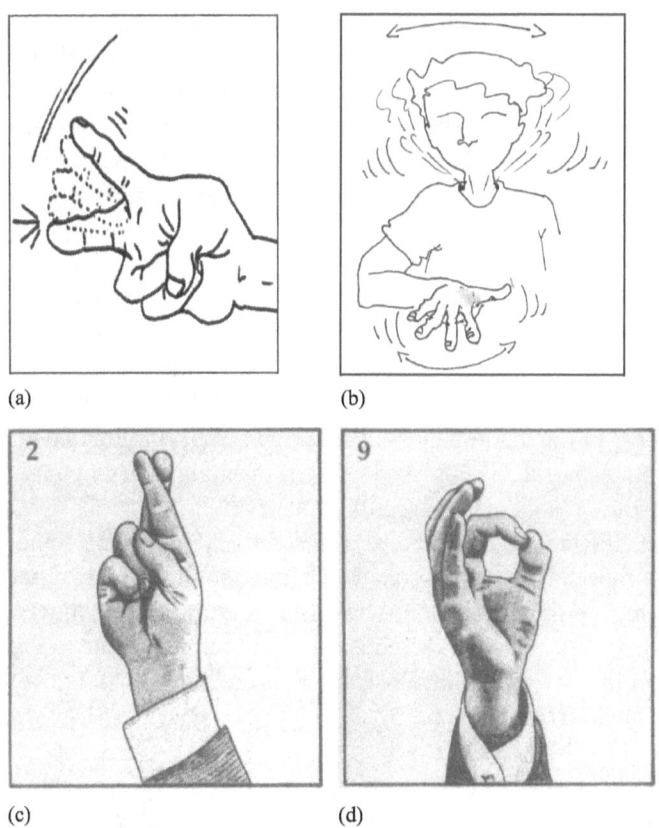

Figure 5.8: Examples of emblems based on metaphors. Illustration (a) is from Payrató (1989/1991), (b) from Saitz and Cervenka (1972), and (c) and (d), from Morris et al. (1979).

(not one of one, as it happens in metonymy), which often involves an abstract domain (the targeted) that is represented by a particular and concrete domain or action (the source).[9] A first sample can be found in the emblems of Figure 5.8.

---

9 Calbris (1980, 1981, 1990, 2011) has written often about this abstract-concrete relationship. Regarding the gesture metaphor, cf. especially Poggi (2007, 2014), with an analysis of rhetorical figures in the emblems of his Italian *gestionario*, and more generally Cienki and Müller (2008) and Müller at. (eds.) (2013, 2014). For multimodal metaphor, see Forceville and Urios-Aparisi (eds.) (2009). On visual metaphor, verbal metaphor, and relevance, see Yus (2009).

In the first example, (8a), we find a frequent emblem that is a gestural metaphor in the prototypical sense: the gesture done with the fingers of the hand imitating the cutting of scissors. While there is no figurative meaning, the gesture is an emblem whose semantic core is 'scissors' (and with usual meanings as 'give me the scissors' or 'do you have the scissors?'). The gesture is based on a metonymy, as just seen in the preceding sub-section: the (simulation of the) action of cutting for the object, the scissors. In a given situational context, the gesture can be done to ask someone for some scissors (as an exhortative or directive act). However, if we add a non-literal meaning, in this case the emblem can have two potential metaphorical uses:

(i) *Tallar* 'cut' in the sense of 'shut up' or 'stop', i.e. to stop the activity being done (as an order or demand that is made to someone). This is the meaning we find, for example, in the institutional advertisement of illustration 5.9 (a) in Figure 5.9. The emblem is also often used with the meaning of 'being brief' or 'reducing the amount of talk' (cf. Poggi 2014: 1488–1489).

(ii) 'Cut' moves towards the meaning of 'criticize': *fer safareig* (English 'air somebody else's dirty laundry') in the phraseology of contemporary Catalan. That is, for example, someone says about someone else that s/he is a person who criticizes too much with a negative connotation; cf. Figure 5.9, illustration (b) below, an example not very "politically correct" from Efron (1970: fig. 66) and Meo-Zilio and Mejía (1980–1983: no. 57).

The gesture in variant (i) is associated above all with an exhortative or directive speech act (to give an order for somebody to stop what s/he is doing). In contrast, variant (ii) is associated with a representative or assertive/asseverative speech act in which we are told something about a person's attributes. In the variant (i) the displacement is softer (or more contiguous or "metonymic") and is based on the polysemy of *tallar* ('cutting') understood as 'shut up' or 'stop'; when something is cut, continuing is not possible. The *blending* (Fauconnier and Turner 2002) that ends up being chosen as relevant is the image of separation, stopping, or breakage of the activity. On the other hand, the image chosen in the variant (ii) is very different, almost the opposite. Now the relevant image in the blending is that of an activity: *criticizing*, perhaps because criticism or gossip was assumed to be common in women's circles (where scissors were also common). The movement of the hand with the scissors opening and closing also remembers, in addition, the movement of the mouth speaking (cf. the resemblance of the gesture with another emblem: *xerraire* / chatty (<I, 105).

Other emblems that can represent actions with a literal meaning may also take non-literal metaphorical senses. A first example is *calor* (*suar*) / heat (to sweat) (<I, 29>), *eixugar el front* with the meaning of wiping off the sweat from

(a) (b)

Figure 5.9: (a) Example of 'cutting' in an institutional advertisement in magazines and newspapers in Catalan: *'talla' els mals rotllos,* in English 'stop the bad (relationship) stuff' (cf. Payrató 1989/1991: 356), and (b) example of 'cutting' as 'criticizing' (Efron 1970: fig. 66).

one's forehead, with the variant cooling off by fanning one's face with a hand collected in Payrató (1989/1991: no. 116), that can take the metaphorical meaning of relief after having gone a difficult situation. A second example is *suïcidi/* suicide (<I, 100>), holding a hand in the shape of a pistol to one's temple, that can take the meaning of 'extreme circumstances,' or 'not being able to withstand something.'

Leaving aside these prototypical examples of metaphorical emblems, if we understand the concept of metaphor in a broad sense, as a symbolic operation, many other emblems also display metaphorical components. For instance in the following examples we find metaphors of different types: in (8b) the oscillating hand means 'more or less'; in (8c) the cross frees somebody from an obligation, and in (8d) the circle means 'perfect, OK.'

In example (8b), the hand swings sideways and vaguely recalls the combined upward-downward swing of the dishes of weighing scale (see <VI, 6>). It has the meaning of 'more or less' and is used as an assessment, usually to answer a question. It belongs to a gesture family in which we find the gesture combined with a similar side-to-side oscillating head gesture (see <VI, 7>, cf. <I, 16> and <I, 17>), all based on an image schema of equilibrium. Both this example and the following ones have a certain degree of iconicity, but metaphor is nevertheless evident. There is now no contiguity between the vehicle of sign and the meaning, as in the metonymic examples of the previous section. Instead, we find a substitution or projection of a mental domain over another. In (8b) the oscillation (of the hand, or in the synonym, of the head) stands in relation to the assessment; in (8c) the cross stands in relation to the freeing of somebody from the obligation to say the truth or to fulfill an oath, and in (8d) the fingers do a circle associated with the meaning of 'perfection.'

Many other emblems are based on metaphorical uses or have metaphorical components: for example, an emblem as usual as the *botifarra*/ forearm jerk (<II, 2>) is often used not as an insult but as a refusal or negation (indeed categorical), in such a way that the mental space or domain of the insult and offense have been qualified or mitigated to the point of refusal or rejection. Furthermore, numerous emblems with a deictic component (for example, meaning 'higher' or 'more', or 'lower' or 'less') are associated with the metaphors of HIGHER IS MORE and LOWER IS LESS. The emblem of 'very good' (<I, 21>) is done with the finger up and the one for 'bad'/ 'suspense' with the finger down (<I, 72>, <VI, 4>). The hands also go downward in the emblem for 'calm' (cf. <I, 28> and <VIII, 11>), while they raise their arms in the 'victory'/ 'win' emblem (<I, 103>).

We find reflections of conceptual metaphors (Lakoff and Johnson 1980) and the image schemes seen above (see 4.1.1) in many emblems that show metaphorical features. Two common cases involve representing the head as a machine and the body (and the head and the mouth) as containers. If the head is a machine, it may be missing a piece or perhaps this piece needs to be screwed or tightened up, as in *boig (bogeria)*/ crazy (madness) (<III, 3>, <VI, 82>), where the index finger rotates at the temple. The head-as-machine may also stop working and needs to be tapped to start again as in *boig (bogeria)*/ crazy (madness) (<III, 4>, <VI, 9>) when the index finger taps the temple. Both examples stand in contrast with the gesture of pointing at the head with the index finger as an example of intelligence or something that requires thinking (<I, 32>). If the head is a container, it can be represented with a full hand having reaching a level of "fullness" (metaphorical, obviously) or of a complete level of anger, tiredness, and annoyance (see Meo-Zilio and Mejía 1980–1983: no. 118.1) If the mouth is a container, it must sometimes be closed by putting the lid on or zipped, so that nothing can escape or spill out (see the examples of emblematic gesture family in Figure 5.3).

5.5.3 Complex combined processes: Metonymy, metaphor and verbal tropes

At the end of subsection 5.5.1 we reviewed the emblem of 'stinking': a gestural metonymy (odor or stink perceived through the nose) that can interpreted metaphorically with the meaning of 'corruption' or 'something shady' instead of the literal 'stinking.' In subsection 5.5.2 we have made a similar observation: the emblem of 'cutting' based on a metonymy (and with the literal meaning organized the semantic core of 'cutting' or 'scissors') can be extended to metaphorical use of 'stopping' and 'criticizing.' These combined metonymy and metaphor processes seem to occur often in the case of emblems: indeed, we illustrate additional examples in Figure 5.10. However, examples in this figure are slightly different: any reference to the initial metonymy has been now been lost, and consequently the conceptual contiguity has also been lost. A metaphor has been built on this initial metonymy, and the only meaning that has persisted is the metaphor, with a substitution of a conceptual field by another, which is based on the figurative sense of the verbal expression. While in some cases the duplicity of gestural meanings persists (literal / metaphorical: 'it is hot' / 'it is a difficult

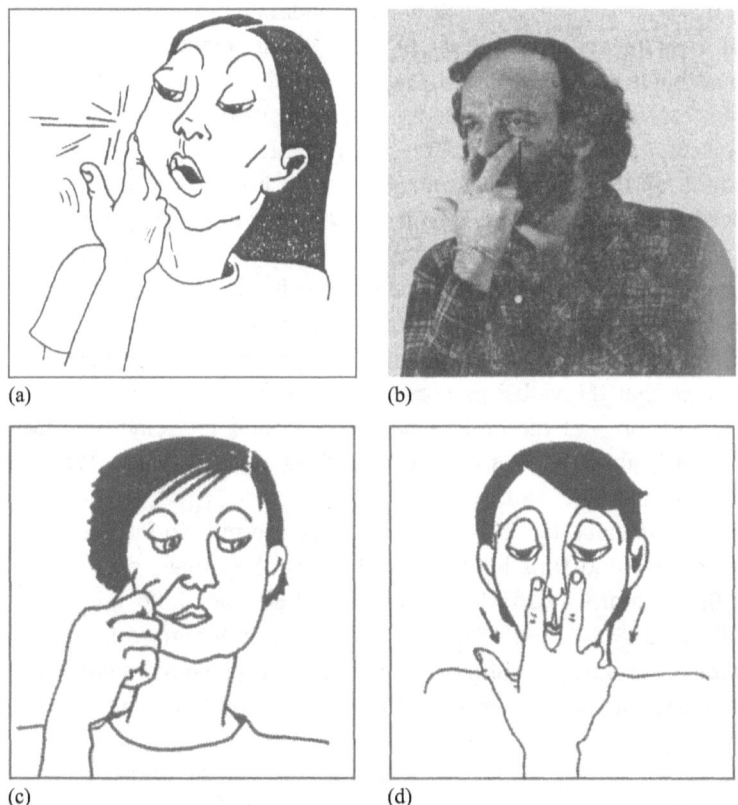

Figure 5.10: Cases of emblematization based on a previous metonymy and a later metaphor. Illustrations (a), (c) and (d) are from Payrató (1989/1991) and (b) is from Meo-Zilio and Mejía (1980–1983).

situation,' 'it stinks' / 'something shady,' 'I see it' / 'I understand it,' 'convicted'/ 'finished,' etc.), only the metaphorical meaning is maintained in others.

In example (10a), we find the case of *ser un caradura* (being cheeky or having no shame), a gesture, like the expression, of Spanish origin, which has replaced an ancient Catalan gesture linked to the expression of *ser un galtes* (being a cheek).[10] Still in use, the Catalan gesture (10c) is based on a metonymy (stretching the cheek or the face of a person, the cheek and the face standing for the entire person through a synecdoche of the part for everything). Example (10a) also has metonymic basis; indeed, it is the same synecdoche (the cheek or the face for the person or his/her character). On this operation, though, another metaphor is incorporated: the hardness of the face (a concrete fact) to which the hand refers when it hits the *barra* (or 'hard face') of the individual. It should be noted that the metaphor is possible only through verbal expression (*ser un caradura*), and that therefore we should speak of multimodal metaphor rather than a strictly gestural or emblematic metaphor. In other words, emblematic gestural symbology is possible in cases like this because of verbal phraseology. However, we cannot always interpret that the emblem is a simple gestural or imagistic version of the phraseology, because in fact presently (synchronously) they are already independent, and because diachronically we do not always know if the expression precedes the gesture, although it is presumed to be in many cases. For example, in the case of the emblem of closing the mouth like a zipper (see <II, 7>) there is no equivalent expression, but the metaphor is obvious.

The interesting example in (10b) or (10d) presumably originates in the Spanish verbal expression *estar a dos velas* (to be with/under two candles), although it is possible that the verbal expression follows the non-verbal one. It is not a Catalan expression, but the gesture has been around for some time (see Amades 1957, <II, 8>), although it is not recognized by many Catalans. We find the process reproduced in Figure 5.11.

The gesture is performed by "placing right index and middle fingers on either side of one's nose and (this is optional) drawing the fingers downward" (Kany 1960: 89); for more illustrations see Kany 1960, Meo-Zilio and Mejía 1980–1983, or Payrató 1989 (cf. <II, 8>, <V, 17>). The gesture is used to convey the fact that someone has run out of money or does not understand something: Sp. *estar a dos velas / quedarse a dos velas* ('to be broke' or 'not to understand

---

10 Cf. 4.2.2, example (1). 'To have a nerve', literally *to have a hard face*; Eng. *to be a rotter/ cheeky*. The index touches one jaw and the thumb the other, with the palm facing inwards (for illustrations see Payrató 1989/1991); this emblem is not in current usage, but has been pointed out in older speakers, particularly in the Balearic Islands.

Sp. *estar/quedarse a dos velas*
(a) 'to be broke'
(b) 'not to understand a word'

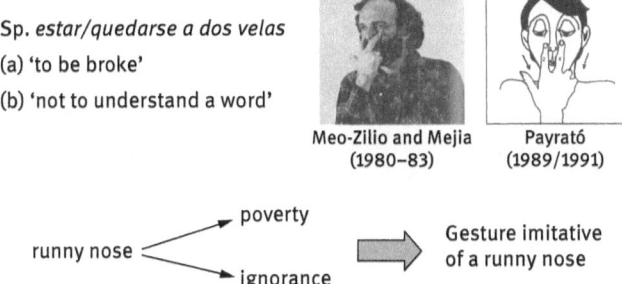

Meo-Zilio and Mejía (1980–83)   Payrató (1989/1991)

runny nose ⟶ poverty
runny nose ⟶ ignorance
⟹ Gesture imitative of a runny nose

Figure 5.11: Processes taking place in the emblem *estar a dos velas*. Illustrations are from Meo-Zilio and Mejía (1980–1983) and Payrató (1989–1991).

a word'; literally 'to be at two candles/sails, to have a runny nose'; Eng. 'to be broke or to be in the dark').

Neither the emblem nor the verbal locution has a clear, well-known origin.[11] The common interpretations are related to one or several of the following images:
(a) The (only) two candles that remain in the altar as minimal illumination (and, metaphorically, poverty).
(b) The two candles placed near the person acting as the bank in some card games (i.e., the only things the player still has after losing a game).
(c) The image of a ship sailing with (only) two sails.
(d) The image of a child with a runny nose, symbolizing poverty or ignorance, depending on the situational context.

In fact the only image that can reasonably contribute to explain the emblem (and not only the idiomatic expression) is the last one, based on a metaphor relating a runny nose with the notion of inadequate resources (e.g., economic, the ability to do something, or mental, the ability to understand something). The metaphor is based, therefore, on the verbal expression, but there is a metonymy (the mucus running down from a person's nose when (s)he cries or sniffs because of having a difficult time or because of being poor) and a metaphor, which carries the full meaning when there is neither talk nor direct references to phraseology.

Moving to the next case, the Catalan/Spanish verbal expression *fer el pilota / hacer el pelota* (literally 'to make the ball/the dough' or 'to be a ball'; Eng. 'to suck up to somebody', 'to be a flatterer') is also interesting because it combines

---

[11] The discussion of these emblems partially reproduces fragments from Payrató (2008).

metonymy, metaphor, phraseology, and homonymy. As a gesture, the flat hand, with the palm facing downward moves up and down, as is illustrated in Figure 5.12.

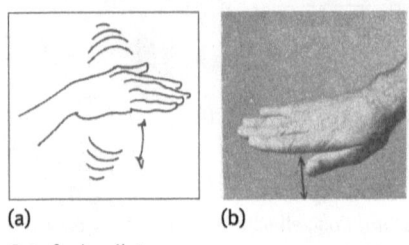

(a)
Cat. *fer la pilota*
Peninsular Sp. *hacer la pelota* ('adular')
Eng. (literally) *to do the ball* ('to flatter')

Figure 5.12: Emblem of *fer la pilota*, with the meaning of 'flattering'. Illustration (a) is from Payrató (1989/1991) and (b) from Meo-Zilio and Mejía (1980–1983).

The Peninsular Spanish expression *ser un pelota / hacer la pelota* or the Catalan expression *ser un pilota / fer la pilota* and their corresponding emblems (based on the action of bouncing a ball) are well known to the speakers of these languages as expressions of adulation, i.e. equivalent to the English 'to flatter' (and its corresponding emblems). However, since the relation between physical actions and mental concepts such as those corresponding to Cat. *ensabonar* (to soap) or *raspallar* (to rub) are clear in many languages and cultures, and the emblems mimic the action of the semantic content of the verb with the metaphor of being a flatterer, what relation can be established between flattering and bouncing a ball? Even the onomatopoeia of the sound that a ball makes when bouncing (Cat. *boing, boing*) can be used to carry the meaning of flattering even if it is in the absence of the gesture and any verbal reference, that is, there is another metonymy between the action of bouncing a ball and the sound it makes. Therefore the conventionality of the action (the sound included) is well established.

To answer the previous question and to clarify these multimodal interrelations can only be done if verbal and non-verbal resources and expressions are put together, synchronically but also diachronically over time. Only in this way can we analyze verbal and non-verbal productions as communicative tools which are used in coordination by interlocutors and which evolve over time, causing mutual influences and changes. The process that takes place in Cat. *fer el pilota o ser un pilota* (literally 'to do a ball' or 'to be a ball', in the sense of flattering someone) is complex, unclear (especially its origin) and is based on the historical evolution and on the phraseology of the language. A simplified drawing is found in Figure 5.13.

5.5 Multimodal tropes in emblematization processes — 169

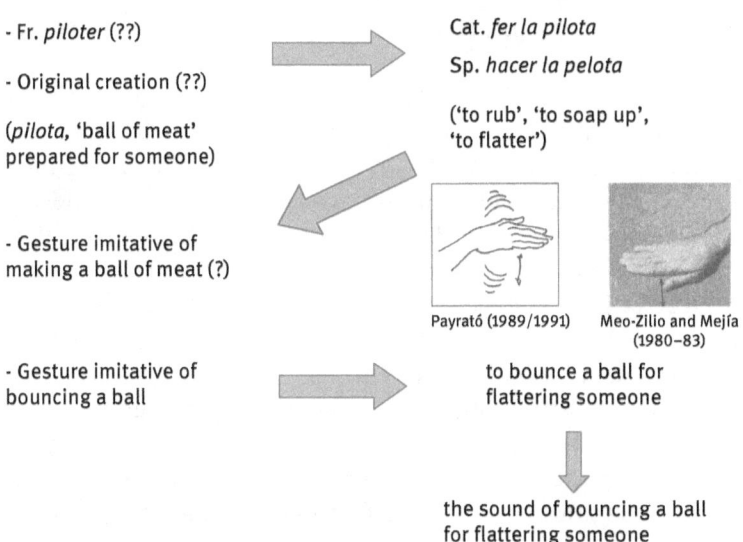

Figure 5.13: Processes of metonymy, metaphor and homonymy in the emblematization of *fer el pilota*. The illustrations are from Payrató (1989/1991) and Meo-Zilio and Mejía (1980–1983).

The example is a paradigmatic case of a language (or variety) dependent emblem, as the process of creation of the gesture depends on the specific variety spoken, and the emblem cannot be exported if the variety or language does not have the corresponding expression and the consequent metaphor or metonymy, in this case to bounce a ball as 'to flatter' (this is why the emblem and the expression are unknown in American Spanish). A deeper analysis should take into account other gestures very probably from the same family, for instance Spanish *hacer la pelotilla* ('to flatter', literally 'to make the little ball'; Eng. 'to toady'; a flat hand moving in circles on one side of the body or above the palm of the other). This emblem most probably predates the other one (the same is true for the two expressions), and imitates the movement of one hand (or the hands) making a small ball of food, the metonymic base for the consequent metaphor for flattering (from the idea of cooking for someone). In this case, metonymy consists in the movement from preparing food to giving food to someone else, upon which the metaphor of preparing someone else's food (concrete act) is extended to being the flatterer of somebody else through the abstraction: SERVING SOMEONE ELSE IS FLATTERING HIM/HER. The semantic notions linked to this family of gestures include caressing, washing someone with soap, rubbing, brushing, or cooking (for somebody), all of which can easily be converted, through a metaphorical change, into the concept of flattering

someone. However, in this example, neither the origin of the verbal expression nor the emblem is clear. A series of points should be borne in mind:
(a) The French lexeme *peloter* ('to flatter') might have been borrowed in Spanish and Catalan, and adapted as *hacer la pelota* in Spanish and *fer la pilota* in Catalan, but the etymology is not clear and the emblem described is not known in French, therefore it must have been created in relation to Spanish or Catalan languages. (In French the emblems for *flatteur* ('flatterer') are based on the images of rubbing or brushing, see Calbris and Montredon 1980: 54.) If this hypothesis turned out to be true, it would be an initial case of homonymy and not of polysemy, but it would not alter the other metonymic and metaphoric displacements.
(b) The homonymy (or polysemy) of *pelota* or *pilota* ('ball'/'dough') in both Spanish and Catalan would have been reproduced in the corresponding expressions, with the creation of the emblems of (first) making a ball of dough, related to the preparation of food (the flat hand moving in circles) and (later) the one of bouncing a ball.
(c) The image of bouncing a ball may have finally been associated more frequently with the meaning of flattering someone or of being a toady/brown-noser/ass-kisser than the image of making dough, as the words *pelota/pilota* are much more frequently used to refer to a ball than to dough.

The analysis clearly suggests that the emblematic gesture of bouncing a ball can be interpreted as the last result of an initial metonymy via the idiomatic expression (*botar la pilota* – > *ser un pilota*, English 'to bounce the ball' – > 'to be a toady'). The process of change conserves the meaning of 'to flatter' and seems to be originally based on the previous polisemy of the word (*pilota*, English 'ball'/'dough') or on the borrowing of the French expression (*peloter*, and the subsequent confusion of homonyms).

5.5.4 Ironic constructions

While in the case of metonymy and metaphor, we find emblematization processes that are based on them, we find in the case of irony multimodal *polyphonic* constructions. In these productions, one voice of the speaker is identified with the verbal mode, and results in an utterance, such as "They are very generous", but another voice by the same speaker is identified with the gestural mode and provides a message that denies or affirms – that contradicts ironically – the content of the first voice (for instance making an emblem related to avarice, cf. <II, 6>, <V, 14>, Figure 2.11 and Meo-Zilio and Mejía (1980–83: no. 21.1). Inversely,

5.5 Multimodal tropes in emblematization processes — 171

in examples (26) and (27), the host of a television show ironically comments on the altruistic nature of inhabitants of a small mountain town (in relation to the amount of people from a large city nearby that regularly visits this small town):[12]

(26) A: *Allà hi ha molta energia positiva*...
                              _____1_____
    There, there is a lot of positive energy...
    1 = emblem of 'money' (<I, 47>, <IV, 7>)

(27) A: *Si venen els de Barcelona*... *energia positiva*...
                                         _____1_____
    If people from Barcelona come... positive energy...
    1 = emblem of 'money' (<I, 47>, <IV, 7>)

While the TV host speaks about the altruism of the small town inhabitants, he simultaneously performs the emblem of 'money' (that we have discussed earlier, cf. Figure 5.7, <I, 47>, <IV, 7> and <VIII, 45>), in such a way that the relevant interpretation is that the inhabitants are not generous but in fact take advantage of the visitors.

Other cases of the same type are for example in obscene jokes (28, 29) or in language games (30):

(28) A: *S'ha acabat la temporada d'esquí!*
                      _____1_____
    The ski season is finished!
    1= emblem of *cardar* ('fucking', cf. <I, 34>, <IV, 16>, <V, 41>)

(29) A: *Aquest cap de setmana volia anar a esquiar*...
                                 _____1_____
    This weekend I wanted to go skiing...
    però al final m'he quedat a casa...
                      _____2_____
    but ultimately I stayed home...
    1 = emblem of *cardar* ('fucking', cf. <I, 34>, <IV, 16>, <V, 41>)
    2 = emblem of *masturbar-se* ('masturbating' <I, 73>)

---

12 *El foraster* (Eng. The Outsider) is a TV show in which the host lives among the inhabitants of a village for a few days. In this episode, the host lives in the village of Guils de Cerdanya (Televisió de Catalunya, TV3, broadcasted on June 7, 2017, available at ccma.cat/tv3/alacarta/el-foraster/guils-de-cerdanya/video/567014; cf. minutes 18, 19, 25, 41, and 48).

(30) A: <u>Baje el pirata, que llaman</u>...
         ___1___   __2__
The pirate comes down, the one called...
1 = deictic emblem of 'coming' (<I, 15>, <VII, I>)
2 = emblem of 'phoning' (<I, 101>, <VIII, 81>)

Examples (28) and (29) rely on the resemblance between the emblem for 'copulate' and the pantomime for skiing; on the other hand, they also rely on association between to be alone and to remain at home, and to hold a penis during masturbation.

The example (30) is a humorous recreation of the first verse of the poet José de Espronceda's "La canción del pirata" ("The Song of the Pirate"), a well-known Spanish poem from the Romantic period. The original text is "Bajel pirata que llaman, por su bravura, el temido" ("A pirate bark ship, the 'dreaded' called/known as"). The *bajel* (bark) becomes "*baje el*" and "*que llaman temido*" (called/known as the 'dreaded') simply "*que llaman*" (they are calling [by phone]). The humorous version is rendered "He should come down, someone is phoning."

Emblems can also be ironic by themselves. Positive evaluation emblems are often used in ironic or sarcastic multimodal constructions: raising the thumb, make the ring or circle with your fingers, or applause. They are examples of frequently used items in this sense, and the figurative sense is interpreted, also in terms of relevance, without any need for accompanying verbal elements. We can therefore apply to exclusively (emblematic) irony the same parameters and principles that have been applied to explain verbal irony (for different theoretical perspectives on verbal irony, see inter alia Ruiz and Alvarado (eds.) 2013). It should be noted that in all these cases the facial expression can provide clues to interpret the meaning and final intention of this type of episode.

5.5.5 Emblems and phraseology

Many emblems are usually associated with a specific phraseology, consisting of statements that are often uttered simultaneously with emblem but which do not verbally materialize the emblem.[13] For example, we have Catalan insult or rejection gestures such as *per aquí es pengen els paraigües* (literally 'here the umbrellas are hung', in the *botifarra*, the forearm jerk, cf. <I, 56>, <II, 2>, <V, 31>), or *puja aquí dalt i balla* (literally 'come up here and dance'), in the *digitus impudicus*

---

[13] Some of the following examples are treated in Payrató (2014b).

(cf. <I, 55>, <II, 3>, <IV, 12>). In conjuration emblems, the gesture and speech can also be expressed simultaneously, as in the case of the fig (cf. <II, 4>, <V, 32>), a gesture of conjuration accompanied by ritual and popular expressions such as Cat. *la figa i la flor / per tu sí, per mi no,* literally 'the fig and the flower / for you yes, for me no,' and *pet de llop que et fot,* literally, '(a type of) mushroom that fucks you.'

Sometimes the verbal expression is a description of the gesture, as a movement understood in purely physical terms: to say 'I'm rubbing my hands' when talking about something joyful; or 'I'm washing my hands' when stating that I'm deliberately ignoring something. In other cases the gesture has promoted verbal expressions that are related to their morphology: for example, in the emblem for robbery (<I, 93>, <V, 23>), Cat. *tocar l'arpa* (literally 'to play the harp').

On the other hand, Catalan contains a large number of verbal expressions that have been established on the basis of gestures (emblematic, pseudo-emblematic or self-adapters). For example, certain body postures are often interpreted in a symbolic, emblematic way, i.e., with a recurring, socially accepted meaning: folded arms, arm over arm or not moving a finger indicate a 'lazy person.'

Regarding the question of the names and denominations of emblems, intercultural differences are evident, even between languages that are close in many ways, such as Catalan and Spanish (typologically, for historical evolution, contact …). The image of a typical sausage (*la botifarra,* cf. <I, 56>, <II, 2>, <V, 31>) gives name to the gesture that in English Morris et al. (1979) call the forearm jerk, and that in Spanish receives the name of a sleeve cut, thus referring to a very different image: *corte de mangas* (a cut of the sleeve). This gesture is called *bras d'honneur* in French, and *banana* in Portuguese because of its similarity with the fruit. A gesture like the Shanghai gesture (cf. <I, 26>, <III, 6> and <V, 28>), has a popular name in Catalan (*pam i pipa*) but not in Castilian Spanish. It has been imported to some countries of South America with the name of *el pito catalán,* English 'Catalan whistle', see Kany 1960, <V, 28>; for other names in English (sixteen names!) and other languages, see Morris et al. (1979: 33–35). The impudent finger has euphemistic names in Catalan (*ditet,* 'the little finger', for example), and a name of *la peineta* ('the hair comb') has recently appeared in Castilian Spanish over the last few years (probably not before the 21st century). In the hair comb gesture, we find the similarity of the movement of the emblem with the object.

Lastly, the intricate relationships between gestural and verbal names have been partly examined in subsection 5.5.3, in cases such as *estar a dos velas / estar a dues veles* ('being with/under or having only two candles') or *fer la pilota / hacer la pelota* ('flattering someone'). In some cases the verbal denomination causes the emblem to appear: for instance in Spanish *me parto* (lit. 'I break up with laughter') or *me parto y me mondo* (lit. 'I break up with laughter and peel myself off'). In some other cases we encounter the reverse process, for example *la botifarra* (sausage) or *pam i pipa* (Shanghai gesture) in Catalan.

5.6 Emblems and interaction: Meaning and functional distribution

In section 4.4 we have analyzed the social distribution of the emblems, and we have focused on the ethnographic analysis of these units, which highlights its cultural roots and diversity. In this section we will see, in complementary terms, how the emblems are integrated in the communicative interactions and the functions that they carry out. Among these, their illocutionary value and the diversity of the manifested diversity of illocutionary force (see 5.6.1 and 5.6.2) are fundamental. The illocutionary value separates what can be understood as co-speech gestures from prototypical emblems, although the boundaries between one and the other cannot be established in a sharp way (see 2.4.2).

As in the case of many other types of gesture, the emblem is not only a semiotic mechanism of creation of meaning, but also an interactive tool:

> Gesture is not simply a way to display meaning but an activity with distinctive temporal, spatial, and social properties that participants not only recognize but actively use in the organization of their interaction. (Goodwin 1986: 47)

Thus, the emblem can also be understood as a pragmatic tool in the service of communicative interaction. Especially valuable is the analysis of the interrelationship between the semantic values of the emblem and its pragmatic functions in communicative interaction (Poggi and Magno Caldognetto 1997, Brookes 2004, Kendon 2004). In fact, even though emblems have been defined and studied as independent of language, the observation of emblems in use in situated contexts show that emblems are often used with talk, in communicative contexts where talk is also present. This consideration leads once more to the need to study verbal and non-verbal elements together, from a unified pragmatic perspective.

The observation of the use of emblems also leads to the consideration of the relationship between them and functional variation. The first observation involves the fact that the use of the emblems is clearly associated to the degree of formality of communicative situations. Although some emblems can be given in all situations (for example, greetings), the overall use of emblems seems to be associated generally with interactive, spontaneous, informal, everyday communication. If we leave aside specialized or technical emblems for special purposes (see 2.3.5), the emblems thus are associated with everyday and rather informal communicative situations. It is true that they do not disappear in formal or even solemn occasions (Efron 1941 already referred to politeness gestures in the Italianized French court). However, formality seems to be regularly associated with the limitation or repression of non-verbal behavior in general – or at least of the minimization of its salience and frequency. This is a feature found in numerous societies, and is probably connected to the idea that gesticulation implies a loss of expressiveness in the verbal channel and goes against a cohesive verbal discourse (see 4.4). If these considerations are correct, it is not surprising that emblems seldom appear or do not occur often in formal situations.

In relation to text types, there are no studies that can substantiate the claim, but it seems quite plausible to hypothesize that emblems appear mostly associated with narrative or instructive texts, or textual sequences, far more often than with descriptive, argumentative, or expository texts.[14]

The use of emblems in relation to situational and contextual variables is also linked to stylistic variables. Speakers' or communicators' gestural use is variable and is associated with their identities, both in (re)creating and expressing a particular identity. Regarding topics and interlocutors, we can assume that, as in other areas of gesture, other forms of variations, such as in terms of familiarity with the topic, degree of involvement in the conversation and the presence of non-native speakers can favor the use of emblems or make them appear more frequently.

5.6.1 Messages conveyed

Kendon (1981a) carried out a comparative analysis of the types of messages conveyed by emblems included in six published repertoires:[15] Efron (1941/1972), for southern Italy (131 gestures); Saitz and Cervenka (1972), for Colombia and the United States (175 and 245 gestures, respectively); Creider (1977), for Kenya (68 gestures); Wylie and Stafford (1977), for France (1977), and lastly Sparhawk (1978) for Iran (123 gestures). The results of these examinations are pretty clear:

---

[14] In the case of the CAP corpus (see Payrató and Fitó (eds.) 2008), the claim could be given for certain, based on the several verifications and reports that have been carried out (see a brief overview on the structure of the corpus in Lloberes and Payrató 2011).

[15] This subsection and some fragments of the following two are based on a reformulation of what is exposed in Payrató (1993).

> This analysis shows that the three broad categories of meaning mentioned – interpersonal control, announcement of one's own current state, and evaluative response to a third person – account for 80% or more of all the gestures listed in the above lists, with the exception of that from Iran, in which they account for 66% of the gestures listed. Gestures concerned with interpersonal control ranked first in frequency in all lists, with the exception of that for Kenya. Gestures concerned with reporting one's own emotional or physical stated ranked second or third most frequent in all six lists. Gestures that appeared merely to serve as labels for objects or actions, however, were *least* frequent in all of the lists, with the exception of that for Iran. (Kendon 1981a: 141)

In a way almost identical to Kendon's (1981a), the 221 gestures of the three established compilations for Catalan (basic repertoire / pseudoemblems / other gestures, see 3.5.2), were gathered according to their contents in one (only) of the five following groups:
(A) Interpersonal control (here reduced exclusively to orders, demands, threats, and insults),
(B) Expressions of one's own physical or mental state,
(C) Evaluative responses to a third person,
(D) Labels for objects or actions, and, finally,
(E) Gestures of conjuration and oaths.

The results obtained from this classification fully confirm the results obtained by Kendon. Setting aside emblems of conjuration and oaths, the least frequent set of emblems in the basic repertory contains labels for objects and actions (14%), while the most frequent set includes gestures of interpersonal control (40%), expressions of one's condition (24%) and evaluative responses (21%). The sum of these three sets constitutes 85% of the basic repertory. Interpersonal control emblems are by far the most numerous, although the absence of gestures of salutation made this category more restrictive than Kendon's original group.

5.6.2 Illocutionary force

As we have seen in the historical review (see chapter 1), the idea that a certain type of gesture goes well beyond what would be a simple complement to verbality and is capable of transmitting an illocutionary value is not new. Although not formulated with these words, Quintilian (see 1.1.1) discussed the pragmatic roles and illocutionary values of autonomous gestures two thousand years ago, which has also been discussed by many authors afterwards. Austin's (1962 [1975]) seminal work on speech acts also foresaw the importance of these values. Austin's words are very clear on that score:

5.6 Emblems and interaction: Meaning and functional distribution — 177

(a) many conventional acts, such as betting or conveyance of property, can be performed in non-verbal ways (19) [...]
(b) actions which are non-linguistic but similar to performative utterances in that they are the performance of a conventional action (69) [...]
(c) we may accompany the utterance of the words by gestures (winks, pointings, shruggings, frowns, etc.) or by ceremonial non-verbal actions. These may sometimes serve without the utterance of any words, and their importance is very obvious (76) [...]
(d) we can for example warn or order or appoint or give or protest or apologize by non-verbal means and these are illocutionary acts (119)

In other proposals to study non-verbality and gesture, the pragmatic roles and illocutionary values of autonomous gestures have been repeatedly discussed, although not always with the same terminology. In fact, there have been some terminological confusions, such as the confusion between the terms *illocutionary*, *perlocutionary* and *performative*, and more particularly, the confusion between the last two. Recent publications have provided new opportunities to clarify the terminology, as for instance, Tessendorf's (2014) analysis of pragmatics and performativity in recurrent gestures, and entries such as *speech act* and the subentry *performative gesture* (under the entry *gesture category*) in the subject index of Müller et al.'s (eds.) (2013, 2014) two volumes.

Remaining outside of the terminological confusion, Kendon had already singled out one of the three terms, the term *performative*, in his review of Morris et al. (1979)'s work to characterize a feature of some emblems:

> There are also two gestures [among the 20 gestures studied by Morris et al.] that have a performative function, in the sense that the performance of the gestures constitutes the actual accomplishment of an act such as searing an oath, making a promise, or making o breaking a promise of friendship. (Kendon 1981a: 141)

However, the development of pragmatic studies after Austin have clearly shown that the key term is neither *performative* nor *perlocutive* (in reference to the effects on the interlocutor recipient), but the term and the concept of *illocution*. Consequently, *illocution* has become the analytic focus of post-Austin pragmatic research. Riley (1976) is most likely the first author who, after Austin's work, explored the illocutionary force of emblems, and Kendon (1988: 136) clearly expressed the point: "[certain non-verbal actions – the so-called *emblems* –] are used singly and as such they are the functional equivalent of a complete speech act." Fein and Kasher (1996: 794), following Austin, have even labeled the kind of (gestural) acts we make:

> Upon reflection, it turns out that Austin's tripartite distinction does not pertain only to speech acts, but to many other intentional acts as well. We assume, then, that there are three things that we do with gestures: *gesticulary*, *ingesticulary* and *pergesticulary* acts.

These three actions are understood to parallel the three dimensions of speech acts distinguished by Austin: the locutionary aspect (with the act of the production of the statement), the illocutionary (and the illocutionary force) and perlocutionary (with the effect on the receptors). Nevertheless, although the acceptance of the illocutionary force of emblems seems clear, it must be stated that we do not yet have consistent descriptions of the use of emblems as equivalent tools to speech acts.[16] Neither do we have comparisons between the use of (properly named) speech acts and the use of emblems. Poggi's and Kendon's studies have broken new ground in this respect, but there is still a long way to go before it is possible to analyze in depth how similar or equivalent communicative mechanisms are coordinated to transmit equivalent or different messages and illocutionary values through verbal, paralinguistic and gestural channels.

5.6.3 Illocutionary types and values

There are clear precedents that are presented as an analysis – or at least as an inventory – of the different illocutionary values that emblems can adopt. Riley (1976: 9) is most likely the first researcher to state it with these words, and proposes the following examples:
[1] *Agreeing* and *disagreeing*, by nodding or shaking one's head;
[2] *Greeting*, by waving and/or by eyebrow flash [...];
[3] *Declining*, e.g. by placing one's hand over a cup or glass when offered more;
[4] *Requesting*, e.g. asking for a cigarette by putting two fingers to one's lips and raising the eyebrows quizzically;
[5] *Commanding*: e.g. a policeman makes a winding motion to tell a motorist with whom he wishes to speak to lower the window of his car;
[6] *Questioning a statement* or *doubting*: often by facial expression [...];
[7] *Reporting ignorance*: e.g. by shrugging or contracting shoulders and throwing up both hands, palms upwards, plus appropriate facial expressions.

Also a clear example is Key's (1977: 7–8) following example:

---

16 See Merz (2010, 2011), specially his comparison of illocutionary functions in sixtenth emblems in Colombia and Germany.

5.6 Emblems and interaction: Meaning and functional distribution

Of interest to the purpose of this study is the occurrence of nonverbal accompaniments with the performative verbs, such as facial expressions, smiles, heads nods, gestures, and vocalizations such as humming, hissing, shushing. Nonverbal acts may actually substitute for the performative verbal ones, as in the following. These may also occur concomitantly with the verbal.

bet = handshake
promise, vow = sign of the cross
warn = tsk, tsk
order = pointing
congratulate = handshake, kiss
condole = silence
forgive, pardon = priest's blessing
apologize = hand gesture
bid = auction gestures
approve = smile, uplifted posture
greet, bid you welcome = smile, outspread hands
concede = shrug
approve = smile, head nod
thank = slight bow

permit = head nod
pronounce guilt = facial expression of disapproval, silence
reprimand = glare
consent, agree = vertical head nod, wink
dare = slit eyes, smirk
censure = frown, finger snap
deny = horizontal head nod
reject = hands raised, palms out
protest = marching, sit-in
dismiss = stand up
toast = lift glass
challenge = throw down glove

Key notices that several acts of this type[17] are often accomplished solely with nonverbal means, without the accompaniment of verbal correlates. This is the usual case, for example, with insults or greetings. Key also points out several contextual situations where it is more frequent or almost required to use non-verbal mechanisms (due to distance, noise, speed, the need to maintain silence, or a crowd) and also includes the case of a vocal emblem (*warn = tsk, tsk*; cf. 2.4.3).

Based on Searle's (1976) classical classification of illocutionary acts, it is not too difficult to find non-verbal actions that fit with each of the categories in the Catalan repertoire:

---

[17] The examples provided by Key are illustrative but they refer to (American) English. It goes without saying that in some cases it is not enough to translate them literally into other languages, without a process of adaptation. Nonetheless, many analogous examples can be found in the different emblem repertoires (cf. 3.3.1 and the sample of appendices (I-VIII) for Catalan and Spanish).

(1) As a confirmation (or assertion), that is, representation or description of a state of affairs or reality, for example the emblems referred to *borratxo/* drunk (<I, 24>, <III, 2>) or *xerraire/* chatty (<I, 105/106/107>, <VI, 5>).
(2) As an exhortation, aimed at changing the recipient's behavior, for example in the case of orders: *apropar-se/* to approach (<I, 14/15>, <VII, 1/2>), *allunyar-se/* to go away (<I, 6/7>), *calma/* calm (<I, 28>), or of requests: *alto/* stop (<I, 8>), *cap/* head (<I, 32>), *demanda/* request (<I, 41/42>).
(3) As a commitment of the issuer to carry out an action, e.g. emblematic gestures of oath (<I, 97>) or of threat (<I, 9/10/11>, <V, 27>).
(4) As an expression of the speaker's psychological state, for example in rejection gestures (<I, 91>), praise (<I, 12>) or insults (<I, 27/55/56>, <IV, 12/18>, <V, 42>, <VII, 10>).
(5) As a declaration, by which a state of affairs of the external world is modified. This last category is restricted, in fact, to rather sporadic and usually very formal situations, but it could be represented, for example, by the religious blessing (<III, 1>) and, in a broad interpretation, by conjuration gestures (<I, 39>, <II, 5>, <V, 32>).

In the case of the Catalan repertoire, these classes, as set forth in Payrató (1993), are represented in different proportions in the three repertoires established: basic repertoire / pseudoemblems / other gestures (see 3.5). Assertive gestures are the most abundant throughout the three sets (47%, 58%, 63%). They constitute representative or assertive acts about the sender, the receiver, or the state of things. Directive gestures, through which the sender signals how the receiver should act, are the second most represented category (particularly in the basic repertory: 29%, 15%, 15%). Expressive gestures, informative of the sender's state of mind, form the third main group (18%, 17%, 15%); the two remaining groups represent only a minimal portion of the three inventories. Commissive gestures (6%, 9%, 6%) are acts in which the sender commits himself to doing something such as promises and threats. Declarative gestures (1%, 3%, 1%), named *declarations* in Searle's original text, alter the condition or status of real things (nominations are the widespread example in everyday life). Only a few gestures of conjuration (invokes) were included in this last class.

The five mentioned categories were not taken as mutually exclusive. On the one hand, the same body action can (occasionally) have several different illocutionary values. On the other hand, some gestures simultaneously perform illocutions whose value and components are astride two categories. Thus, invitations and threats constitute at the same time attempts to direct the receiver's behavior and commitments regarding the sender; therefore they were considered to fit into directive and commissive categories. In a similar way, gestures of mockery and insult were thought to be both assertive and expressive.

Together with the concrete percentages of the sharp tripartite distribution, the most striking aspect in the analysis is the different proportion of assertive and directive gestures throughout the three inventories, in contrast with the uniformity of the remaining ones (expressive, commissive, and declarations). Moreover, the disproportions show two clear and complementary trends. Whereas assertive gestures are on the increase in the non-basic repertories (47%, 58%, 63%), directive gestures decrease in a clear way – they make up almost half the productions in the basic repertory (29%, 15%, 15%). What this suggests is that the directive actions considered in this group (basically, orders, demands, and threats) tend to be understood and be conventionalized more steadily than the assertive ones.

One can also observe other similar trends with regards to interactive value. While label emblems remain constant throughout the three repertories (14%, 15%, 15%), interpersonal control emblems are the main category only in the basic repertory (40%), decreasing in the other compilations (25%, 15%). The opposite trend is revealed in the evaluative responses emblems (21%, 18%, 33%), and still more in the emblems of expression of one's own physical or mental state (24%, 37%, 33%). The data seem now to suggest that in the filters between the three repertories, certain kinds of gestures are more likely to be 'stopped' than others: in particular, those which (as a message) convey comments either to other people or about one's own condition in contrast with those that constitute signs of interpersonal control.

5.6.4 Illocution and functions: An example

In an ethnographic study of the relationship between identity, communication, and social exclusion among people with disabilities, Moyer et al. (in preparation) have examined the situated communicative practices of a group of people experiencing severe dysarthria, a speech disorder caused by the neuronal connections to the articulatory muscles, as a result of acquired brain injury in Catalonia, Spain. Moyer et al. have identified how each participant affected with severe speech impairment and varying degrees of physical impairment, develops their own emerging multimodal "home-developed"[18] communicative

---

18 We borrow and adjust the notion of home-developed signs from Goldin-Meadow's (2003) term "homesign" which she attributes to the signs invented by deaf children of hearing

system that relies on their semi-intelligible speech and motor abilities. These multimodal "home" communication systems often include well-known emblematic gestures (e.g. emblem of drinking, or emblem of wiping the sweat from one's forehead) and "home-developed" conventionalized gestures that have stable meanings and shapes across time (e.g. the gesture of touching one's ear becomes the name of a dog whose ear was bitten when it was a puppy). A singular phenomenon of these "home" communicative systems is the appearance of combination of emblems that form emblematic phrases and/or create distinct meanings.[19]

For instance, Fernando is a man is his mid thirties who became quadriplegic as a result of a traumatic brain injury in a motorcycle accident. Unable to move his arms and legs, he combines the production of a few vowels and syllabic spacings with an extensive range of vocalizations, head movements, and facial expressions to communicate multimodally. Together with his family and carers, he has developed a repertoire of emblematic gestures that includes 1) licking his upper lip to indicate that he likes something; 2) sticking his tongue out to indicate he does not want something; 3) moving his tongue to the left to communicate "yes;" 4) and moving his tongue to the right to communicate "no."

Alan, on the other hand, is a young man in his mid twenties who recurrently combines multiple emblems together. Alan suffers from spastic tetraparesis (weakness in all four limbs), also a result of brain injury endured in a motorcycle accident. Alan has full movement of his left arm, which he constantly uses to produce gestures. For example, a speech therapist asks Alan about the name of his dog during a therapy session. Alan, however, has two dogs. In the next turn, Alan answers the question by using two sequentially combined gestures. He first indicates the concept of "mine" by repeatedly

---

parents who have not been exposed to a conventional sign language. Here, we use it to underscore the fact that speech-impaired individuals in Moyer et al. develop their own sign systems idiosyncratically and ad hoc, as opposed to being taught Catalan or Spanish Sign Language.

19 Combinations of two or three emblems are also found in the everyday communication of non-impaired speakers, as in combinations of deictic emblems that are exhortative or express mental states; for instance, "you + come," "I + there?" or "No, (we all) + later + yes". Several authors also document combinations of two or more emblems when the verbal channel is temporarily blocked or limited: Meo-Zilio (1983) describes a combination of an emblem and a time signal, and Poyatos (2002) describes multiple emblems and phrasal emblems; cf. also Kendon (1992) and Haviland (2007). In binary combinations, the structure follows a theme / comment construction (and thus known information / new information), similar to that of everyday, colloquial verbal constructions. It may be possible that this phenomenon is related to protolanguages, such as those indicated by Bickerton (1990: §5), with sequences of two or three words or signs without morphology or syntax (in children under two years, in the initial stages of pidgins, and in chimpanzees who learn sign languages).

touching his chest with his hand in a pointing down shape with the index finger extended. After that, he raises his index and middle fingers to indicate the quantity of two.

Alan has a few emblems that he combines recurrently to produce new meanings that allow him to carry out multiple actions and express a wide range of stances. One such emblem is wiping one's sweat (<I, 29>), which Payrató (1989/1991) documents with the meaning of 'it is hot' or 'sweating.' Alan uses it metaphorically with a core meaning of 'working hard.' A few minutes after the combined emblematic sequence of "mine" + "two," the speech therapist reminds him that there are some speech exercises he should have done but has not done. Alan combines two gestures to produce a turn with the approximate meaning of 'I forgot / I didn't know / it went past me / it was too complicated.' He first rolls his eyes and then wipes the (metaphoric) sweat of his forehead.

As the therapy session continues, Alan is reluctant to continue with the speech therapy exercises as he becomes physically tired of uttering words, which requires great effort on his part because of his severe dysarthria. After the speech therapist praises him for his efforts, Alan combines multiple gestures to convey, teasingly, that the speech therapist should have mercy on him and cut him some slack. First, Alan grabs and releases the speech therapist' hand, and second, he wipes the sweat off his forehead. A few exercises later and after more enthusiastic praise by his mother and speech therapist, Alan produces a third example of combining the emblem of wiping the forehead sweat with other gestures to create another distinct meaning in his multimodal turn. On this third occasion, Alan combines a pronounced eyebrow movement with the wiping of his forehead sweat and laughter to convey jokingly that he did last speech exercise fantastically well.

Fernando's and Alan's use of "home-developed" emblems to create a wide range of meanings, speech acts, and utterances, illustrate how people with severe speech impairments, their families/caretakers, and clinicians develop their own particular multimodal communicative systems. Indeed, these "home" systems include many gestures that have stable shapes and meaning. Some of these conventionalized gestures are widely used and some others have become conventionalized by speech-impaired people and their families and clinicians. Regardless of how the gestures have become signs with stable meanings and shapes across interactions and time, people with severe speech impairment use and combine them in ways that are clearly not depictive/illustrative/spontaneous. Because these are idiosyncratic and are mostly comprehensible to impaired individuals and the people who routinely interact with them, home "emblems" differ from technical repertoires, such as the sport repertoire discussed early in section 3.3.2. At the same time, "home" emblems are clearly not fully grammatical signs, such as the sign languages of the deaf, which are segmentable/ decomposable and combinable to create words and syntactic structures (see 2.4.4). However, they nonetheless resemble the initial stages of homesigns developed by children of hearing parents (Goldin-Meadow 2003) and even the incipient stages of the development of sign languages (Senghas et al. 2005).

Finally, we would like to note that one of the challenges in emblem research in the 21st century is that a more precise typology of the functions of the emblem as a speech act and a more detailed analysis of how the emblem is integrated in conversational or interactive flow remain to be done. We will review this and other related issues in the conclusions in following chapter.

6 Conclusions and final remarks

In this last chapter, we discuss the most important aspects of current research on emblems as well as some challenges of future research, particularly in relation to a general theory of language from a pragmatic perspective (6.1). This theory should be framed within the context of multimodal communication, and should include an applied research dimension that encompasses language teaching, lexicography, and the numerous areas of intercultural pragmatics (6.1.1). In addition, we synthesize here our proposal of conceptualizing the emblems according to three basic dimensions that have been examined throughout the book:
(a) A cognitive dimension, in which we underscore how emblems are constructs that result from the pairing of a gestural form with a meaning (6.2).
(b) An ethnographic dimension that highlights emblems as sociocultural displays in which the cognitive pairing has become recurrent and conventionalized within a social group (6.3).
(c) A pragmatist dimension that emphasizes how emblems are pragmatic tools with an illocutionary force that is manifested in communicative interactions (6.4).

Many years ago, Adam Kendon, one of the greatest scholars and strongest proponent of gesture studies, and very likely the most prolific, versatile and quoted, stated that "[t]o study emblematic gestures is, perhaps, to study a rather minor mode of human communication. Yet, as we have tried to suggest, it is a mode that appears to raise a number of issues of great relevance for a full theory of human symbolic action" (Kendon 1981a: 159). Throughout this book, we have endeavored to illustrate the (great) importance of these minor phenomena. A pragmatic theory cannot put aside this type of symbolic action, so present in social interaction – that is why we use the term *symbolic interaction*. Neither can stylistics, both in production and interpretation, and that is why we speak of *pragmastylistics*. The gestures by which we live, those that give title to this book, are a minor corner of human communication, but every corner serves nonetheless to give a unique perspective, often much more interesting and theoretically productive than we might have guessed or imagined.

6.1 The research on emblems: Present and future: Pragmatic theory and multimodality

As illustrated by recent studies (cf. McNeill (ed.) 2000, Kendon 2004, Müller et al. (eds.) 2013, 2014), it is reasonable to argue that a theory of gesture must be included within a pragmatic theory of linguistic and communicative use if we assume that gesture should be conceived as a component of the linguistic utterance (or French *énonciation*). Indeed, in our case, we believe that recent emblem research shows that its analysis cannot be independent from linguistic analysis, and vice versa; the analysis of the linguistic use cannot be independent from the analysis of the gestural units that are associated with and that share a common meaning – often a common interdependent meaning – with the linguistic units.

The complexity of communicative behavior calls for a generous and comprehensive approach, which cannot be, therefore, any other way but multimodal, since the creation of meanings and their interpretation is done through different channels and modalities. Human communication is multimodal and relies on the *co*-sharing of cognitive contents and the *co*-participating in social interaction. Seen from the reverse angle, a pragmatic theory cannot forget the non-verbal dimension without falling into an unjustified reductionism. In other words, these circumstances are an invitation "to take into consideration the irremediable indexicality of linguistic resources, as well as the systematic and methodic use of embodied resources" (Mondada 2013: 579).

Emblems have been studied quite often in a self-enclosed way, without relating them to other communicative modes, especially verbal ones. On occasion it seemed that it was a type of (absurd) retaliation as a response to the discipline of linguistics' lack of interest. Consequently, the autonomous or independent-from-talk quality of emblems was emphasized. However, instead of promoting progress in emblem studies, these rather autarchic attitudes and research approaches have contributed to leaving emblem analysis without a general pragmatic, semiotic and communicative theory (based on language use, rather than in structures or systems). In turn, emblem research was further marginalized or at least not considered in areas external to the study of gesture, especially in the field of language sciences. As Wharton argues (2022: 384), we would expect that "[r]esearchers into gesture should no more ignore pragmatics than those working in pragmatics should ignore the study of gesture." This is the research direction that we propose, which is very evident in Senft's (2014) pragmatic manual and indeed has some earlier precedents, for example the work by Archer, Ajmer, and Wichmann (2012). These authors "present the first current handbook on pragmatics (not encyclopedic) with several chapters on prosody, gesture, and non-verbal communication, consequently recognizing the appropriatenes of these topics for the pragmatic theory. Empirical research on gesture may apport many evidences for pragmatic theorization, and inversely pragmatic interpretation theories can illuminate and frame contextually many gestural phenomena" (Payrató and Tessendorf 2014: 1536–1537).

The benefits of integrating the study of emblems within a pragmatic theory are in many ways evident. The greatest benefit is the need to unify and coordinate theories that, in the simplest possible way, explain the complexity that we find in communicative practice. Conversely, the benefits of multimodal analysis for a pragmatic theory are equally clear. The communicative practices and the processes of creation and interpretation of meaning are not only *multilingual* (they are not confined to one language, and for that reason the concept of *translanguaging* is justified), but they are also *multimodal*: communicative competence is manifested in the practical ability to combine different modalities (verbal, vocal, and gestural) in face-to-face interactions and in written productions (with text and images). Whether in human-to-human or human-machine conversation, a debate, a comic or magazine, or in cinema, theater, and opera, multimodality has become so ever-present in our everyday life, that a pragmatic theory that does not incorporate multimodality is unthinkable. Unfortunately, the lagging-behind theoretical gap has direct consequences, for example, in the design of grammatical models, in the fields of pragmastylistics and politeness, and in the conception of the communicative repertoire of individuals and social groups. What traditional linguistics had considered verbal texts are in fact *communicative discourses*, and therefore the pragmatics of verbality must go hand in hand with the pragmatics of multimodality. It is not a purely terminological issue but of concepts and research programs. A theory of linguistic use is necessarily a theory of communicative use. Again, the limits of pragmatics are not the limits of "language" understood as a grammar or ability, but the limits of culture and communication, the limits of the creation of meaning in social interaction, through different modalities and their intersection.

The first and most general conclusion of this study and the approach to research that we argued in this book is that emblem research is an excellent laboratory to deepen our knowledge of human communication. In particular, it is an excellent field to help develop an empirically based pragmatic theory of communicative multimodality, which at the same time does not neglect its cognitive and sociocultural bases.

6.1.1 A note on applications

Multimodality is also evident in applied research areas, understood as areas of confluence between theory and practice where specific communication problems or questions must be resolved. The applied area that has been developed the most within emblem research is lexicography, as illustrated in our review of gestural lexicography in section 3.4. From traditional dictionaries to current online collections, the need to have explicit emblem repertoires has been constant, and has also been extended to a neighboring field: second language teaching (and their subsequent repertoires).

In the case of second language teaching, the introduction of dictionaries can be traced, as we have seen, at least to Brault (1963) for French and Green (1968) for Spanish – Spanish being a language that enjoys a good tradition and vitality in this regard.[1] An interesting anecdote of Green's book is Gregory Bateson's quote opening:

> "D:: Daddy, when they teach us French at school, why don't they teach us to wave our hands?
> F:: I don't know. I'm sure I don't know. That is probably one of the reasons why people find learning languages so difficult."

In the French tradition, Calbris and Montredon (1986) already devoted a section to comment on several "Suggestions pour cours de langue" (4–5), and indeed many later compilations have been carried out with didactic goals. If we compare previous and contemporary research, an argument can be made about the need of future research to move towards analyses of less-described languages, and more importantly, towards intercultural comparisons. Furthermore, it is necessary to improve the pedagogical resources used in the education in order to facilitate the learning of these units. One tool that may facilitate learning is new technologies, for example, the so-called *talking faces* (facial animation techniques based on three-dimensional models and image-based techniques).

---

1 See subsequent works by Coll, Gelabert and Martinell (1990) and Cestero (1999), among others. Some dictionaries are designed according to the receptor, for example Takagaki et al.'s (1998) for Japanese speakers, as Martinell and Ueda's (eds.) (1990). Martinell and Ueda's dictionary can be consulted online and with videos for each emblem (cf. Appendix VIII): http://gamp.c.u-tokyo.ac.jp/~ueda/gestos/. Brief collections of Peninsular and/or American Spanish emblems designed to facilitate second learning are also available online, as for instance, the British newspaper The Guardian series "Learn Spanish Gestures" (which, nonetheless, contains several errors and inaccuracies): https://www.theguardian.com/travel/series/learn-spanish.

In this area, computational progress is fundamental in order to improve automatic production and recognition of emblems that are based on multimodal systems that combine speech (and prosody) and gesture. These systems can also play an important role in communication pathology research, another area where emblem research – disorders of interpretation and production of emblematic gestures – can offer information that is useful to psycholinguistic and neuro-linguistic work.

Other applications coming out of emblem research are found in the fields of literature and translation (cf. Poyatos 2008, 2013), both in terms of how emblems are reflected in literature (i.e. how they appear described or suggested), and in terms of translation difficulties. Both fields raise numerous questions about interculturality and, in particular, about intercultural pragmatics. Both fields are also intimately related to pragmastylistics, particularly a pragmastilistics of orality, since it is an irreducible multimodal pragmastylistics (see Payrató's 2017 proposal).

Throughout this book we have illustrated the need to create an explicit and shared methodology for emblem empirical studies. Such a need is even more urgent in all the applied fields of emblem studies. Beyond unit categorization and classification, for which we have a degree of consensus, the establishment of emblem repertoires, as seen in the third chapter of the book, calls for a common method, with explicit protocols and preferably with surveys of both coding (production) and decoding (interpretation). This is the only way to ensure, on the one hand, that the elaborated repertoires are reliable and representative, and on the other, that they are suitable for contrastive and intercultural pragmatic studies.

6.2 Emblems as cognitive constructions

The contributions from cognitive science to the study of gesture and nonverbal communication have been numerous throughout the last quarter of 20th century, and particularly David McNeill's work (1992, 2000, 2005b). However, in the specific case of the study of the emblems, the analysis models used do not seem to have benefited much from cognitive theories, perhaps because of the isolation of the studies mentioned above. As a synthesis of what has been proposed in previous chapters, we believe that cognitive science theoretical contributions to emblem analysis are numerous:
(1) The categorization of gesture as a *prototype* allows a more reasonable and explanatory conception of this phenomenon than previous conceptualizations that posited gestures in terms of fixed, immovable, and self-excluding

features in which empirical data did not fit. Empirical data should not be forced to fit into unmovable categories and theoretical models. Rather, a more flexible categorization should be developed to capture the "flexibility" – a flexibility of gradation and multifunctional units – that empirical studies of emblems have recurrently shown.

(2) The categorization of the emblem as a *prototypical category* is consistent with the first point, about gesture as a conceptual domain. Gesture emblematization can be understood as a process aimed at a prototypical ideal, with a number of (also ideal) characterizing features and exemplars. However, the features of the ideal prototype or exemplar may not always be fulfilled in practice. A feature of an actual occurrence of an emblem will vary in the extent to which it comes close to the feature of that prototypical emblem. Furthermore, the actual occurrence will share more or less features with the prototype exemplar. Thus, each occurrence presents different degrees of prototypicity. The phenomenon in (1) and (2) is parallel to what we find in other types of categorizations, and to grammatical categories in linguistics.

(3) From a cognitive point of view, the emblem can be considered as a construction that combines or matches a gestural form with meaning (usually a non-natural, symbolic meaning). This is the case in the origin of the emblematization process: a non-autonomous co-speech gesture that is often based on practical actions or image schemas undergoes a process that makes it completely autonomous from verbal language. This process is accompanied by the development and reinforcement of a recurrent meaning and a variable degree of social diffusion.

(4) Variants of the (same) emblem and differentiation between emblems can be determined according to a *family resemblance* model. A first emblem may be connected directly to a second one because of specific features, and the second one may share some features with other emblems, but not all. The result is the "air" of the members of family that occurs between a family of emblems: interconnected units but not in the same way or for the same characteristics. The family-like model explains the relationships between emblems (and their variants) in the repertoire of each community or social group better than other more rigid models that are based in traditional semantic and structuralist conceptions.

(5) It is easy to discover many *image schemes* that explain – or at least help to explain – the origin of emblems, on the one hand, and on the other, explain how emblematic gestures work autonomously. These image schemes can be discovered easily, particularly in very obvious and simple cases. Examples of schemes are CONTAINER (very often referring to the head and the mind in

emblems, and their properties), PATH (for example in deictic emblems or in directive emblems of distance, approach, separation), VERTICALITY (also in deictic emblems), and in other cases related to CONTACT, CYCLE, PAIRING, etc. The same applies to *mimetic* schemes from actions that are typically human (EAT, WALK, SEAT, etc.)

(6) Related to *image* and *mimetic schemes*, we often find tropes or cognitive operations in the emblem formation: *metonymic* (contiguity), *metaphorical* (substitution) and combined (metaphors from metonymy, for example). In addition, some combinations can only be explained if we also take into account verbal expressions (utterances or phraseology) that are often at the origin of the emblem (or sometimes from which they are derived, in a reverse direction). Emblems are presented as genuine *multimodal cognitive constructions*, which combine a gestural expression with a verbal one (and with a particular prosody).

(7) The use of emblems is often associated to cases of irony (or sarcasm), which require the recipient to make inferences to interpret them. If we add to this fact the need to distinguish ostensive (communicative) stimuli of countless other signals, it makes sense to argue that a principle of *relevance* intervenes in the use of the emblems, and that emblems should be considered as achieving an optimal degree of relevance from a cognitive perspective. Relevance is thus presumed in the cognitive domain as well as in the pragmatic and communicative domains (see 6.4).

All these points are to be explored and deepened in future research on emblems in order to develop more accurate explanations of the cognitive nature of these units.

6.3 Emblems as sociocultural displays

The emblems are socioculturally conventionalized items, that is, they are units that belong to a sociocultural group or specific speech/communication community. In this group, they have been born (or have been imported from other groups) and have been disseminated, both in a passive sense (interpretive knowledge of the emblem) and in an active sense (production or use).

From an ethnographic perspective, an emblem is an item in the communicative repertoire of a particular individual and, by extension, of the repertoire of a community. On the one hand, the emblem has biological roots and can be conceived as an (ethological) display. On the other hand, at the same time, it has sociocultural roots, and is a sample or a "cultural" product of a specific community: it is patterned or modeled as the typical speech events or acts of this community are.

Edward Sapir, one of the linguistic anthropologists that we could consider as the father of the ethnographic tradition, already discussed the gesture and its sociocultural background. In a somewhat enigmatic quote, which has been reproduced in many later works and that is very suitable for emphasizing the sociocultural component of emblematic gestures, Sapir (1927: 556) argues that:

> A very good example of another field for the development of unconscious cultural patterns is that of gesture. Gestures are hard to classify and it is difficult to make a conscious separation between that in gesture which is merely of individual origin and that which is referable to the habits of the group as a whole. In spite of these difficulties in conscious analysis, we respond to gestures with an extreme alertness and, one might almost say, in accordance with an elaborate and secret code that is written nowhere, known by none, and understood by all. But this code is by no means referable to simple organic responses. On the contrary, it is as finely certain and artificial, as definitely a creation of social tradition, as language or religion or industrial technology. Like everything else in human conduct, gesture roots in the reactive necessities of the organism, but the laws of gesture, the unwritten code of gestured messages and responses, is the anonymous work of an elaborated social tradition. (Sapir 1927: 556)

When Sapir notes that it is difficult to separate what is purely individual (for example an exclusive gestural discourse of an individual) from what we associate with the habits of a group, and establishes a clear precedent of the Bourdieu's (1977) concept of *habitus* and also points to the difference between gesticulation or coverbal gestures (in McNeill's sense) and emblematic gestures, that is to say, *conventionalized* gestures, with shared patterns or standards and with systematic meanings within a community.

As in the cognitive field, reviewed above, there is also much research to develop in relation to the emblems in the ethnographic field. The creation of repertoires, for example, is a logical and important task if we consider that it is the base of numerous applications, such as lexicographical or pedagogical. However, it requires shared foundations and methodologies, because otherwise, it is not possible to develop comparisons that are fundamental for pragmatic intercultural studies. Furthermore we believe that numerous works have shown that ethnographic analysis is the only one that, as a paradigm of qualitative methodology, can reveal the accurate value of an emblem within communicative interaction (cf. 4.4 and Sherer's and Brookes' works). Ethnographic analysis is the most effective method for unraveling the pragmatic functions that the emblems develop in each sociocultural group, and that are associated with all types of variation (ethnic, dialectal, geographical, social, and functional) that are inherent to any communicative community.

6.4 Emblems as pragmatic tools

Emblems can be understood as pragmatic mechanisms that make it possible to carry out or realize the human ability to communicate in the form of action. This emblematic communicative act has many analogies with speech acts. The main analogy resided on the fact that an emblem has illocutionary force, which differentiates it from other gestures. Every gesture is "pragmatic" in a general semiotic sense, since gestures are signs. However, only some signs (either gestures or linguistic utterances) have an illocutionary force and are capable of becoming a communicative act or action. An illustrator or a co-speech gesture does not have it if we consider it in isolation and without any associated with speech, just as it does not have the phone [k] or the morf [-ness]. A greeting gesture or a directive emblem are communicative acts on their own, like utterances such as: *Hello! Hey!* Or *Come over here!* Many emblems are also performative (Kendon 1981a): they carry out the action that they express. Consequently, they are equivalent to performative verbal expressions (for instance, greetings, insults, orders, demands and requests) and can be combined with such verbal expressions, creating multimodal constructions (cf. Enfield 2009, Mondada 2013, 2016, and Alturo et al. 2016).

Based on their illocutionary value, emblems can be classified in a similar way as conventional speech acts: declarative or assertive, expressive, commissive, directive, among the most common, and declarations, in more formal situations (or technical and specific). More detailed research and analyses remain to be done in order to examine how non-verbal illocutionary acts are related to verbal ones, how they may complement or excluded one another in different speaking communities (intercultural pragmatics) and in different situational contexts (pragmastylistics or functional/interactional pragmatics).

Likewise, more in-depth research is needed on the principles or maxims that control (linguistic and non-linguistic) communicative use and that are applied to each situation. When do emblems appear with linguistic utterances and when do they appear in a completely independent fashion? If we consider that the principle of relevance should be taken into account not only in linguistic but also in non-verbal production – particularly in emblem production, which can be considered halfway between linguistic and non-verbal – how do interlocutors modify the inferences that they make depending on the simultaneous combination of verbal and non-verbal elements in a communicative act? To what extent does the combination of verbal and non-verbal elements occur because it is *optimal*, that is, economically and efficiently from the point of view of a pragmatics of optimality?

We know now that some pragmatic phenomena, which have traditionally been studied only in the verbal sphere, have an indisputable non-verbal correlate in oral communication. Obvious cases are deixis, politeness, discursive coherence and stylistic issues (for instance expressiveness), which rely on multiple non-verbal mechanisms, often involving emblems. How are a *situated* multimodal production and interpretation achieved in a particular context? The answers to this question and to the previous ones are not just worth pursuing in pragmatics, but they have strong psycholinguistic and neuro-linguistic implications, particularly in regard to production and interpretation models of speech and gesture.

It will not come as a surprise to any of the readers of this book that the most powerful questions often lead to the most complex and challenging answers. What constitutes an emblem or an emblematic gesture is a specific and limited question on an area of knowledge that is largely general and difficult to delimit: how to build a sociopragmatic theory of human communication. If we imagine ourselves on a PATH in metaphors as LIFE IS A JOURNEY and GAINING (KNOWLEDGE) IS TO TRAVEL, the emblematic gestures by which we live offer us a journey – more or less long and more or less exotic – associated with the discovery of new knowledge about the human ability to communicate for the benefit of social interaction.

Appendices

The following appendices contain samples of emblems from communities with native speakers of Catalan and Spanish, extracted from Payrató (1989/1991, 1993), Amades (1957), Mascaró (1981), Cardona (1953–54), Kany (1960), Saitz and Cervenka (1972) and Meo-Zilio and Mejía (1980–83). The last appendix (VIII) incorporates links to video recordings of emblems (Martinell and Ueda (eds.) 1990).

Appendix I
Basic repertory of Catalan emblems

Basic repertoire of Catalan emblems (Number, Catalan keywords, English (approximate) equivalent keywords, and brief verbal description), which is based on Payrató (1993). The illustrations corresponding to each gesture can be consulted in Payrató (1989/1991), with online access to:

http://www.tdx.cat/handle/10803/1687;jsessionid=46B9A98A31F4448A1B0EC16CE6BEF2E0.tdx2)

<1> Adonar-se'n (Oblit). **To realize (Slip)**. Strike palm to forehead.
<2> Adulador. **Toady**. Flat hand moves up and down.
<3> Afanyar-se ("Ràpid!"). **To hurry ("Quickly!")**. Extended fingers beckon.
<4> Afirmació (Acord). **Affirmation (Agreement)**. Tilt head forwards and backwards.
<5> Alerta. **Alert**. Index finger pulls lower eyelid.
<6> Allunyar-se ("Ves-te'n!"). **To go away ("Get out!")**. Joined fingers open outwards.
<7> Allunyar-se ("Ves-te'n!", "Marxem!"). **To go away ("Get out!", "Let's go!")**. Snap fingers.
<8> Alto. **Stop**. Raised hand, palm extended away from body.
<9> Amenaça ("Et pegaré!"). **Threat ("I'll bash you!")**. Open hand moves obliquely.
<10> Amenaça (Avís). **Threat (Warning)**. Waggle index finger.
<11> Amenaça (Provocació). **Threat (Provocation)**. Shake upraised fist.
<12> Apreciació (Dona, Figura). **Appraisal (Woman, Figure)**. Hand traces curves.
<13> Apreciació ('Pitram'). **Appraisal ('Big-bosomed')**. Hands twist in front of chest.
<14> Apropar-se ("Vine!"). **To approach ("Come here!")**. Extended fingers fold to down turned palm.
<15> Apropar-se ("Vine!"). **To approach ("Come here!")**. Extended fingers fold to up turned palm.
<16> Aproximadament (Dubte, Desconeixement). **Approximately (Doubt, Ignorance)**. Side to side motion with head.
<17> Aproximadament (Regular). **Approximately (Regular)**. Flat hand undulates side to side.
<18> Autostop. **Hitch-hiker**. Outward movement of fist, thumb extended.

<19> Barrut (Galtes, Caradura). **Cheeky (Rotter, Cad)**. Palm lightly slaps cheek.
<20> Bé (Perfecte, "D'acord!"). **All right (Perfect, "O.K.!")**. Index finger and thumb form circle.
<21> Bé (Perfecte, "D'acord!"). **All right (Perfect, "O.K.!")**. Thumb extended upwards from fist.
<22> Beure. **To drink**. Thumb moves towards mouth.
<23> Boig (Bogeria). **Mad (Madness>**. Index finger rotates at temple (or taps temple).
<24> Borratxo (Borratxera). **Drunk (Drunkenness)**. Finger or thumb taps end of nose.
<25> Burla (Llengotes). **Taunt (Tongue out)**. Extend tongue.
<26> Burla (Pam i pipa). **Taunt (Thumb one's nose)**. With thumb to nose, open hand waves.
<27> Cabró. **Cuckold**. Index and small finger extended upwards.
<28> Calma. **Calm**. Open hands, palms down, move up and down.
<29> Calor (Suar). **Heat (To sweat)**. Hand wipes forehead.
<30> Caminar. **To walk**. Index and middle fingers move forwards and backwards.
<31> Cansament. **Tiredness**. Exhale while inflating cheeks.
<32> Cap (Intel·ligència, Idea). **Head (Intelligence, Idea)**. Index finger touches forehead or temple.
<33> Cardar. **To fuck**. Move index finger in and out of closed hand.
<34> Cardar (Fotre). **To fuck (To fuck up)**. Arms in 'ski' position move in pulling motion.
<35> Claus (Obrir). **Keys (To open)**. Closed hand shakes keys from side to side.
<36> Complicitat (Avís). **Complicity (Warning)**. Open and close one eye.
<37> Compte (Escriure). **Bill (To write)**. Hand zigzags in air.
<38> Comptes (Pagar, Cobrar). **Account (To pay, To charge)**. Index finger or fist beats palm.
<39> Conjur (Atracció bona sort). **Conjuration (Hoping for good luck)**. Cross index and middle fingers.
<40> Continuïtat (Repetició). **Continuity (Repetition)**. Rotate extended index finger.
<41> Demanda. **Request**. Cup hand before the body.
<42> Demanda (Reclam). **Request (Call)**. Open hand raised above head.
<43> Desafiament (Provocació). **Challenge (Provocation)**. Stretch upper body and head forward.
<44> Descuit (Parla). **Slip (Speech)**. Cover mouth with hand.
<45> Desentendre's. **To ignore**. Sharp up and down movement of arm.

Appendix I Basic repertory of Catalan emblems — **199**

<46> Detingut (Emmanillat). **Arrested (Handcuffed)**. Fists touching each other side by side.
<47> Diner(s). **Money (Cash)**. Rub thumb and index finger.
<48> Dubte (Desconeixement, Impotència). **Doubt (Ignorance, Impotence)**. Open hand extended, shrug shoulders.
<49> Efeminat (Marica). **Effeminate person (Queer)**. Open hand falls backwards.
<50> Embarassada. **Pregnant woman**. Hand(s) making a semicircle before stomach.
<51> Enfrontament. **Confront**. Index fingers touching tips.
<52> Exclamació (Èmfasi). **Exclamation (Emphasis)**. Shake hand up and down before the body.
<53> Fàstic. **Disgust**. Mouth opens in convulsive grimace (as if to vomit).
<54> Forçut (Mascle). **Strong male (Macho)**. Raise and bend arm at side.
<55> Fot-et (Dit impúdic). **Fuck you (Raised finger)**. Extend middle finger from fist.
<56> Fot-et (Botifarra). **Fuck you (Forearm jerk)**. Bend one arm while slapping its bicep with the other hand.
<57> Fotografia. **Photograph**. Thumbs and index fingers imitate camera.
<58> Fred. **Cold**. Hands rub arms.
<59> Fuita. **Flight**. Slap hands with an up and down movement.
<60> Fumar. **(To smoke)**. Index and middle fingers form a 'V' at the mouth.
<61> Gens (Mínim). **A tiny little bit (Minimum)**. Thumb nail to index finger.
<62> Gras (Obessitat). **Fat (Obesity)**. Hands vibrate before stomach.
<63> Hora. **Hour**. Index finger taps wrist.
<64> Indiferència (Dubte, Desconeixement). **Indifference (Doubt, Ignorance)**. Lips frown.
<65> Indiferència (Desconeixement). **Indifference (Ignorance)**. Frown and shrugged shoulders.
<66> Innocència. **Innocence**. Extend open hands before body.
<67> Interrogació. **Question**. Head tilted back, hands open.
<68> Invitació (Passar, "Endavant!"). **Invitation (To pass, "Come in!")**. Open hand moves from front to side of body.
<69> Llegir. **To read**. Open hands together before body.
<70> Llegir (Mirar). **To read (To look at)**. Open hand held before body.
<71> Lloança ("Excel·lent!"). **Praise ("Excellent!")**. Kiss joined fingertips, and hand pulls away.
<72> Malament. **Badly**. Extended thumb points down.
<73> Masturbació (Home). **Masturbation (Man)**. Half opened hand moves up and down.)

<74> Menjar. **To eat**. Joined fingertips move towards mouth.
<75> Molt (Ple). **A lot (Full)**. Upwardly pointed fingertips touch and separate.
<76> Negació. **Negation**. Head turns from side to side.
<77> Negació. **Negation**. Extended index finger moves from side to side.
<78> Panxa (Tip, Gana, Mal de panxa). **Belly (To be full, Hunger, Stomach ache)**. Open palm pressing against stomach.
<79> Pas ("Separeu-vos!"). **Way ("Make way!")**. Extended arms, palms facing outwards, separate laterally.
<80> Passar ("Circulin!"). **To pass ("Move along!")**. Extended hand moves back and forth.
<81> Picar-se (Drogaaddicte). **To inject (Drugaddict)**. Extended index finger presses upper forearm.
<82> Plorar. **To cry**. Fists rub eyes.
<83> Pobresa (Escurat). **Poverty (Ruined)**. Pull trouser pockets inside-out.
<84> Poc. **Little**. Index finger and thumb show space between them.
<85> Por (Acollonit). **Fear (Frightened)**. Thumb and index finger vibrate at throat.
<86> Prec. **Suplication**. Hands held in prayer move back and forth.
<87> Presumir. **To boast**. Straighten body and raise shoulders.
<88> Prou (Final). **Enough (End)**. Palm down hands held side by side separate laterally.
<89> Prou (Final, Res). **Enough (End, Nothing)**. Upheld hands side by side separate laterally.
<90> Pudor. **Stink**. Thumb and index finger pinch nose.
<91> Rebuig ("Prou!"). **Repulse ("Enough!")**. Arm extended with open hand.
<92> Recordar (Idea). **To remember (Idea)**. Index finger held at temple, moves away.
<93> Robar. **To steal**. Fingers rotate and fold.
<94> Satisfacció (Guanyador, Victòria). **Satisfaction (Winner, Victory)**. Upheld fists shake.
<95> Sentir (Escoltar). **To hear (To listen to)**. Index finger points to ear.
<96> Silenci. **Silence**. Vertical index finger in front of the lips.
<97> Sinceritat (Jurament). **Sincerity (Oath)**. Palm pressed to chest.
<98> Son (Dormir). **Sleepy (To sleep)**. Head rests laterally on hands.
<99> Sorpresa. **Surprise**. Bulging eyes, raised eyebrows.
<100> Suïcidi. **Suicide**. Hand held in 'pistol form' points to temple.
<101> Telèfon. **Telephone**. Fist pressing the ear.
<102> Unió (Entesa). **Union (Understanding)**. Extended index fingers held side by side.

<103> Victòria. **Victory**. Index and middle finger form a 'V'.
<104> Vista (Veure-hi, Mirar). **Vision (To see, To look at)**. Index finger points to the eye.
<105> Xerraire. **Chatty**. Extended fingers and thumb beneath open and close.
<106> Xerraire (Bocamoll). **Chatty (Gossip)**. Index finger touches tip of tongue.
<107> Xerraire (Parlar). **Chatty (To talk)**. Open relaxed hand rotates before mouth.
<108> Xuclat (Prim, Malalt). **Gaunt (Thin, Ill)**. Hand pulls cheeks toward mouth.

Appendix II
Catalan emblems. Sample of Amades (1957)

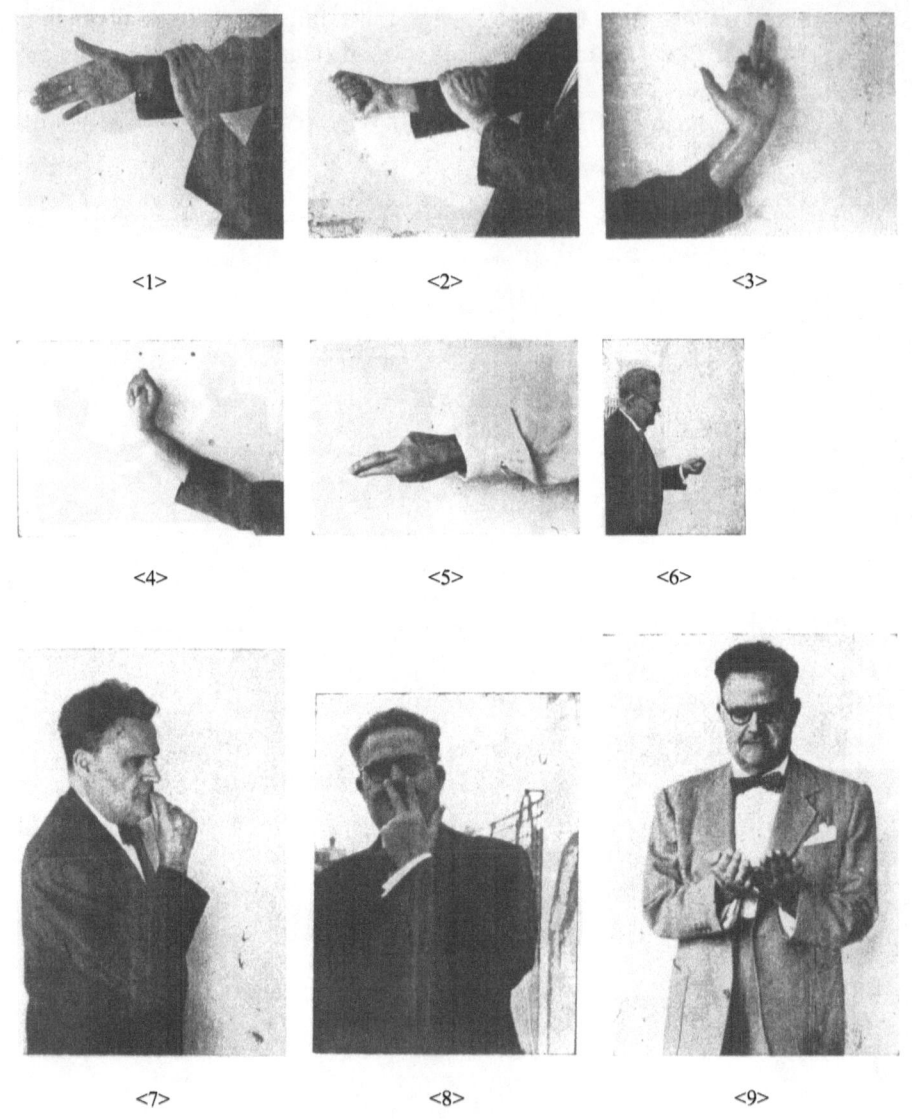

Appendix II Catalan emblems. Sample of Amades (1957) — **203**

<10>

<11>

<12>

- <1> Anar-se'n. **Leave speedily**
- <2> Botifarra (b). **Forearm jerk (b)**
- <3> Botifarra (a). **Forearm jerk (a)**
- <4> Figa. **Fig**
- <5> Jurament. **Swearing**
- <6> Avarícia. **Avarice, miserliness**
- <7> Callar. **Shut up**
- <8> Diner (no tenir diners). **Money (not to have money)**
- <9> Llegir. **To read**
- <10> Borratxera. **Drunkenness**
- <11> Pam i pipa. **Mockery**
- <12> Ell. **He**

Appendix III
Catalan emblems. Sample of Mascaró (1981)

<1> Jurament. **Swearing**
<2> "Està pitof", "està torrat." **To be drunk (lit. 'to be toasted')**
<3> "És boig", "està tocat del bolet". **Crazy (lit. 'to have one's hat tilted /bent')**
<4> "És boig", "està tocat del bolet". **Crazy (lit. 'to have one's hat tilted /bent')**
<5> Gest de mofa i d'insult "llengotes". **Mockery and insult gesture (lit. 'long tongues')**
<6> Gest de mofa i d'insult "pam i pipa". **Mockery and insult gesture (lit. 'palm and pipe')**
<7> Unió, casament, complicitat. **Union, marriage, complicity**

Appendix IV
American Spanish gestures (Venezuela). Cardona (1953–1954)

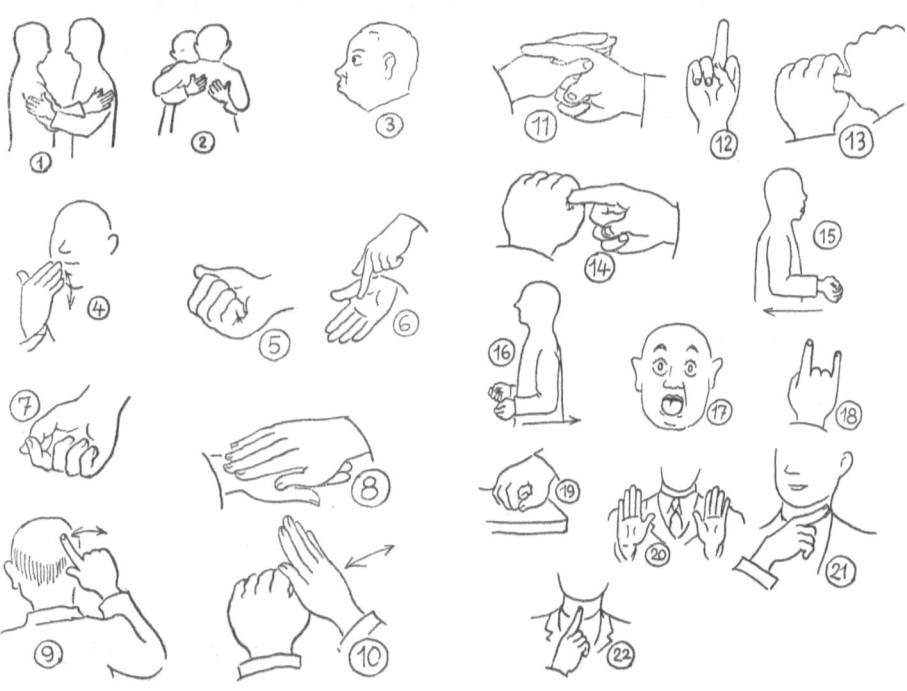

<1>   Para saludar. **To greet**
<2>   Abrazos de Año Nuevo. **New Year hugs**
<3>   Para señalar. **To point**
<4>   Para indicar comida. **To signal food**
<5–7>   Para indicar dinero. **To signal money**
<8>   Para formalizar un trato o convenio. **To formalize/seal a deal or an agreement**
<9>   Gesto de negación. **Negation gesture**
<10–15> Gestos vulgares y escatológicos de negación, repudio o rechazo. **Vulgar and scatological gestures of negation, repudiation or rejection**
<16>   Gesto vulgar para indicar el coito. **Vulgar gesture for intercourse**

<17>   Para indicar sorpresa. **To signal surprise**
<18–19> Gestos supersticiosos contra la guiña o mal de ojo. **Superstitious gestures against evil eye or cursing/spell-casting wink**
<20>   Gesto de inhibición. **Gesture of inhibition**
<21–22> Para indicar despido de un empleo, ruptura de relaciones, muerte, etc. **To signal that one is being fired, relationship breakup, death, etc.**

Appendix V
American Spanish gestures. Kany (1960)

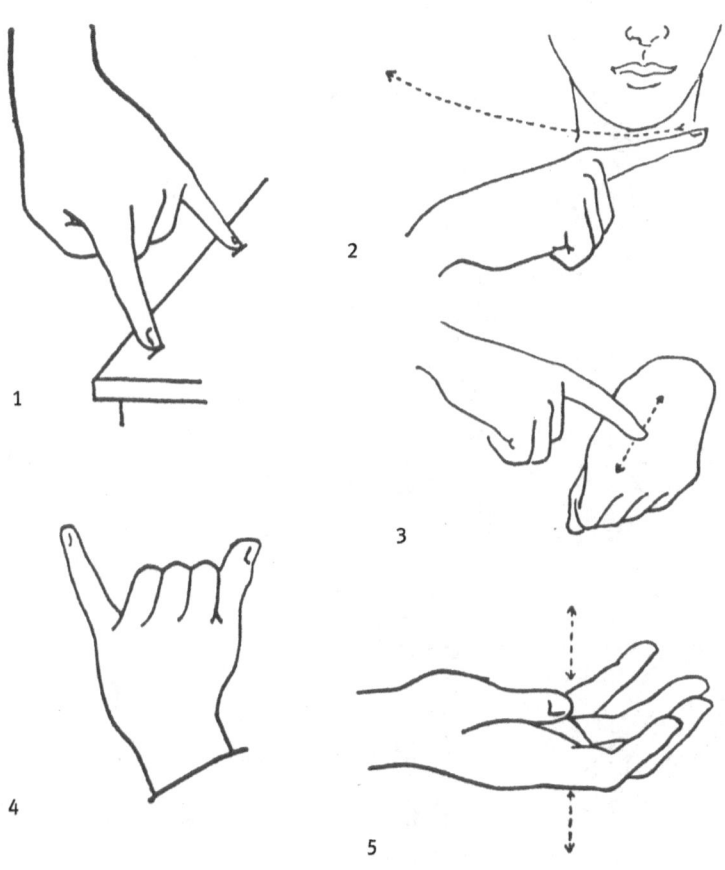

1. *cuernos.* 2. *matar.* 3. *negro.* 4. *flaco.* 5. *huevón.*

208 —— Appendix V American Spanish gestures. Kany (1960)

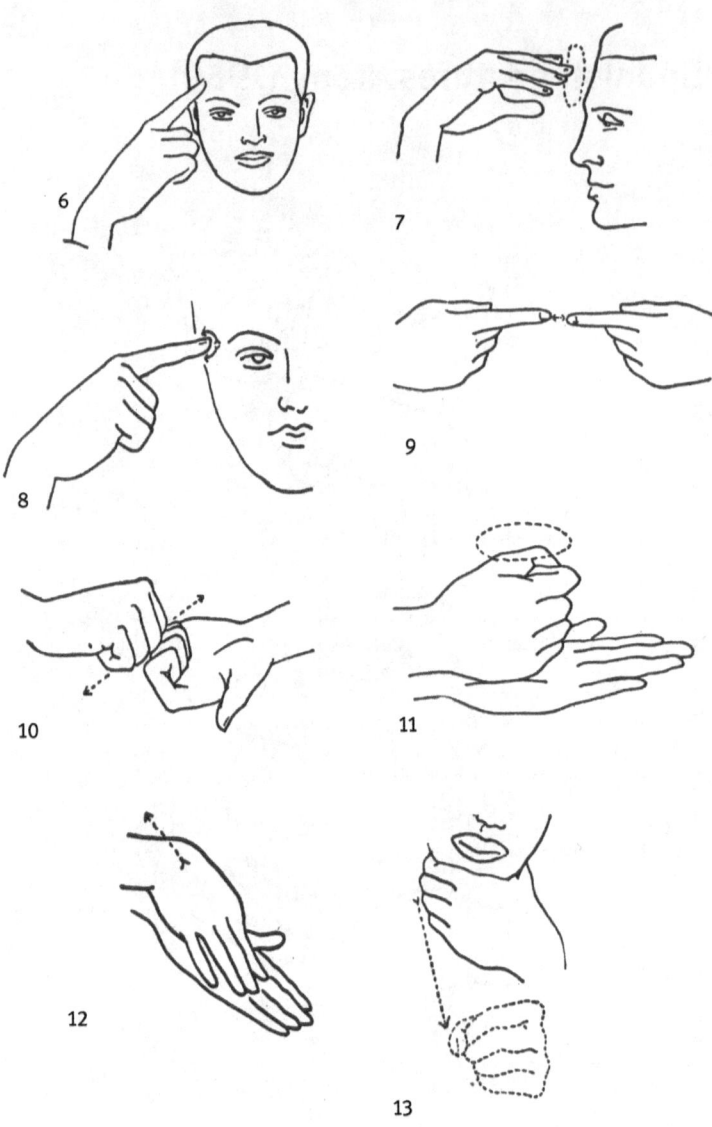

6, 7, 8. *loco*. 9. *de punta*. 10, 11, 12, 13. *rabia*.

Appendix V American Spanish gestures. Kany (1960)

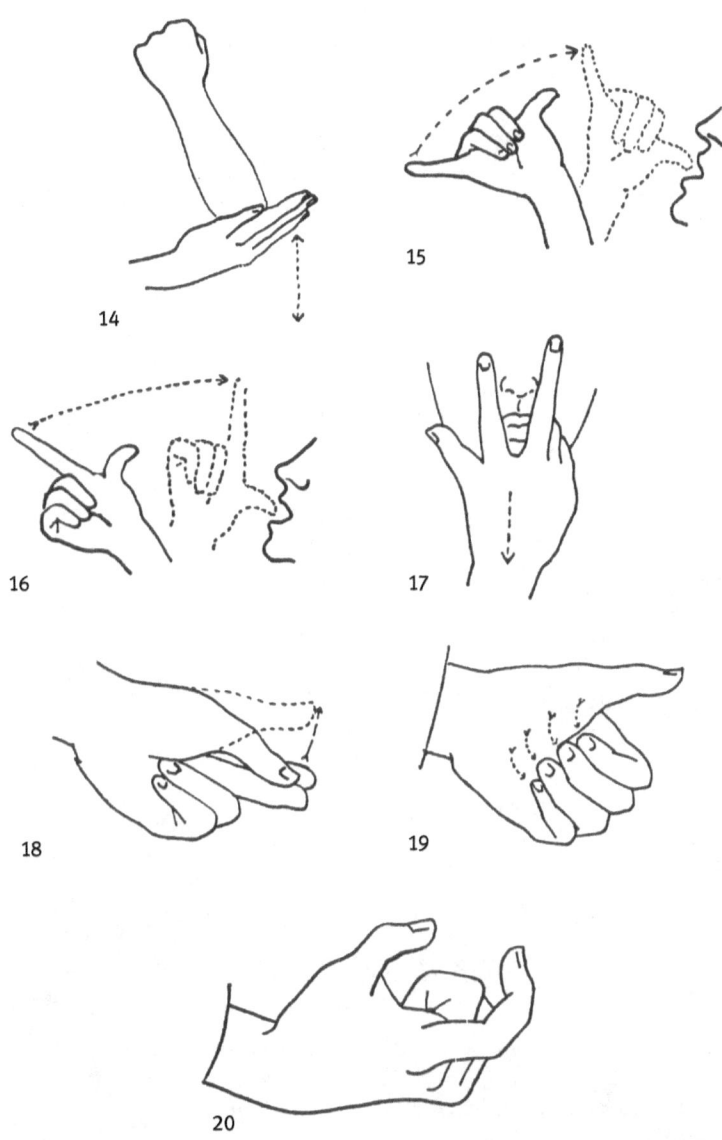

14. *codo.* 15, 16. *beber.* 17. *a dos velas.* 18,19,20. *dinero.*

Appendix V American Spanish gestures. Kany (1960)

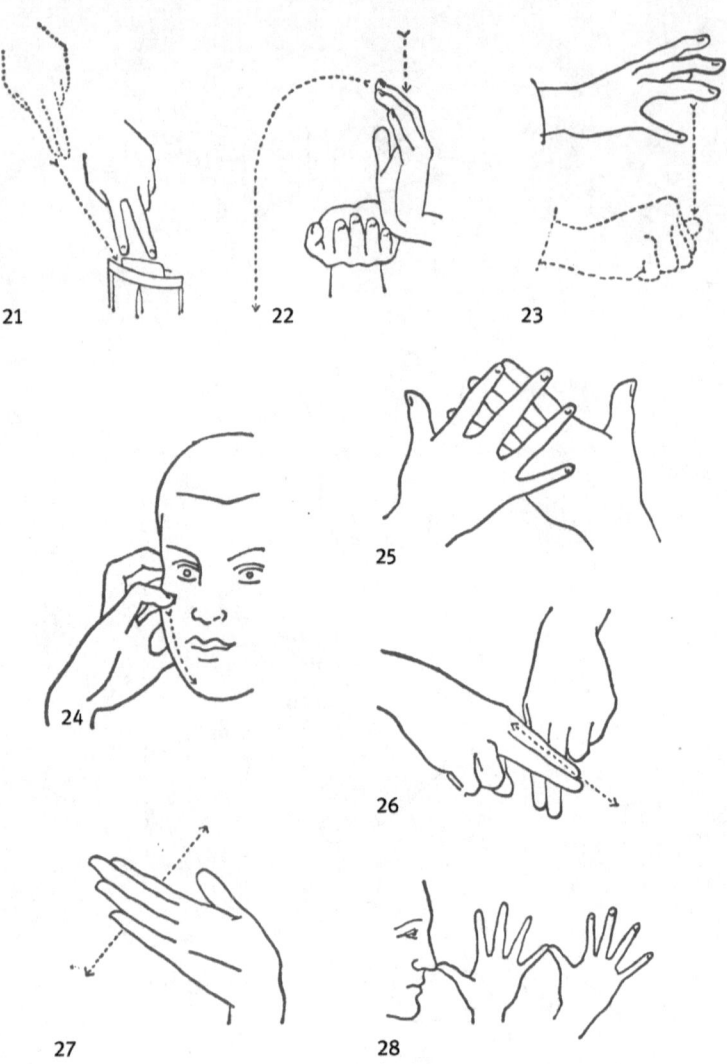

21. *tomador de dos.* 22. *clavarse el dinero.* 23,24. *robar.* 25, 26. *cárcel.*
27. *pegar.* 28. *pito catalán.*

Appendix V American Spanish gestures. Kany (1960) — 211

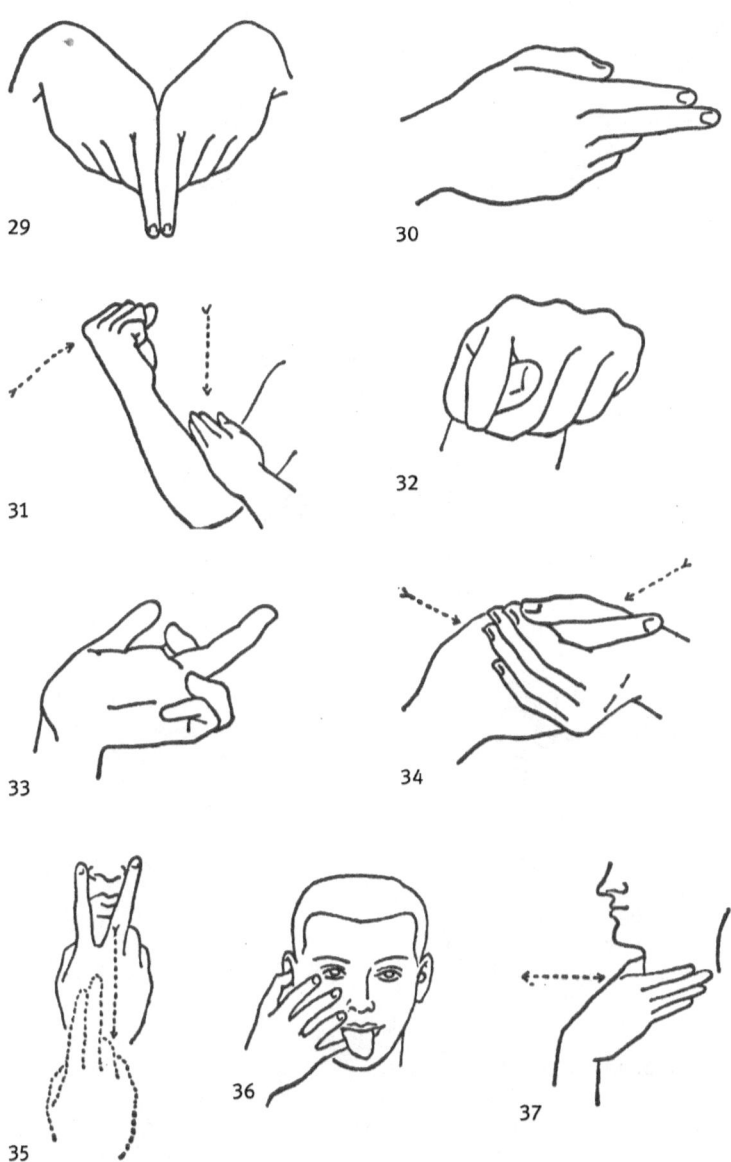

29, 30. *juntarse*. 31. *corte de managa*. 32, 33. *higa*. 34. *pistola*.
35. *violin*. 36. 4 *violines*. 37. *mentada*.

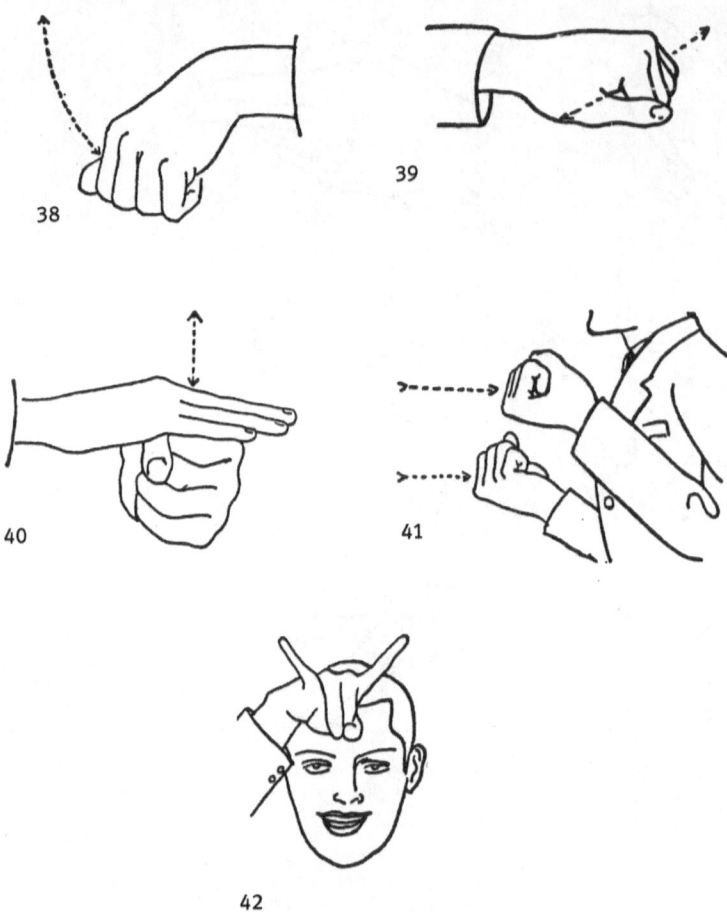

38, 39, 40, 41. *copular*. 42. *cornudo*.

<1>   Cuernos. **Horns**
<2>   Matar. **Killing**
<3>   Negro. **Black**
<4>   Flaco. **Thin**
<5>   Huevón. **Slacker**
<6–8>   Loco. **Crazy**
<9>   De punta. **To be annoyed at someone (lit. 'at end')**
<10–13> Rabia. **Rage**
<14>   Codo. **Elbow**
<15, 16> Beber. **Drinking**

Appendix V American Spanish gestures. Kany (1960)

<17>   A dos velas. **Poor (lit. 'having only two candles')**
<18–20> Dinero. **Money**
<21>   Tomador de dos. **(Heavy) drinker/drunk**
<22>   Clavarse el dinero. **To steal money**
<23, 24> Robar. **Stealing**
<25, 26> Cárcel. **Prison**
<27>   Pegar. **Hitting**
<28>   Pito catalán. **Catalan whistle (sign of mockery)**
<29, 30> Juntarse. **Getting together, union**
<31>   Corte de mangas. **Forearm jerk**
<32, 33> Higa. **Fig**
<34>   Pistola. **Gun**
<35>   Violín. **Offense gesture (lit. 'violin')**
<36>   Cuatro violines. **Offense gesture (lit. 'four violins')**
<37>   Mentada. **Offense gesture (usually associated with insulting the other person's mother)**
<38–41> Copular. **Intercourse**
<42>   Cornudo. **Horned/ cuckold**

Appendix VI
American Spanish emblems (Colombian). Sample of Saitz and Cervenka (1972)

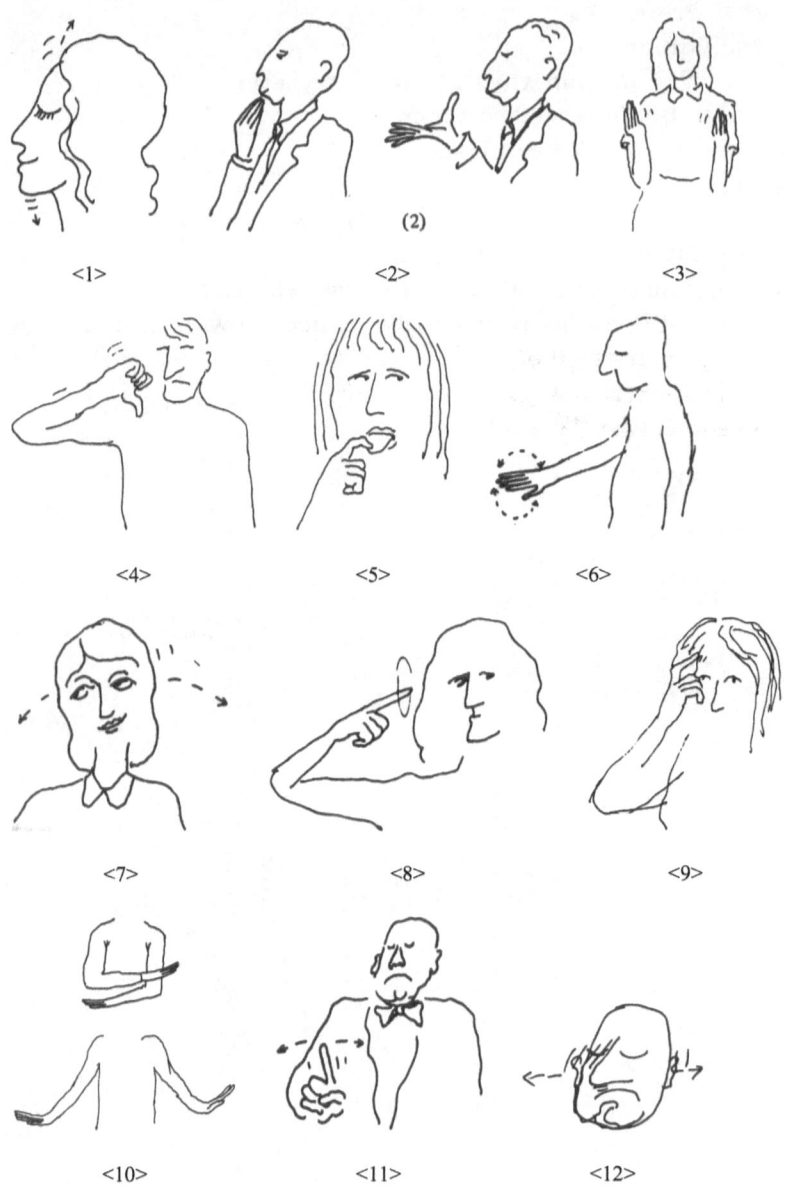

<1>	**Agreement** [and **Yes**]
<2>	**Approval**
<3>	**Crowd**
<4>	**Disapproval**
<5>	**Gossip**
<6–7>	**More or less**
<8–9>	**Insanity**
<10>	**Termination**
<11>	**No**
<12>	**No**

Appendix VII
Spanish emblems. Sample of Meo-Zilio and Mejía (1980–1983)

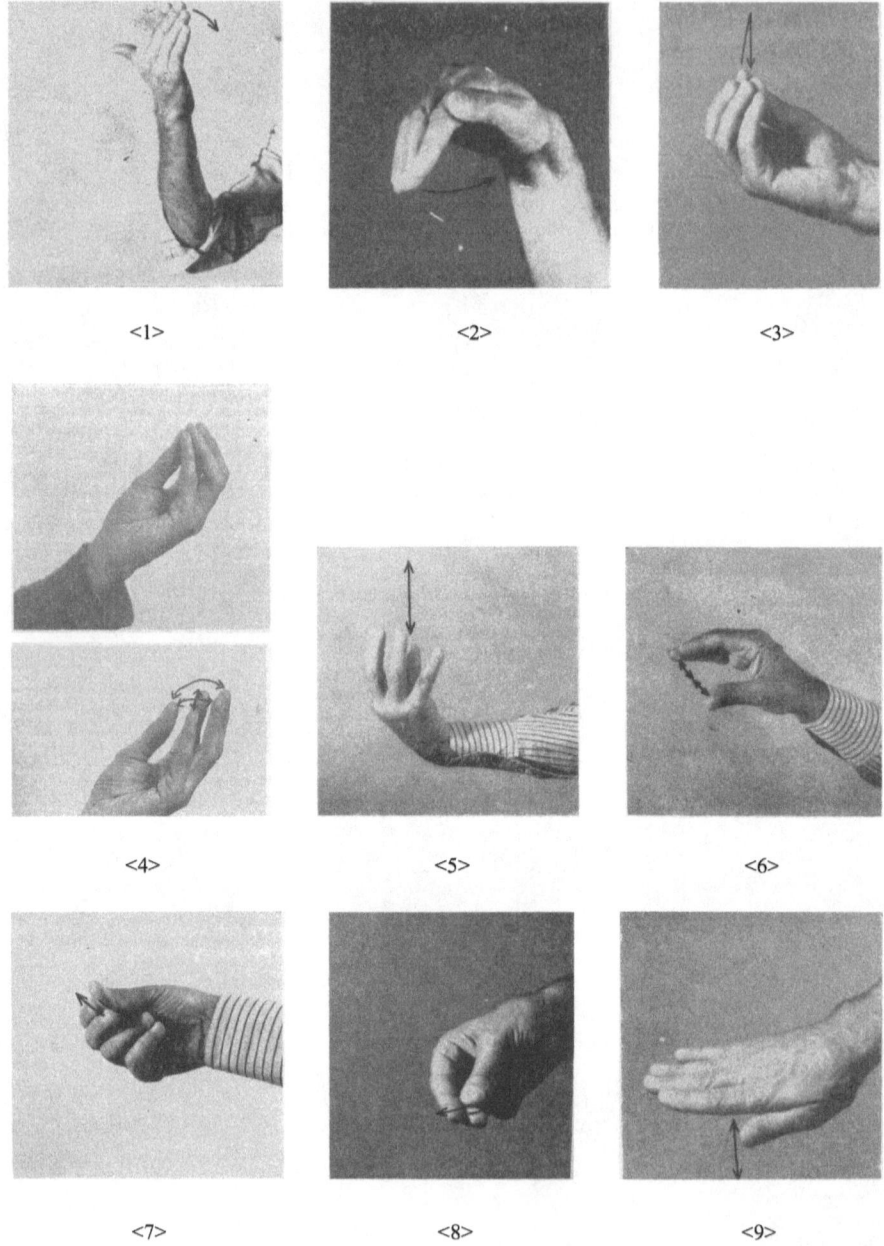

Appendix VII Spanish emblems. Sample of Meo-Zilio and Mejía (1980–1983) — **217**

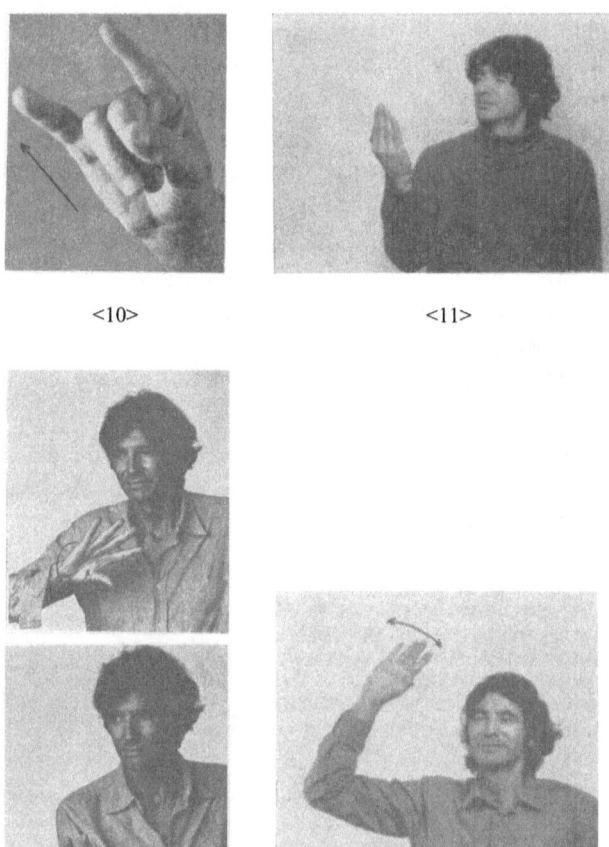

<1–2> Acercarse [orden de ... ; invitación a ...]. **Come close [order to ... ; invitation to ...]**
<3> Cantidad [gran ...]. **Quantity [a great ...]**
<4> Miedo (temor, canguelo); miedoso (temeroso, medroso); Temer y similares. **Fear (dread, jitters); fearful (frightened, scared); To fear and similar meanings**
<5> Huevón (pelotudo, boludo), torpe (incapaz y similares). **Slacker (bum, deadbeat, lit. 'with big testicles') clumsy/sloppy (incompetent and similar meanings)**

<6> Hablador (que habla demasiado, charlatán, parlanchín y similares). **Talkative (that talks too much, charlatan, chatterbox and similar meanings)**

<7–8> Dinero en general. **Money en general**

<9> Adulador (adulón y similares) **Flatterer (toady/brown-noser/ass-kisser and similar meanings)**

<10> Conjuros de repulsión del mal agüero. **Spells for rejecting bad omens**

<11> Ver [no ...] (Ver mal); miope (corto de vista, cegato y similares). **Seeing [not seeing] (seeing poorly); short-sighted (short-sighted, shut-eyed, and similar meanings)**

<12> "¡Basta!" ("¡Se acabó!" y similares). **"Enough!" ("It's over!") and similar meanings)**

<13> Robo (Hurto, estafa); ladrón (caco, estafador); robar (hurtar, estafar) y similares. **Robbery (Theft, scam); thief (crook, burglar); to rob (to steal, scam and similar meanings)**

<14> Saludos. **Greetings**

Appendix VIII
Other samples of emblems (links to illustrations and videos)

– Emblemas españoles. Martinell and Ueda (eds.) (1990)
  https://lecture.ecc.u-tokyo.ac.jp/~cueda/gakusyu/gestos/index.html

Included gesture list:
<1>   Acercarse. **To come closer**
<2>   Alegrarse del mal ajeno. **To rejoice/feel schadenfreude, lit. 'to rejoice when bad things happen to others'**
<3>   Allí. **There**
<4>   Antes. **Before**
<5>   Aquí. **Here**
<6>   Asco. **Disgust**
<7>   ¡Basta ya! **Enough!**
<8>   Beber. **Drinking**
<9>   Borracho. **Drunk**
<10> Buena idea. **Good idea**
<11> Cálmate. **Calm down**
<12> Caminar. **Walking**
<13> Cara dura. **Cheeky**
<14> ¡Circulen, circulen! **Move along, move along!**
<15> Comer. **Eating**
<16> Contar. **Counting numbers**
<17> Correr. **Running**
<18> Corta el rollo. **Cut it out**
<19> Cuenta. **Bill/ check**
<20> ¡Cuidado! **Watch out!**
<21> Desengaño. **Disapointment**
<22> Después. **Later/ afterwards**
<23> Deténgase. **Stop**
<24> Dormir. **Sleeping**
<25> Dos dedos. **A bit (lit. 'two fingers')**
<26> Estudiar. **Studying**
<27> Gire. **Turn around**
<28> Gran extensión. **Large area**
<29> Hablar. **Talking**

<30> Harto. **Fed up**
<31> Hola. **Hello**
<32> Impaciente. **Impatient**
<33> Indiferencia. **Indifference**
<34> Lagarto, lagarto. **Sneaky/cagey** (lit. 'lizzard, lizzard')
<35> Levántese. **Stand up**
<36> ¡Lo conseguí! **I did it!**
<37> Loco. **Crazy**
<38> Más o menos. **More or less**
<39> Manos a la obra. **Let's get started/ let's get our hands dirty** (lit. 'hands on the work')
<40> Manos sobre mano. **Nothing done/ iddle hands** (lit. 'one hand over the other')
<41> ¡Mira! **Look!**
<42> Mitad. **Half**
<43> Mucha gente. **A lot of people**
<44> Mucho. **A lot**
<45> Mucho dinero. **A lot of money**
<46> Muy alto. **Very tall**
<47> Muy bajo. **Very short**
<48> Muy bien. **Very good**
<49> Muy delgado. **Very thin**
<50> Muy gordo. **Very fat**
<51> Nada. **Nothing**
<52> No. **No**
<53> No oír. **Not hearing**
<54> No saber. **Not knowing**
<55> No ver. **Not seeing**
<56> Nosotros. **We**
<57> Números. **Numbers**
<58> Ojalá. **I wish!/ I hope so!**
<59> Oler mal. **To stink**
<60> Olvidarse. **Forgetting**
<61> Pedir. **Asking for**
<62> Poco. **Little**
<63> Por estas. **I swear to you on these** (lit. 'on these')
<64> ¡Qué sed! **I'm so thirsty!**
<65> ¡Qué calor! **It's so hot!**
<66> ¡Qué dolor! **It's so painful!**
<67> ¡Qué frío! **It's so cold!**

<68> ¡Qué hambre! **I'm so hungry!**
<69> ¡Qué miedo! **I'm scared!/ it's so scary!**
<70> ¡Qué pereza! **What a drag!**
<71> Quizá. **Maybe**
<72> Rico. **Rich/ delicious**
<73> Sacar la lengua. **Sticking tongue out (sign of mockery)**
<74> Sí. **Yes**
<75> Siéntese. **Sit down**
<76> Siga recto. **Keep going straight ahead**
<77> ¡Silencio! **Silence!**
<78> Sorpresa. **Surprise**
<79> Sudar. **Sweating**
<80> Suicidarse, matar. **Committing suicide, killing**
<81> Telefonear. **Making a phone call**
<82> ¡Toca madera! **Knock on wood!**
<83> Tú. **You (2nd person singular pronoun)**
<84> Unidos. **Together/ united**
<85> ¡Vete! **Leave!/ go away!**
<86> Vosotros. **You (2nd person plural pronoun)**
<87> ¡Ya está listo! **Ready!**
<88> ¡Ya lo tengo! **I got it!**
<89> Yo. **I**

– Emblemas españoles y brasileños. Nascimento (2008):
  http://elies.rediris.es/Language_Design/LD10/LD_10_01_Nilma_Pazeado.pdf

References

Adams, Florence A. F. 1891. *Gesture and Pantomimic Action*. New York: Edgar S. Werner.
Aldrete, Gregory S. 1999. *Gestures and acclamations in Ancient Rome*. Baltimore: The John Hopkins University Press.
Alturo, Núria, Ignasi Clemente, and Lluís Payrató. 2016. Notes for a multilingual and multimodal functional discourse grammar. In Marta Fernández-Villanueva and Konstanze Jungbluth (eds.), *Beyond Language Boundaries. Multilingual Use in Multilingual Contexts*, 3–33. Berlin: De Gruyter Mouton.
Amades, Joan. 1957. El gest a Catalunya. *Anales del Instituto de Lingüística* VI. 88–148.
Andrén, Mats. 2014. Gestures in Northern Europe: children's gestures in Sweden. In Cornelia Müller, Alan Cienki, Ellen Fricke, Silva H. Ladewig, David McNeill, and Jana Bressem (eds.), *Body – language – communication: An international handbook on multimodality in human interaction* (vol. 2), 1282–1289. Berlin: De Gruyter Mouton.
Archer, Dawn, Karin Aijmer, and Anne Wichmann. 2012. *Pragmatics. An advanced resource book for students*. London: Routledge.
Arndt, H. and R. W. Janney. 1987. *InterGrammar: Toward an integrative model of verbal, prosodic and kinesic choices in speech*. New York: Mouton de Gruyter.
Austin, John L. 1962 [2nd. edn. 1975]. *How to do things with words*. Cambridge, MA: Harvard University Press.
Austin, Gilbert. 1806. *Chironomia [. . .]*. London. Reprint [1966]: Carbondale and Edwardsville: Southern Illinois University Press.
Axtel, Roger E. 1991. *Gestures. The do's and taboos of body language around the world*. New York: Wiley.
Bacon, Albert M. 1985. *A Manual of Gestures in Oratory*. Chicago: S. C. Griggs.
Bacon, Francis. 1640. *Of the Advancement and Proficiency of Learning. Book VI*. Oxford: Young and Forrest.
Barakat, Robert A. 1973. Arabic gestures. *Journal of Popular Culture* 6. 749–787.
Barakat, Robert A. 1975. *The Cistercian Sign Language. A study in non-verbal communication*. Kalamazoo, Michigan: Cistercian Publications.
Basto, Cláudio. 1938a. A linguagem dos gestos em Portugal (Esbozo etnográfico). *Revista Lusitana* 36. 5–72.
Basto, Cláudio. 1938b. Os gestos com a cabeça. *Mémorias da Academia das Ciências de Lisboa III*. 129–155.
Bäuml, Betty J. and Franz H. Bäuml. 1975. *A dictionary of gestures*. Metuchen: Scarecrow Press.
Bavelas, Janet Beavin, Nicole Chovil, Linda Coates, and Lori Roe. 1995. Gestures specialized for dialogues. *Personality and Social Psychology Bulletin* 21. 394–405.
Bavelas, Janet Beavin, Nicole Chovil, Douglas A. Lawrie, and Allan Wade. 1992. Interactive gestures. *Discourse Processes* 15. 469–489.
Bell, Charles. 1806. *Essays on the Anatomy of Expression in Painting*. London: Longman, Hurst, Rees, and Orme.
Bernadó, Jordi and Francesc Prat. 1980. Sobre els signes fònics usats en les relacions home-bèstia. *Treballs de Sociolingüística Catalana* 3. 117–133.
Bickerton, Derek. 1990 *Language and species*. Chicago: Chicago University Press.
Birdwhistell, Ray L. 1970 *Kinesics and context: Essays on body motion communication*. Philadelphia: University of Pennsylvania Press.

Blutner, Reinhard. 2013. Pragmatics in Optimality Theory. In Frank Liedtke and Cornelia Schulze (eds.), *Beyond words. Content, context, and inference*, 33–58. Berlin: De Gruyter Mouton.
Bohle, Ulrike. 2014. Contemporary classification systems. In Cornelia Müller, Alan Cienki, Ellen Fricke, Silva H. Ladewig, David McNeill, and Jana Bressem (eds.) *Body – Language – Communication: An International Handbook on Multimodality in Human Interaction* (vol. 2), 1453–1461. Berlin: De Gruyter Mouton.
Bonaiuto, Marino and Tancredi Bonaiuto. 2014. Gestures and body language in Southern Europe. Italy. In Cornelia Müller, Alan Cienki, Ellen Fricke, Silva H. Ladewig, David McNeill, and Jana Bressem (eds.), *Body – language – communication: An international handbook on multimodality in human interaction* (vol. 2), 1240–1253. Berlin: De Gruyter Mouton.
Bonet, Juan Pablo. 1620. *Reduction de las letras y arte para enseñar a ablar los mudos*. Madrid: Francisco Abarca de Angulo.
Bonifacio, Giovanni. 1616. *L'Arte de' Cenni* [...]. Vicenza: Francesco Grossi.
Bourdieu, Pierre. 1977. *Outline of a theory of practice*. Cambridge: Cambridge University Press (French original: *Esquisse d'une theorie de la pratique, precedé de trois etudes d'ethnologie kabyle*. 1972. Paris: Droz).
Boutet, Dominque and Simon Harrison. 2014. Gestures in Western Europe: France. In Cornelia Müller, Alan Cienki, Ellen Fricke, Silva H. Ladewig, David McNeill, and Jana Bressem (eds.), *Body – language – communication: An international handbook on multimodality in human interaction* (vol. 2), 1272–1282. Berlin: De Gruyter Mouton.
Brault, Gerald J. 1963. Kinesics and the classroom: some typical French gestures. *The French Review* 36. 374–382.
Bressem, Jana and Cornelia Müller. 2014a. A repertoire of German recurrent gestures with pragmatic functions. In Cornelia Müller, Alan Cienki, Ellen Fricke, Silva H. Ladewig, David McNeill, and Jana Bressem (eds.), *Body – language – communication: An international handbook on multimodality in human interaction* (vol. 2), 1575–1591, Berlin: De Gruyter Mouton.
Bressem, Jana and Cornelia Müller. 2014b. The family of away gestures: negation, refusal, and negative assessment. In Cornelia Müller, Alan Cienki, Ellen Fricke, Silva H. Ladewig, David McNeill, and Jana Bressem (eds.), *Body – language – communication: An international handbook on multimodality in human interaction* (vol. 2), 1592–1604. Berlin: De Gruyter Mouton.
Brewer, W. D. 1951. Patterns of gesture among the levantine Arabs. *American Anthropologist* 53. 232–237.
Broide, N. 1977. Israeli emblems: Israeli communicative units: Emblem repertoire of "Sabras" (Israeli natives) of Eastern European descent. Dissertation, University of Tel Aviv.
Brookes, Heather J. 2001. O clever 'He's streetwise'. When gestures become quotable: the case of the clever gesture. *Gesture* 1. 167–184.
Brookes, Heather J. 2004. A repertoire of South African quotable gestures. *Journal of Linguistic Anthropology* 14. 186–224.
Brookes, Heather J. 2005. What gestures do: some communicative functions of quotable gestures in conversations among Black urban South Africans. *Journal of Pragmatics* 37. 2044–2085.
Brookes, Heather J. 2011. Amangama amathathu 'The three letters': The emergence of a quotable gesture (emblem). *Gesture* 11, 194–218.
Brookes, Heather J. 2014a. Gestures in South Africa. In Cornelia Müller, Alan Cienki, Ellen Fricke, Silva H. Ladewig, David McNeill, and Jana Bressem (eds.), *Body – language – communication: An international handbook on multimodality in human interaction* (vol. 2), 1147–1153. Berlin: De Gruyter Mouton.

Brookes, Heather J. 2014b. Gesture and taboo: a cross-cultural perspective. In Cornelia Müller, Alan Cienki, Ellen Fricke, Silva H. Ladewig, David McNeill, and Jana Bressem (eds.), *Body – language – communication: An international handbook on multimodality in human interaction* (vol. 2), 1523–1530. Berlin: De Gruyter Mouton

Brookes, Heather and Victoria Nyst. 2014. Gestures in the Sub-Saharan region. In Cornelia Müller, Alan Cienki, Ellen Fricke, Silva H. Ladewig, David McNeill, and Jana Bressem (eds.), *Body – language – communication: An international handbook on multimodality in human interaction* (vol. 2), 1154–1161. Berlin: De Gruyter Mouton.

Brown, Penelope. 2014. Gestures in native Mexico and Central America: The Mayan cultures. In Cornelia Müller, Alan Cienki, Ellen Fricke, Silva H. Ladewig, David McNeill, and Jana Bressem (eds.), *Body – language – communication: An international handbook on multimodality in human interaction* (vol. 2), 1206–1215. Berlin: De Gruyter Mouton.

Brun, Theodore. 1969. *The international dictionary of sign language: A study of human behaviour.* London: Wolfe.

Bühler, Karl. 1933. *Ausdruckstheorie. Das System an der Geschichte aufgezeigt.* Jena: Verlag von Gustav Fischer. Spanish translation: *Teoría de la expresión. El sistema explicado por su historia.* 1980. Madrid: Alianza.

Bulwer, John. 1644. *Chirologia: or the Natvrall Langvage of the Hand* and *Chironomia: or the Art of Manuall Rhethoricke.* London: T. Harper, 1644. Re-edition by James W. Cleary (ed.). 1974. Carbondale and Edwadsville: Southern Illinois University Press.

Burgoon, Judeek, Laura K. Guerrero, and Cindy H. White. 2013. The codes and functions of nonverbal communication. In Cornelia Müller, Alan Cienki, Ellen Fricke, Silva H. Ladewig, David McNeill, and Sedinha Tessendorf (eds.), *Body – language – communication: An international handbook on multimodality in human interaction* (vol. 1), 609–626. Berlin: De Gruyter Mouton.

Calbris, Geneviève. 1980. Étude des expressions mimiques conventionnelles françaises dans le cadre d'une communication non verbal. *Semiotica* 29. 245–346.

Calbris, Geneviève. 1981. Étude des expressions mimiques conventionnelles françaises dans le cadre d'une communication non verbale testées sur des Hongrois. *Semiotica* 35. 125–156.

Calbris, Geneviève. 1990. *The semiotics of French gestures.* Bloomington: Indiana University Press.

Calbris, Geneviève. 2003. From cutting an object to a clear cut analysis. *Gesture* 3. 19–46.

Calbris, Geneviève. 2011. *Elements of meaning in gesture.* Amsterdam and Philadelphia: John Benjamins.

Calbris, Geneviève and Jacques Montredon. 1986. *Des gestes et des mots pour le dire.* Paris: Clé International.

Cardona, Miguel. 1953–54. Gestos o ademanes habituales en Venezuela. *Archivos venezolanos de folklore* II, 3. 159–166.

Cavé, Christian, Isabelle Guaitella, and Serge Santi (eds.). 2001. *Oralité et gestualité. Interactions et comportements multimodaux dans la communication.* Paris: L'Harmattan.

Chauvin, Carole. 1999. Jeux chorégraphiques enfantins de la région rhône-alpine. Gestualité et spatialité. *Géolinguistique* 8. 253–276.

Cestero, Ana María. 1999. *Repertorio básico de signos no verbales del español.* Madrid: Arco Libros.

Cicero, Marcus Tullius. 2001. *On the Ideal Orator [De Oratore, 55 BC].* New York: Oxford University Press.

Cienki, Alan J. 2005. Image schema and gesture. In Beate Hampe (ed.), *From perception to meaning: Image schemas in cognitive linguistics*, 421–442. Berlin: De Gruyter Mouton.
Cienki, Alan J. 2014. Cognitive linguistics: spoken language and gesture as expressions of conceptualization. In Cornelia Müller, Alan Cienki, Ellen Fricke, Silva H. Ladewig, David McNeill, and Sedinha Tessendorf (eds.), *Body – language – communication: An international handbook on multimodality in human interaction* (vol. 1), 182–201. Berlin: De Gruyter Mouton.
Cienki, Alan J. and Cornelia Müller. 2008. *Metaphor and gesture*. Amsterdam and Philadelphia: John Benjamins.
Cienki, Alan J. and Cornelia Müller. 2014. Ways of viewing metaphor in gesture. In Cornelia Müller, Alan Cienki, Ellen Fricke, Silva H. Ladewig, David McNeill, and Sedinha Tessendorf (eds.), *Body – language – communication: An international handbook on multimodality in human interaction* (vol. 2), 1766–1781. Berlin: De Gruyter Mouton.
Cleary, James W. 1974. Editor's Preface. In John Bulwer [1644] *Chirologia: Or the natural language of the hand [. . .]*. London (Reprint: Carbondale and Edwardsville: Southern Illinois University Press.
Clemente, Ignasi. 2015. *Uncertain futures: Communication and culture in childhood cancer treatment*. Oxford and New York: Wiley Blackwell.
Cocchiara, Giuseppe. 1932. *Il linguaggio del gesto*. Turin: Bocca. Reprint [1977] Palermo: Sellerio.
Coll, Josep, Maria José Gelabert, and Emma Martinell. 1990. *Diccionario de gestos con sus giros más usuales*. Madrid: Edelsa/Edi6.
Collet, Peter and Josephine Chilton. 1981. Laterality in negation. Are Jakobson and Vavra Right? *Semiotica* 35. 57–70.
Collet, Peter and Alberta Contarello. 1987. Gesti di assenso e di dissenso. In Pio E. Ricci-Bitti (ed.), *Comunicazione e gestualità*, 69–85. Milan: Franco Angeli.
Condillac, Étienne Bonnot de. 1746. *Essai sur l'Origine des Connaissances Humaines [...]*. Paris: Pierre Mortier. Re-edited in 1973. Auvers-sur-Oise: Galiléee.
Condon, William S. 1976. An analysis of behavioral organization. *Sign Language Studies* 13. 285–318.
Contarello, Alberta. 1980. *Differenze ed uniformità culturali nel comportamento e nella comunicazione non verbale*. Bologna: Patron.
Cortelazzo, Manlio. 1969. *Avviamento critico allo studio della dialettologia italiana. I. Problemi e metodi*. Pisa: Pacini.
Cosnier, Jacques. 1985. L'évaluation de la gestualité communicative en 1985. *Bulletin d'Audiophonologie* 5–6. 687–700.
Creider, Chet A. 1977. Towards a description of East African gestures. *Sign Language Studies* 14. 1–20.
Creider, Chet A. 1986. Interlanguage comparisons in the study of the interactional use of gesture. Progress and prospects. *Semiotica* 62. 147–163.
Cresollius, Ludovico. 1620. *Vacationes Autumnales sive: De Perfecta Oratoris Actione et Pronunciatione*. Paris: Lutetiae Parisiorum.
Critchley, Macdonald. 1939. *The language of gesture*. London: Arnold (Reprint [1971] New York: Haskell).
Croft, William and D. Allan Cruse. 2004. *Cognitive linguistics*. Cambridge: Cambridge University Press.
Cuenca, Maria-Josep. 2011. Catalan interjections. In Lluís Payrató and Josep M. Cots (eds.), *The pragmatics of Catalan*, 173–211. Berlin: De Gruyter.

Dahan, Gelisand and Jacques Cosnier. 1977. Sémiologie des quasi-linguistiques français. *Psychologie Médicale* 9. 2053–2072.
Danguitsis, Constantin. 1943. *Étude descriptive du dialecte de Démirdési (Brousse, Asie Mineure)*. Paris: G.-P. Maisonneuve.
Darwin, Charles. 1872. *The Expression of the Emotions in Man and Animals*. London: J. Murray.
Davidson, Levette J. 1950. Some current folk gestures and sign languages. *American Speech* 25. 3–9.
Delacroix, Henri. 1924. *Le langage et la pensée*. Paris: Alcan.
Delaporte, Yves and Emilky Shaw. 2009. Gesture and signs through history. *Gesture* 9. 35–60.
Devereux, George. 1949. Some Mohave gestures. *American Anthropologist* 51. 325–326.
Diadori, Pierangela. 1990. *Senza parole: 100 gesti degli italiani*. Roma: Bonacci.
Du Bois, John W. 1991. Transcription design principles for spoken discourse research. *Pragmatics* 1. 71–106.
Du Bois, John W., Susanna Cumming, Stephan Schuetze-Coburn, and Danae Paolino. 1992. Discourse transcription. *Santa Barbara Papers in Linguistics* 4. 1–225.
Duchenne, Guillaume B. 1862. *Mecanisme de la physiognomie humaine ou analyse électrophysiologique de l'expression des passions. Avec un atlas composé de 74 figures électrophysiologiques photographiés*. Paris: Ve Jules Renouard, Libraire.
Dutsch, Dorota. 2013. The body in rhetorical delivery and in theater: an overview of classical works. In Cornelia Müller, Alan Cienki, Ellen Fricke, Silva H. Ladewig, David McNeill, and Sedinha Tessendorf (eds.), *Body – language – communication: An international handbook on multimodality in human interaction* (vol. 1), 329–342. Berlin: De Gruyter Mouton.
Eastman, Carol M. and Sh. Yahya Ali Omar. 1985. Swahili gestures: comments (vielezi) and exclamations (viingizi). *Studies in African Linguistics* 9. 95–99.
Eco, Umberto. 1976. *A theory of semiotics*. Bloomington: Indiana University Press.
Efron, David. 1941. *Gesture and environment*. New York: King's Crown.
Efrón, David. 1970. *Gesto, raza y cultura*. Buenos Aires: Ediciones Nueva Visión.
Efron, David. 1972 [1941]. *Gesture, race and culture. A tentative study of the spatio-temporal and "linguistic" aspects of the gestural behavior of eastern Jews and southern Italians in New York City, living under similar as well as different environmental conditions*. The Hague: Mouton.
Eibl-Eibesfeldt, Irenaus. 1972. Similarities and differences between cultures in expressive movements. In Robert A. Hinde (ed.), *Non-verbal communication*, 297–312. Cambridge: Cambridge University Press.
Eibl-Eibesfeldt, Irenaus. 1977. Patterns of greetings in New Guinea. In Stephen. A. Wurm (ed.), *New Guinea area languages and language study* (vol. 3), 209–247. Canberra: Australian National University.
Eismann, Wolfgang. 1983. Russische Gesten im Sprachunterricht. In Ruprecht S. Baur (ed.), *Materialen zur Landeskunde der Sowjetunion* (vol. 1), 93–109. München: Sagner.
Ekman, Paul. 1970. Apreciación retrospectiva. In David Efron, *Gesto, raza y cultura*, 13–20. Buenos Aires: Nueva Visión.
Ekman, Paul. 1980. Three classes of non-verbal behavior. In W. von Raffler-Engel (ed.), *Aspects of non-verbal behavior*, 89–102. Lisse: Swets and Zeitlinger.
Ekman, Paul and Wallace V. Friesen. 1969. The repertoire of non verbal behavior: categories, origins, usage and coding. *Semiotica* 1. 49–98.
Ekman, Paul and Wallace V. Friesen. 1972. Hand movements. *Journal of Communication* 22. 353–374.
Ellyson, Steve L. and John F. Dovidio (eds.). 1985. *Power, dominance, and nonverbal behavior*. New York: Springer.

Enfield, Nick J. 2009. *The anatomy of meaning. Speech, gesture, and composite utterances.* Cambridge: Cambridge University Press.
Engel, Johann Jakob. 1876. *Ideen zu einer Mimik: Mit erläuternden Kupfertafeln.* Berlin: Mylius.
Essegbey, James. 2014. Gestures in West Africa: left hand taboo in Ghana. In Cornelia Müller, Alan Cienki, Ellen Fricke, Silva H. Ladewig, David McNeill, and Jana Bressem (eds.), *Body – language – communication: An international handbook on multimodality in human interaction* (vol. 2), 1161–1169. Berlin: De Gruyter Mouton.
Fauconnier, Gilles and Mark Turner. 2002. *The way we think. Conceptual blending and the mind's hidden complexities.* New York: Basic Books.
Fein, Ofer and Asa Kasher. 1996. How to do things with words and gestures in comics. *Journal of Pragmatics* 26. 793–808.
Feldman, Sandor S. 1959. *Mannerisms of speech and gestures in everyday life.* New York: International Universities Press.
Ferguson, Charles. 1964. Intervention in the discussion session. In Thomas A. Sebeok, Alfred S. Hayes, and Mary Catherine Bateson (eds.), *Approaches to semiotics*, 175. London: Mouton.
Feyereisen, Pierre. 2013. Psycholinguistics of speech and gesture: Production, comprehension, architecture. In Cornelia Müller, Alan Cienki, Ellen Fricke, Silva H. Ladewig, David McNeill, and Sedinha Tessendorf (eds.), *Body – language – communication: An international handbook on multimodality in human interaction* (vol. 1), 156–168. Berlin: De Gruyter Mouton.
Feyereisen, Pierre, Michèle Van de Wiele, and Fabienne Dubois. 1988. The meaning of gestures: what can be understood without speech? *Cahiers de Psychologie Cognitive/ European Bulletin of Cognitive Psychology* 8. 3–25.
Fitó, Jaume. 2009. El gest i la dixi d'espai en textos instructius. *Caplletra* 46. 9–42.
Flachskampf, Ludwig. 1938. Spanische Gebärdensprache. *Romanische Forschungen* LII, 205–258. Spanish translation: El lenguaje de los gestos españoles. Ensayos y Estudios (Berlín) I/4, 248–279 (Offprint: 1941).
Flórez, Luis (dir.). 1982. *Atlas lingüístico-etnográfico de Colombia* (vol. III). Bogotá: Instituto Caro y Cuervo.
Forceville, Charles J. and Eduardo Urios-Aparisi (eds.). 2009. *Multimodal metaphor.* Berlin – New York: Mouton de Gruyter.
Forment, Mar. 1996. La gestualidad hispánica y la gestualidad oriental: dos códigos diferentes para dos culturas distintas. *Actas del Cuarto Congreso de Hispanistas de Asia.* Seoul. 791–797.
Fornés, M. Antònia and Mercè Puig. 2008. *El porqué de nuestros gestos. La Roma de ayer en la gestualidad de hoy.* Barcelona: Octaedro – Edicions UIB.
Freedman, Norbert. 1972. The analysis of movement behavior during the clinical interview. In Aron Wolfe Siegman and Benjamin Pope (eds.), *Studies in dyadic communication*, 153–175. New York: Pergamon Press.
Fricke, Ellen. 2013. Towards a unified grammar of gesture and speech: A multimodal approach. In Cornelia Müller, Alan Cienki, Ellen Fricke, Silva H. Ladewig, David McNeill, and Sedinha Tessendorf (eds.), *Body – language – communication: An international handbook on multimodality in human interaction* (vol. 1), 733–754. Berlin: De Gruyter Mouton.
Galhano-Rodrigues, Isabel. 2014. Gestures in Southwest Europe: Portugal. In Cornelia Müller, Alan Cienki, Ellen Fricke, Silva H. Ladewig, David McNeill, and Jana Bressem (eds.), *Body – language – communication: An international handbook on multimodality in human interaction* (vol. 2), 1259–1266. Berlin: De Gruyter Mouton.

Geeraerts, Dirk. 1989. Prospects and problems of prototype theory. *Linguistics* 27. 587–612.
Geeraerts, Dirk and Hubert Cuykens (eds.). 2007. *The Oxford handbook of cognitive linguistics*. Oxford: Oxford University Press.
Geiger, Pauk and Richard Weiss. 1950. *Atlas der schweizerischen Volkskunde*. Zürich: Schweizerische Gesellschaft für Volkskunde.
Gilbert, Austin. 1806. *Chironomia or, a Treatise on Rhetorical Delivery*. London: W. Bulmer, and Co. Re-edited in 1966. Carbondale and Edwardswille: Southern Illinois University Press.
Givens, David B. 1977. Shoulder shrugging: a densely communicative expressive behavior. *Semiotica* 19. 13–28.
Goffman, Erving. 1963. *Behavior in Public Places: Notes on the Social Organization of Gatherings*. New York: Free Press.
Goldin-Meadow, Susan. 2003. *The resilience of language: What gesture creation in deaf children can tell us about how all children learning language*. New York and Hove: Psychology Press.
Goldziher, Ignaz. 1886. Materialen zur kenntis der Almohadeubewegung in Nord Afrika. *Zeitschrift der Deutschen Morgenländischen Gesellschaft* 41. 30–140.
Goosens, Louise. 1990. Metaphtonymy: the interaction of metaphor and metonymy in expressions of linguistic action. *Cognitive Linguistics* 1. 323–340.
Gratiolet, Louis Pierre. 1865. *De la physiognomie et des mouvements d'expression*. Paris: Hetzel.
Grice, Henry P. 1957. Meaning. *Philosophical Review* 66. 377–388.
Grice, Henry P. 1975. Logic and conversation. In P. Cole and J. Morgan (eds.), *Syntax and semantics 3. Speech acts*, 41–58. New York: Academic Press.
Grigorjeva, Svetlana A., Nikolay V. Grigorjev, and Grigory E. Kreydlin. 2001. *Slovari Jazyka Russkih Zhestov [The Dictionary of Russian Gestures]*. Wiener Slawistischer Almanac, 49. Moscow/Vienna: Jazyki russkoj kultury.
Goodwin, Charles. 1986. Gesture as a resource for the organization of mutual orientation. *Semiotica* 62. 29–49.
Graziano, Maria. 2014. Gestures in Southern Europe: children's pragmatic gestures in Italy. In Cornelia Müller, Alan Cienki, Ellen Fricke, Silva H. Ladewig, David McNeill, and Jana Bressem (eds.), *Body – language – communication: An international handbook on multimodality in human interaction* (vol. 2), 1253–1258. Berlin: De Gruyter Mouton.
Green, Jerald R. 1968. *A gesture inventory for the teaching of Spanish*. Philadelphia: Chilton Books.
Gruber, Mayer I. 1980. *Aspects of nonverbal communication in the ancient Near East*. Rome: Institutum Pontificium Biblicum.
Guidetti, Michèle. 2003a. Pragmatic aspects of conventional gestures in young French children. In Monica Rector, Isabella Poggi, and Nadine Trigo (eds.), *Gestures: Meaning and use*, 39–44. Porto: Ediçoes Universidade Fernando Pessoa.
Guidetti, Michèle. 2003b. *Pragmatique et psychologie du développement. Comment communiquent les jeunes enfants*. Paris: Belin.
Gullberg, Marianne. 1998. *Gesture as a communication strategy in second language discourse: A study of learners of French and Swedish*. Lund: Lund University Press.
Gullberg, Marianne. 2012. Bilingual multimodality in language documentation data. *Language Documentation and Conservation Special Publication* 3. 46–53.
Gullberg, Marianne. 2013. Bilingualism and gesture. In Tej K. Bhatia and William C. Ritchie (eds.), *The handbook of bilingualism and multilingualism* (2nd edn.), 417–438. New Jersey: Blackwell.
Hacks, Charles. 1892. *Le geste*. Paris: Marpon et Flammarion.

Hamalian, Leo. 1965. Communication by gesture in the Middle East. *ETC. A Review of General Semantics* 22. 43–49.
Hanna, Barbara E. 1996. Defining the emblem. *Semiotica* 112. 289–358.
Harrison, Phyllis A. 1983. *Behaving Brazilian: A comparison of Brazilian and North American social behavior.* Rowley: Newbury House Publishers.
Harrison, Simon. 2014a. Gestures in industrial settings. In Cornelia Müller, Alan Cienki, Ellen Fricke, Silva H. Ladewig, David McNeill, and Jana Bressem (eds.), *Body – language – communication: An international handbook on multimodality in human interaction* (vol. 2), 1413–1419. Berlin: De Gruyter Mouton.
Harrison, Simon. 2014b. Head shakes: Variation in form, function, and cultural distribution of a head movement related to "no". In Cornelia Müller, Alan Cienki, Ellen Fricke, Silva H. Ladewig, David McNeill, and Jana Bressem (eds.), *Body – language – communication: An international handbook on multimodality in human interaction* (vol. 2), 1496–1501. Berlin: De Gruyter Mouton.
Haviland, John B. 2004. Gesture. In A. Duranti (ed.), *A companion to linguistic anthropology*, 197–221. Malden: Blackwell.
Haviland, John B. 2007. Gesture. In Alessandro Duranti (ed.), *A Companion to Linguistic Anthropology*, 197–221. Oxford: Blackwell.
Hayes, Francis C. 1940. Should we have a dictionary of gestures? *Southern Folklore Quarterly* 4. 239–245.
Hayes, Francis C. 1951. Gestos o ademanes folklóricos. *Folklore Américas* 11. 15–21.
Hayes, Francis C. 1957. Gestures: a working bibliography. *Southern Folklore Quarterly* 21. 218–317.
Hayes, Francis C. 1959 Guía para el que recoge ademanes o gestos. *Folklore Americas* 19. 1–6.
Hécaen, Henri. 1967. Approche sémiotique des troubles du geste. *Language* 5. 67–83.
Hou, Shumeng and Wing Chee So. 2014. Gestures in China: universal and culturally specific characteristics. In Cornelia Müller, Alan Cienki, Ellen Fricke, Silva H. Ladewig, David McNeill, and Jana Bressem (eds.), *Body – language – communication: An international handbook on multimodality in human interaction* (vol. 2), 1233–1240. Berlin: De Gruyter Mouton.
Jakobson, Roman 1972. Motor signs for 'yes' and 'no'. *Language in Society* 1. 91–96 (Original: [1970] *Jazyk i celovek*).
Johnson, Harold G., Paul Ekman and Wallace V. Friesen. 1975. Communicative body movements: American emblems. *Semiotica* 15(4). 335–353.
Johnson, Mark. 1987. *The body in the mind. The bodily basis of meaning, imagination and reason.* Chicago: Chicago University Press.
Johnson, Robert. 1977. An extension of Oregon sawmill sign language. *Current Anthropology* 18. 353–354.
Johnson, Sahnny. 1985. *Japanese nonverbal communication.* Rowley: Newbury.
Jorio, de Andrea. 1832. *La mimica degli antichi investigata nel gestire napoletano.* Naples: Stamperia del Fibreno (Reprint: [1964] Naples: Associazione napoletana per i monumenti e il paesaggio).
Jorio, Andrea de. 2000. *Gesture in Naples and gesture in Classical Antiquity.* A translation of *La mimica degli antichi investigata nel gestire napoletano*, with an Introduction and Notes by Adam Kendon. Bloomington: Indiana University Press.
Kany, Charles Emil. 1960. *American-Spanish euphemisms.* Berkeley: University of California Press.
Kaulfers, Walter Vincent. 1931 Curiosities of colloquial gestures. *Hispania* 14. 249–264.
Kaulfers, Walter Vincent. 1932. A handful of Spanish. *Education* 52. 423–428.

Kendon, Adam. 1972. Some relationships between body motion and speech: an analysis of an example. In Aaron Siegman and Benjamin Pope (eds.), *Studies in dyadic communication*, 177–210. Elmsford, NY: Pergamon Press.
Kendon, Adam. 1980. Gesticulation and speech: two aspects of the process of utterance. In M. R. Key (ed.), *The relationship of verbal and nonverbal communication*, 207–227. The Hague: Mouton.
Kendon, Adam. 1981a. Geography of gesture. *Semiotica* 37. 129–163.
Kendon, Adam. 1981b. Introduction: Current issues in "nonverbal communication." In A. Kendon (ed.), *Nonverbal communication, interaction, and gesture: Selections from Semiotica*, 1–53. Berlin/Boston, Germany: De Gruyter.
Kendon, Adam. 1982. The study of gesture. Some observations on its history. *Recherches Sémiotiques / Semiotic Inquiry* 2. 45–62.
Kendon, Adam. 1983. Gesture and speech: how they interact. In J.M. Wiemann and R.P. Harrison (eds.), *Nonverbal interaction*, 13–45. Beverly Hills: Sage.
Kendon, Adam. 1984. Did gesture have the hapiness to escape the curse at the confusion of Babel? In A. Wolfgang (ed.), *Nonverbal behavior. Perspectives, applications, intercultural insights*, 75–114. Lewiston: Hogrefe.
Kendon, Adam. 1985. Some uses of gesture. In Deborah Tannen and Muriel Saville-Troike (eds.), *Perspectives on silence*, 215–234. Norwood, NJ: Ablex Publishing Corporation.
Kendon, Adam. 1986. Some reasons for studying gesture. *Semiotica* 62. 3–28.
Kendon, Adam. 1987. On gesture: its complementary relationship with speech. In Aron W. Siegman and Stanley Feldstein (eds.), *Nonverbal behavior and communication* (2nd. edn.), 65–97. Hillsdale: L. Erlbaum.
Kendon, Adam. 1988a. How gestures can become like words. In Fernando Poyatos (ed.), *Cross-cultural perspectives in nonverbal communication*, 131–141. Toronto: C.J. Hogrefe.
Kendon, Adam. 1988b. *Sign languages of Aboriginal Australia: Cultural, semiotic and communicative perspectives*. Cambridge: Cambridge University Press.
Kendon, Adam. 1990. Gesticulation, quotable gestures, and signs. In Michael Moerman and Masaichi Nomura (eds.) *Culture embodied*, 53–77. Osaka: National Museum of Ethnology.
Kendon, Adam. 1992. Some recent work from Italy on quotable gestures ('emblems'). *Journal of Linguistic Anthropology* 2. 72–93.
Kendon, Adam. 1995. Gestures as illocutionary and discourse structure markers in Southern Italian conversation. *Journal of Pragmatics* 23(3). 247–279.
Kendon, Adam. 2000. Language and gesture: unity or duality? In D. McNeill (ed.), *Language and gesture*, 47–63. Cambridge: Cambridge University Press.
Kendon, Adam. 2002. Some uses of the head shake. *Gesture* 2. 147–182.
Kendon, Adam. 2004. *Gesture: Visible action as utterance*. Cambridge: Cambridge University Press.
Kendon, Adam. 2013. Exploring the utterance roles of visible bodily action: A personal account. In Cornelia Müller, Alan Cienki, Ellen Fricke, Silva H. Ladewig, David McNeill, and Sedinha Tessendorf (eds.), *Body – language – communication: An international handbook on multimodality in human interaction* (vol. 1), 7–28. Berlin: De Gruyter Mouton.
Kendon, Adam. 2017. Reflections on the "gesture-first" hypothesis of language origins. *Psychonomic Bulletin Review* 24. 163. https://doi.org/10.3758/s13423-016-1117-3.
Key, Mary R. 1977. *Nonverbal communication. A research guide and bibliography*. Metuchen: Scarecrow.
Kirch, Max S. 1987. *Deutsche Gebärdensprache*. Hamburg: Buske.

Kita, Sotaro. 1990. The temporal relationship between gesture and speech: A study of Japanese-English bilinguals. University of Chicago MA thesis.
Kita, Sotaro. 2009. Cross-cultural variation of speech accompanying gesture: a review. *Language and Cognitive Processes* 24. 145–167.
Kita, Sotaro (ed.). 2003. *Pointing: Where language, culture, and cognition meet*. Hillsdale, NJ: L. Erlbaum Associates.
Kita, Sotaro and James Essegbey. 2001. Pointing left in Ghana. How a taboo on the use of the left hand influences gestural practice. *Gesture* 1. 73–95.
Kita, Sotaro and Asli Özyürek. 2003. What does cross-linguistic variation in semantic coordination of speech and gesture reveal? Evidence for an interface representation of spatial thinking and speaking. *Journal of Memory and Language* 47. 16–32.
Kleiber, Georges. 1990. *La sémantique du prototype*. Paris: Presses Universitaires de France.
Kleinpaul, Rudolf. 1888. *Sprache ohne Worte. Idee einer allgemeinen Wissenschaft der Sprache*. Leipzig: W. Friedrich. Reprinted in 1972. The Hague: Mouton.
Kreidlin, Grigori E. 2001. Towards the general semantic typology of emblematic gestures: the case of the Russian body language. In Christian Cavé, Isabelle Guaïtella and Serge Santi (eds.), *Oralité et gestualité. Interactions et comportements multimodaux dans la communication*, 245–248. Paris: L'Harmattan.
Kreidlin, Grigori E. 2004. The Russian dictionary of gestures. In Cornelia Müller and Roland Posner (eds.), *Semantics and pragmatics of everyday gestures*, 173–193. Berlin: Weidler.
Kreydlin, Grigory E. 2010. Lexicography of gestures and their nominations (dictionaries and database systems). In Olga Karpova and Faina Kartashkova (eds.), *New trends in lexicography. Ways of registrating and describing lexis*, 90–98. Newcastle upon Tyne: Cambridge Scholars Publishing.
Kreydlin, Grigory E. 2014. Gestures in Northeast Europe: Russian, Poland, Croatia, the Czech Republic, and Slovakia. In Cornelia Müller, Alan Cienki, Ellen Fricke, Silva H. Ladewig, David McNeill, and Jana Bressem (eds.), *Body – language – communication: An international handbook on multimodality in human interaction* (vol. 2), 1289–1299. Berlin: De Gruyter Mouton.
Kress, Gunther and Theo Van Leeuwen. 2001. *Multimodal discourse*. London: Arnold.
Krout, Maurice H. 1942. *Introduction to social psychology*. New York: Harper. (Symbolism. New York: Harper. (Symbolism. [1971]. In Haig A. Bosmajian (ed.), *The rhetoric of nonverbal communication*, 15–32. Glenview, IL: Scott, Foresman).
Krüger, Reinhard. 2004. Fare le corna and the invention of a novel: Théophile Gautiers Gettatura (1857) and De Jorio's Mimica degli antichi (1832) or, problems of a gesture-etymology. In Cornelia Müller and Roland Posner (eds.), *Semantics and pragmatics of everyday gestures*. Berlin: Weidler.
La Barre, Weston. 1947. The cultural basis of emotions and gestures. *Journal of Personality* 16. 49–68.
La Barre, Weston. 1964. Paralinguistics, kinesics, and cultural anthropology. In T. A. Sebeok, A. S. Hayes and M. C. Bateson (eds.), *Approaches to semiotics*, 191–220. The Hague: Mouton.
Lacroix, J.M. and Y. Rioux. 1978. La communication non-verbale chez les bilingues. *Canadian Journal of Behavioural Sciences* 10. 130–140.
Ladewig, Silva H. 2014a. Recurrent gestures. In Cornelia Müller, Alan Cienki, Ellen Fricke, Silva H. Ladewig, David McNeill, and Jana Bressem (eds.), *Body – language – communication: An international handbook on multimodality in human interaction* (vol. 2), 1558–1574. Berlin: De Gruyter Mouton.

Ladewig, Silva H. 2014b. The cyclic gesture. In Cornelia Müller, Alan Cienki, Ellen Fricke, Silva H. Ladewig, David McNeill, and Jana Bressem (eds.), *Body – language – communication: An international handbook on multimodality in human interaction* (vol. 2), 1605–1618. Berlin: De Gruyter Mouton.

Ladewig, Silva H. 2014c. Creating multimodal utterances: The linear integration of gestures into speech. In Cornelia Müller, Alan Cienki, Ellen Fricke, Silva H. Ladewig, David McNeill, and Jana Bressem (eds.), *Body – language – communication: An international handbook on multimodality in human interaction* (vol. 2), 1662–1667. Berlin: De Gruyter Mouton.

Laikin, Paul. 1963. *A hand guide to language, with a guide to famous international hand gestures*. New York: Sloves and Frey.

Lakoff, George. 1987. *Women, fire, and dangerous things*. Chicago: Chicago University Press.

Lakoff, George and Mark Johnson. 1980. *Metaphors we live by*. Chicago: Chicago University Press.

Lamedica, Nico. 1982. Variazioni significative di gesti omologhi in due repertori gestuali dell'Italia meridionale. *Bulletino filosofico (Università della Calabria)* 1. 97–129.

Lefevre, Romana. 2011. *Rude hand gestures of the world*. San Francisco: Chronicle Books.

Leite de Vasconcellos, José. 1925. *A figa. Estudo de etnografia comparativa, precedido de algumas palavras a respeito do 'sobrenatural' na medicina popular portuguesa*. Porto: Araujo and Sobrinho.

Leite de Vasconcellos, José. 1938 A linguagem dos gestos. *Mémorias da Academia das Ciências de Lisboa* V. 454–491.

Levelt, Willem J. M. 1989. *Speaking: From intention to articulation*. Cambridge, MA: MIT Press.

Levinson, Stephen C. 1983. *Pragmatics*. Cambridge: Cambridge University Press.

Levy, Elena T. and David McNeill. 1992. Speech, gesture, and discourse. *Discourse Processes* 15. 277–301.

Lewandowska-Tomaszczyk, Barbara. 2007. Polysemy, prototypes, and radial categories. In Dirk Geeraerts and Hubert Cuykens (eds.), *The Oxford handbook of cognitive linguistics*, 139–169. Oxford: Oxford University Press.

Lloberes, Marina and Lluís Payrató. 2011. Pragmatic coherence as a multimodal feature: illustrative cospeech gestures, events, and states. In Lluís Payrató and Josep M. Cots (eds.), *The pragmatics of Catalan*, 215–246. Berlin/New York: De Gruyter Mouton.

Lynn, Ulrike. 2011. Keep in touch – a dictionary of contemporary physical contact gestures in the Mid-Atlantic region of the United States. Technische Universität Berlin PhD dissertation. On line: http://opus4.kobv.de/opus4-tuberlin/frontdoor/index/index/docId/3484.

Lynn, Ulrike. 2014. Gestures in dictionaries: physical contact gestures. In Cornelia Müller, Alan Cienki, Ellen Fricke, Silva H. Ladewig, David McNeill, and Jana Bressem (eds.), *Body – language – communication: An international handbook on multimodality in human interaction* (vol. 2), 1502–1511. Berlin: De Gruyter Mouton.

Lyons, John. 1972. Human language. In Robert A. Hinde (ed.), *Non-verbal communication*, 49–85. Cambridge: Cambridge University Press.

Mallery, Garrick. 1881a. The gesture speech of man. *Proceedings of the American Association for the Advancement of Science* 30. 283–313.

Mallery, Garrick. 1881b. *Sign language among North American Indians (compared with that among other peoples and deaf-mutes)*. Washington, Annual Reports of the Bureau of American Ethnology (Reprint: [1972] The Hague: Mouton).

Mallery, Garrick. 1891. Greeting by gesture. *Popular Science Monthly* Feb.-March. 477–490.

Marañón, Gregorio. 1937. *Psicología del gesto*. Santiago de Chile: Cultura.
Maricchiolo, Fridanna, Stefano De Dominicis, Uberta Ganucci Cancelleri, Angiola Di Conza, Augusto Gnisci, and Marino Bonaiuto. 2014. Co-speech gestures: structures and functions. In Cornelia Müller, Alan Cienki, Ellen Fricke, Silva H. Ladewig, David McNeill, and Jana Bressem (eds.), *Body – language – communication: An international handbook on multimodality in human interaction* (vol. 2), 1461–1473. Berlin: De Gruyter Mouton.
Martí, Joan. 1992. Apunts sobre la comunicació no verbal dels algueresos. *Revista de l'Alguer* 3. 33–50. Catalan version (revised and amplified) of the chapter Nonverbale Kommunikation: die Gestik, in Joan Martí [1986] *L'Alguer. Kulturanthropologische Monographie einer sardischen Stadt*, 337–364. Berlin: Reimer.
Martinell, Emma and Hiroto Ueda (eds.). 1990. *Diccionario de gestos españoles. Versión internet*. https://lecture.ecc.u-tokyo.ac.jp/~cueda/gakusyu/gestos/index.html#[[Inicio]].
Mascaró, Jaume. 1981. Notes per a un estudi de la gestualitat catalana. *Serra d'Or* 259. 25–28.
Mathon, Céline. 1969. Pour une semiologie du geste en Afrique Occidentale. *Semiotica* 3. 245–255.
Mauss, Marcel. 1973. Techniques of the body. *Economy and Society* 2. 70–88 (French original: [1935] Techniques du corps, *Journal de Psychologie Normal et Patholigique* XXXII. 271–293).
McClave, Evelyn Z. 2000. Linguistic functions of head movements in the context of speech. *Journal of Pragmatics* 32. 855–878.
McClave, Evelyn Z., Helen Kim, Rita Tanner and Milo Mileff. 2007. Head movements in the context of speech in Arabic, Bulgarian, Korean, and African-American Vernacular English. *Gesture* 7. 343–390.
McNeill, David. 1985. So you think gestures are nonverbal? *Psychological Bulletin* 92. 350–371.
McNeill, David, Levy, Elena T., and Laura L. Pedelty. 1990. Speech and gesture. In Geoffrey R. Hammond (ed.), *Cerebral control of speech and limb movements*, 203–256. Amsterdam: North Holland.
McNeill, David. 1992. *Hand and mind. What gestures reveal about thought* (2nd. edn.) Chicago: Chicago University Press.
McNeill, David. 2000. Introduction. In David McNeill (ed.), *Language and gesture*, 1–10. Cambridge: Cambridge University Press.
McNeill, David. 2005. *Gesture and Thought*. Chicago and London: University of Chicago Press.
McNeill, David. 2013. Gesture as a window onto mind and brain, and the relationship to linguistic relativity and ontogenesis. In Cornelia Müller, Alan Cienki, Ellen Fricke, Silva H. Ladewig, David McNeill, and Sedinha Tessendorf (eds.), *Body – language – communication: An international handbook on multimodality in human interaction* (vol. 1), 28–54. Berlin: De Gruyter Mouton.
McNeill, David (ed.). 2000. *Language and gesture*. Cambridge: Cambridge University.
Meissner, Martin and Stuart B. Philpott. 1975. A dictionary of sawmill workers' signs. *Sign Language Studies* 9. 309–347. https://muse.jhu.edu/article/507165/pdf.
Meo-Zilio, Giovanni. 1961a. El lenguaje de los gestos en el Uruguay. *Boletín de Filología (Universidad de Chile)* XIII. 75–163.
Meo-Zilio, Giovanni. 1961b. *El lenguaje de los gestos en el Río de la Plata*. Montevideo.
Meo-Zilio, Giovanni. 1983. El lenguaje de los gestos en el dominio hispanófono: comportamientos morfosintácticos y derivacionales. In A. David Kossof et al. (eds.), *Actas del VIII Congreso de la Asociación Internacional de Hispanistas* II. 305–315. Madrid: Istmo.

Meo-Zilio, Giovanni. 1987. Expresiones 'lingüísticas' concomitantes con expresiones gestuales en España e Hispanoamérica. *Diálogos hispánicos de Amsterdam* 6. 65–79.
Meo-Zilio, Giovanni. 1990. Gestos de procedencia italiana en el Plata. *Río de la Plata* 10. 83–95.
Meo-Zilio, Giovanni and Silvia Mejía. 1980–1983. *Diccionario de gestos. España e Hispanoamérica*, vol. 1 (1980) and vol. 2 (1983). Bogotá: Instituto Caro y Cuervo.
Merz, Andreas. 2010. Embleme im interkulturellen Vergleich. Eine Untersuchung zur Bedeutung von 16 Emblemen in Kolumbien und Deutschland. Diplomarbeit. Leipzig: Universität Leipzig. http://www.qucosa.de/fileadmin/data/qucosa/documents/12638/Diplomarbeit.pdf
Merz, Andreas. 2011. Gesten im interkulturellen Vergleich – eine kontrastive Analyse der Bedeutungen von zwei Emblemen in Kolumbien und Deutschland. *Lebende Sprachen* 56. 51–64. https://doi.org/10.1515/les.2011.003.
Meyer, Christian. 2014. Gestures in West Africa: Wolof. In Cornelia Müller, Alan Cienki, Ellen Fricke, Silva H. Ladewig, David McNeill, and Jana Bressem (eds.), In *Body – language – communication: An international handbook on multimodality in human interaction* (vol. 2), 1169–1175. Berlin: De Gruyter Mouton.
Mittelberg, Irene. 2010. Geometric and image-schematic patterns in gesture space. In Vyvyan Evans and Paul Chilton (eds.), *Language, cognition, and space: The state of the art and new directions*, 351–385. London: Equinox.
Mittelberg, Irene and Linda R. Waugh. 2009. Metonymy first, metaphor second: a cognitive-semiotic approach to multimodal figures of thought in co-speech gesture. In Charles J. Forceville and Eduardo Urios-Aparisi (eds.): *Multimodal metaphor*. 329–356. Berlin: De Gruyter – Mouton.
Mittelberg, Irene and Linda R. Waugh. 2014. Gestures and metonymy. In Cornelia Müller, Alan Cienki, Ellen Fricke, Silva H. Ladewig, David McNeill, and Jana Bressem (eds.), In *Body – language – communication: An international handbook on multimodality in human interaction* (vol. 2), 1747–1766. Berlin: De Gruyter Mouton.
Moerman, Michael. 1990. Studying gestures in social context. In Michael Moerman and Masaichi Nomura (eds.), *Culture embodied*, 5–52. Osaka: National Museum of Ethnology.
Moerman, Michael and Masaichi Nomura (eds.). 1990. *Culture embodied*. Osaka: National Museum of Ethnology.
Monahan, B. 1983. *A dictionary of Russian gesture*. Ann Arbor: Hermitage.
Mondada, Lorenza. 2013. Multimodal interaction. In Cornelia Müller, Alan Cienki, Ellen Fricke, Silva H. Ladewig, David McNeill, and Sedinha Tessendorf (eds.), *Body – language – communication: An international handbook on multimodality in human interaction* (vol. 1), 577–589. Berlin: De Gruyter Mouton.
Mondada, Lorenza. 2016. Challenges of multimodality: language and the body in social interaction. *Journal of Sociolinguistics* 20(3). 336–366.
Morris, Desmond, Peter Collett, Peter Marsh, and Marie O'Shaughnessy. 1979. *Gestures. Their origins and distribution*. London: Jonathan Cape.
Moyer, Melissa, Ignasi Clemente, Gema Rubio, and Marta Giménez (in preparation). Social inclusion and the impact of Voiceitt on identity and talk in persons with acquired brain injury. Barcelona: Universitat Autònoma de Barcelona.
Müller, Cornelia. 2004. The palm-up-open-hand. A case of a gesture family? In Cornelia Müller and Roland Posner (eds.), *Semantics and pragmatics of everyday gestures*, 233–256. Berlin: Weidler.
Müller, Cornelia. 2010. Wie Gesten bedeuten. Eine kognitive-linguistische und sequenzanalytische Perspektive". *Sprache und Literatur* 41. 37–68.

Müller, Cornelia. 2014. Ring-gestures across cultures and times: dimensions of variation. In Cornelia Müller, Alan Cienki, Ellen Fricke, Silva H. Ladewig, David McNeill, and Jana Bressem (eds.), *Body – language – communication: An international handbook on multimodality in human interaction* (vol. 2), 1511–1522. Berlin: De Gruyter Mouton.
Müller, Cornelia and Gerald Speckmann. 2002. Gestos con una Valoración Negativa en la Conversación Cubana. *DeSignis* 3. 91–103. Buenos Aires: Gedisa.
Müller, Cornelia, Alan Cienki, Ellen Fricke, Silva H. Ladewig, David McNeill, and Jana Bressem (eds.) 2014. *Body – language – communication: An international handbook on multimodality in human interaction* (vol. 2). Berlin: De Gruyter Mouton.
Müller, Cornelia, Alan Cienki, Ellen Fricke, Silva H. Ladewig, David McNeill and Sedinha Tessendorf (eds.). 2013. *Body – language – communication: An international handbook on multimodality in human interaction* (vol. 1). Berlin: De Gruyter Mouton.
Müller, Cornelia and Roland Posner (eds.). 2004. *The semantics and pragmatics of everyday gestures*. Berlin: Weidler.
Munari, Bruno. 1963. *Supplemento al dizionario italiano*. Milan: Muggiani.
Munari, Bruno. 1994. *Il dizionario dei gesti italiani*. Roma: AdnKronos Libri.
Nascimento, Nilma. 2008. Inventario de emblemas gestuales españoles y brasileños. *Language Design* 10. 5–75. http://elies.rediris.es/Language_Design/LD10/LD_10_01_Nilma_Pazeado.pdf.
Newbury, Kendra. 2011. Gesture and language shift on the Uruguayan-Brazilian border. In Gale A. Stam and Mika Ishino (eds.), *Integrating Gestures: the Interdisciplinary Nature of Gesture*, 231–241. Amsterdam: Benjamins.
Nogué, Neus and Lluís Payrató. 2007. Multimodal person deixis from multimodal corpora. Poster communication, 10th International Pragmatics Conference, Göteborg.
Núñez, Rafael E. and Eve Sweetser. 2006. With the future behind them: convergent evidence from aymara language and gesture in the crosslinguistic comparison of spatial construals of time. *Cognitive Science* 30(3). 401–450.
Ott, Edward A. 1902. *How to gesture*. New York: Hinds and Noble.
Padilla, Manuel. 2003. Perspectivas pragmáticas sobre los saludos. *Interlingüística* 14. 815–828.
Papas, William. 1972. *Instant Greek* (10th edn., 1981). Athens: Papas.
Pasquinelli, Barbara. 2005. *Gesto ed Espressione*. Milano: Electa.
Paura, Bruno and Marina Sorge. 2002. *Comme te l'aggia dicere? Ovvero l'arte gestuale a Napoli*. Napoli: Intra Moenia.
Payrató, Lluís. 1988. *Català col·loquial. Aspectes de l'ús corrent de la llengua catalana* (2nd. edn., 1990). València: Universitat de València.
Payrató, Lluís. 1989. *Assaig de dialectologia gestual. Aproximació pragmàtica al repertori d'emblemes del català de Barcelona*. Universitat de Barcelona PhD dissertation. Publicacions de la Universitat de Barcelona, 1991. http://www.tdx.cat/handle/10803/1687;jsessionid=46B9A98A31F4448A1B0EC16CE6BEF2E0.tdx2.
Payrató, Lluís. 1993. A pragmatic view on autonomous gestures: A first repertoire of Catalan emblems. *Journal of Pragmatics* 20. 193–216.
Payrató, Lluís. 2001. Methodological remarks on the study of emblems: The need for common elicitation procedures. In Christian Cavé, Isabelle Guaïtella and Serge Santi (eds.), *Oralité et gestualité. Interactions et comportements multimodaux dans la communication*, 262–265. Paris: L'Harmattan.

Payrató, Lluís. 2003. What does 'the same gesture' mean? Emblematic gestures from some cognitive-linguistic theories. In Monica Rector, Isabella Poggi and Nadine Trigo (eds.), *Gestures: Meaning and use*, 73–81. Porto: Ediçoes Universidade Fernando Pessoa.

Payrató, Lluís. 2004. Notes on pragmatic and social aspects of everyday gestures. In Cornelia Müller and Roland Posner (eds.), *Semantics and pragmatics of everyday gestures*, 103–113. Berlin: Weidler.

Payrató, Lluís. 2006. Breus apunts introductoris per a un projecte de dialectologia catalana del gest. *Miscel·lània Joan Veny*, 309–322. Barcelona: Publicacions de l'Abadia de Montserrat.

Payrató, Lluís. 2008. Past, present, and future research on emblems in the Hispanic tradition: Preliminary and methodological considerations. *Gesture* 8. 5–21.

Payrató, Lluís. 2009. Non-verbal communication. In Jef Verschueren and Jan-Ola Östman (eds.), *Key notions for pragmatics*, 163–194. Amsterdam and Philadelphia: John Benjamins.

Payrató, Lluís. 2013a. *El gest nostre de cada dia*. Barcelona: Publicacions de l'Abadia de Montserrat.

Payrató, Lluís 2013b. Textos, estils i multimodalitat: cap a una pragmaestilística del text multimodal. In Lluís Payrató, Neus Nogué, and Núria Alturo (eds.) *Estil i estils. Teoria i aplicacions de l'estilística*, 51–86. Barcelona: Agrupación de Editores y Autores Universitarios.

Payrató, Lluís. 2014a. Emblems or quotable gestures: structures, categories, and functions. In Cornelia Müller, Alan Cienki, Ellen Fricke, Silva H. Ladewig, David McNeill, and Jana Bressem (eds.), *Body – language – communication: An international handbook on multimodality in human interaction* (vol. 2), 1474–1481. Berlin: De Gruyter Mouton.

Payrató, Lluís. 2014b. Gestures in Southwest Europe: Catalonia. In Cornelia Müller, Alan Cienki, Ellen Fricke, Silva H. Ladewig, David McNeill, and Jana Bressem (eds.), *Body – language – communication: An international handbook on multimodality in human interaction* (vol. 2), 1266–1272. Berlin: De Gruyter Mouton.

Payrató, Lluís. 2017. Pragmatics and multimodality. A reflection on pragmastylistics. In Rachel Giora and Michael Haugh (eds.), *Doing pragmatics interculturally. Cognitive, philosophical, and sociopragmatic perspectives*, 293–312. Berlin: De Gruyter Mouton.

Payrató, Lluís and Jaume Fitó (eds.). 2008. *Corpus audiovisual plurilingüe*. Barcelona: Publicacions i Edicions de la Universitat de Barcelona.

Payrató, Lluís and Sedinha Tessendorf. 2014. Pragmatic gestures. In Cornelia Müller, Alan Cienki, Ellen Fricke, Silva H. Ladewig, David McNeill, and Jana Bressem (eds.), *Body – language – communication: An international handbook on multimodality in human interaction* (vol. 2), 1531–1539, Berlin: De Gruyter Mouton.

Peirce, Charles S. 1931–1958. *Collected papers of Charles Sanders Peirce*. Cambridge, MA: Harvard University Press.

Perelló, Jorge and Juan Frigola. 1987. *Lenguaje de signos manuales*. Barcelona: Editorial Científico Médica.

Pérez, Faustino. 2000. *Diccionario de gestos dominicanos*. Santo Domingo: F. Pérez.

Perkins, Michael. 2007. *Pragmatic impairment*. Cambridge: Cambridge University Press.

Piderit, Theodor. 1867. *Wissenschaftliches System der Mimik und Physiognomik*. Detmold: Klingenberg.

Pike, Kenneth L. 1967. *Language in relation to a unified theory of the structure of human behavior*. The Hague: Mouton.

Pitrè, Giuseppe. 1989. *Usi, costumi, crecenze e pregiudizi del popolo siciliano*. Palermo: Pedone-Laurel.

Poggi, Isabella. 1981. *Le interiezioni: Uso del linguaggio e analisi della mente*. Torino: Boringhieri.

Poggi, Isabella. 1983. 'La mano a borsa': analisi semantica di un gesto emblematico olofrastico. In Grazia Attili and Pio E. Ricci-Bitti (eds.), *Comunicare senza parole. La communicazione non-verbale nel bambino e nell'interazione sociale tra adulti*, 219–238. Roma: Bulzoni (2nd edn., 1984).

Poggi, Isabella. 1987. Frasi e parole con la voce e con le mani. In Isabella Poggi (ed.) *Le parole nella testa. Guida a un'educazione linguistica cognitivista*, 329–337. Bologna: Mulino.

Poggi, Isabella. 2002. Symbolic gestures: the case of the Italian gestionary. *Gesture* 2. 71–98.

Poggi, Isabella. 2004. The Italian gestionary. Meaning representation, ambiguity, and context. In Cornelia Müller and Roland Posner (eds.), *Semantics and pragmatics of everyday gestures*, 73–88. Berlin: Weidler.

Poggi, Isabella. 2007. *Mind, hands, face and body: A goal and belief view of multimodal communication*. Berlin: Weidler.

Poggi, Isabella. 2014. Semantics and pragmatics of symbolic gestures. In Cornelia Müller, Alan Cienki, Ellen Fricke, Silva H. Ladewig, David McNeill, and Jana Bressem (eds.), *Body – language – communication: An international handbook on multimodality in human interaction* (vol. 2), 1481–1496. Berlin: De Gruyter Mouton.

Poggi, Isabella (ed.). 1987. *Le parole nella testa. Guida a un'educazione linguistica cognitivista*. Bologna: Mulino.

Poggi, Isabella and Emanuela Magno Caldognetto. 1997. *Mani che parlano. Gesti e psicologia della comunicazione*. Padova: Unipress.

Poggi, Isabella and Marina Zomparelli. 1987. Lessico e grammatica nei gesti e nelle parole. In Isabella Poggi (ed.), *Le parole nella testa. Guida a un' edicazione cognitivista*, 291–328. Bologna: Mulino.

Posner, Roland. 2003. Everyday gestures as as result of ritualization. In Monica Rector, Isabella Poggi, and Nadine Trigo (eds.), *Gestures: Meaning and use*, 217–229. Porto: Ediçoes Universidade Fernando Pessoa.

Posner, Roland, Reinhard Krüger, Thomas Noll, and Massimo Serenari (eds.). In preparation. *The Berlin dictionary of everyday gestures*. Berlin: Weidler.

Poyatos, Fernando. 1970. Kinésica del español actual. *Hispania* LIII. 444–452.

Poyatos, Fernando. 1975. Gesture inventories: fieldwork methodology and problems. *Semiotica* 13. 199–227.

Poyatos, Fernando. 1976. *Man beyond words. Theory and methodology of nonverbal communication*. Oswego: New York State English Council.

Poyatos, Fernando. 1980. Interactive functions and limitations of verbal and nonverbal behaviors in natural conversation. *Semiotica* 30. 211–244.

Poyatos, Fernando. 1983. *New perspectives in nonverbal communication. Studies in cultural anthropology, social psychology, linguistics, literature and semiotics*. Oxford: Pergamon.

Poyatos, Fernando. 1988. The communicative status of human audible movements: before and beyond paralanguage. *Semiotica* 70. 265–300.

Poyatos, Fernando (ed.). 1988. *Cross-cultural perspectives in nonverbal communication*. Toronto: C.J. Hogrefe.

Poyatos, Fernando. 2008. *Textual translation and live translation: The total experience of non-verbal communication in literature, theater and cinema*. Amsterdam and Philadelphia: John Benjamins.

Poyatos, Fernando. 2013. Body gestures, manners, and postures in literature. In Cornelia Müller, Alan Cienki, Ellen Fricke, Silva H. Ladewig, David McNeill, and Sedinha Tessendorf (eds.), *Body – language – communication: An international handbook on multimodality in human interaction* (vol. 1), 287–300. Berlin: De Gruyter Mouton.

Quintilian, Marcus Fabius. 1969. *The Institutio Oratoria of Quintilian [De Institutione Oratoria, 95 AD]*. New York: Putnam.

Rabanales, Ambrosio. 1954–55. La somatolalia. *Boletín de Filología* VIII. 355–378.

Raffler-Engel, Walburga Von. 1971. Cultural differences in the acquisition of nonverbal behavior. *Word* 1/2/3. 195–204.

Raffler-Engel, Walburga Von. 1976. Linguistic and kinesics correlates in code switching. In William C. McCormack and Stephen A. Wurm (eds.), *Language and man: Anthropological issues*, 269–286. The Hague: Mouton.

Rector, Monica. 1986 Emblems in Brazilian culture. In Paul Bouissac, Michael Herzfeld, and Roland Posner (eds.), *Iconicity. Essays on the nature of culture*, 447–462. Tübingen: Stauffenburg.

Rector, Monica. 2014. Gestures in South America: Spanish and Portuguese. In Cornelia Müller, Alan Cienki, Ellen Fricke, Silva H. Ladewig, David McNeill, and Jana Bressem (eds.), *Body – language – communication: An international handbook on multimodality in human interaction* (vol. 2), 1175–1181. Berlin: De Gruyter Mouton.

Rector, Monica, Isabella Poggi and Nadine Trigo (eds.). 2003. *Gestures: Meaning and use*. Porto: Ediçoes Universidade Fernando Pessoa.

Rector, Monica and Salvatore Trigo. 2004. Body signs: Portuguese communication on three continents. In Cornelia Müller and Roland Posner (eds.), *Semantics and pragmatics of everyday gestures*, 195–204. Berlin: Weidler.

Rector, Monica and Aluizio R. Trinta. 1985. *Communicaçao nao-verbal: A gestualidade Brasileira*. Petrópolis: Vozes.

Reinach, Salomon. 1924. L'histoire des gestes. *Revue Archéologique*. 64–79.

Reiter, Sabine. 2014. Gestures in South American indigenous cultures. In Cornelia Müller, Alan Cienki, Ellen Fricke, Silva H. Ladewig, David McNeill, and Jana Bressem (eds.), *Body – language – communication: An international handbook on multimodality in human interaction* (vol. 2), 1182–1193. Berlin: De Gruyter Mouton.

Ricci Bitti, Pio E. 1992. Facial and manual components of Italian symbolic gestures. In Fernando Poyatos (ed.), *Advances in nonverbal communication*, 187–196. Amsterdam and Philadelphia: John Benjamins.

Riley, Philip. 1976. Discoursive and communicative functions of non-verbal communication. In *Mélanges pédagogiques*. 1–18. Université de Nancy II: CRAPEL.

Rohlfs, Gerhard. 1959 [1960]. Influence des élements autochtones sur les langues romanes (Problèmes de géographie linguistique). *Actes du Colloque International de Civilisations, Littératures et Langues Romanes*, 240–247. Bucarest: Commission nationale roumaine pour l'UNESCO.

Rosch, Eleanor. 1978. Principles of categorization. In Eleanor Rosch and Barbara B. Lloyd (eds.), *Cognition and categorization*, 27–48. Hillsdale, NJ: Lawrence Erlbaum.

Ross, Brian H. and Valerie S. Makin. 1999. Prototype versus exemplar models in cognition. In Robert J. Sternberg (ed.), *The nature of cognition*, 205–241. Cambridge: MIT.

Rosell i Vilar, Pere Màrtir. 1930. *La raça*. Barcelona: Catalònia.

Ruesch, Jurgen and Weldon Kees. 1956. *Non-verbal communication: Notes in the visual perception of human relations*. Berkeley: University of California Press.

Ruiz, Leonor and M. Belén Alvarado (eds.). 2013. *Irony and humor: From pragmatics to discourse*. Amsterdam and Philadelphia: John Benjamins.

Safadi, Michaela and Carol A. Valentine. 1988. Emblematic gestures among Hebrew speakers in Israel. *International Journal of Intercultural Relations* 12. 327–361.
Safadi, Michaela and Carol A. Valentine. 1990. Contrastive analysis of American and Arab nonverbal and paralinguistic communication. *Semiotica* 82. 269–292.
Saint-Jacques, Bernard. 1972. Quelques aspects du langage gestuel en japonais. In Jacqueline M.C. Thomas and Lucien Bernot (eds.), *Langues et techniques. Nature et societé. I. Approche Linguistique*, 391–394. Paris: Klincksieck.
Saitz, Robert L. and Edward J. Cervenka. 1972. *Handbook of gestures: Colombia and the United States*. The Hague: Mouton.
Sanders, Robert E. 1980. Principles of relevance: a theory of the relationship between language and communication. *Communication and Cognition* 13. 77–95.
Sanders, Robert E. 1985. The interpretation of nonverbals. *Semiotica* 55. 195–216.
Sandoval, Richard. 2014. Gestures in native Northern America: bimodal talk in Arapaho. In Cornelia Müller, Alan Cienki, Ellen Fricke, Silva H. Ladewig, David McNeill, and Jana Bressem (eds.), *Body – language – communication: An international handbook on multimodality in human interaction* (vol. 2), 1215–1226. Berlin: De Gruyter Mouton.
Santi, Serge, Isabelle Guaïtella, Christian Cavé and Gabrielle Konopczynski (eds.). 1998. *Oralité et gestualité. Communication multimodale, interaction*. Paris: L'Harmattan.
Santi, Serge and Martha Ruiz. 1998. Stratégies gestuelles en espagnol et en français de sujets bilingues en situation d'interview. In Serge Santi, Isabelle Guaïtella, Christian Cavé, and Gabrielle Konopczynski (eds.), *Oralité et gestualité. Communication multimodale, interaction*, 421–426. Paris: L'Harmattan.
Sapir, Edward. 1927. The unconscious patterning of behavior in society. Original in Ethel S. Dummer (ed.), *The unconscious: A symposium*, 114–142. New York: Knopf. [Reprint in David G. Mandelbaum (ed.), *Selected writings of Edward Sapir in language, culture and personality* 958, 544–559. Berkeley: University of California Press].
Saville-Troike, Muriel. 1982. *The ethnography of communication. An introduction*. Oxford: Blackwell (3rd edn., 2003).
Scheflen, Albert E. and Alice Scheflen. 1972. *Body language and the social order*. Oxford: Prentice Hall.
Scherer, Klaus R. 1977. Die Funktionen des nonverbalen Verhaltens im Gespräch. In Dirk Wegner (ed.), *Gesprächanalysen*, 275–297. Hamburg: Buske.
Scherer, Klaus R. and Paul Ekman (eds.). 1982. *Handbook of methods in nonverbal behavior research*. Cambridge: Cambridge University Press.
Schmitt, Jean-Claude. 1990. *La raison des gestes dans l'Occident médiéval*. Paris: Gallimard.
Schmitt, Jean-Claude (ed.). 1984. *Gestures. History and anthropology*. London: Harwood Academic Publishers.
Schmitt, Reinhold. 2005. Zur multimodalen Struktur von turn-taking. *Gesprächsforschung – Online Zeitschrift zur verbalen Interaktion* 6. 17–61.
Schneller, Raphael. 1988. The Israeli experience of cross-cultural misunderstanding: insights and lessons. In Fernando Poyatos (ed.), *Cross-cultural perspectives in nonverbal communication*, 153–173. Toronto: C.J. Hogrefe.
Schönherr, Beatrix. 2014. Categories and functions of posture, gaze, face, and body movements. In Cornelia Müller, Alan Cienki, Ellen Fricke, Silva H. Ladewig, David McNeill, and Jana Bressem (eds.), *Body – language – communication: An international handbook on multimodality in human interaction* (vol. 2), 1333–1341. Berlin: De Gruyter Mouton.

Schuler, Edgar A. 1944. V for victory: a study in symbolic social control. *The Journal of Social Psychology* 19. 283–299.
Searle, John R. 1976. A classification of illocutionary acts. *Language in Society* 5. 1–23.
Searle, John R. 1979. *Expression and meaning. Studies in the theory of speech acts.* Cambridge: Cambridge University Press.
Seckendorff, Gustav Anton von. 1816. *Vorlesungen über Deklamation und Mimik.* Braunschweig.
Senft, Gunter. 2014. *Understanding pragmatics.* London: Routledge.
Senghas, Richard J., Ann Senghas, and Jennie E. Pyers. 2005. The emergence of Nicaraguan Sign Language: questions of development, acquisition, and evolution. In Sue T. Parker, Jonas Langer, and Constance Milbrath (eds.), *Biology and knowledge revisited: From neurogenesis to psychogenesis,* 287–306. London: Lawrence Erlbaum Associates.
Serenari, Massimo. 2003. Examples from the Berlin dictionary of everyday gestures. In Monica Rector, Isabella Poggi, and Nadine Trigo (eds.), *Gestures: Meaning and use,* 111–117. Porto: Ediçoes Universidade Fernando Pessoa.
Serenari, Massimo. 2004. The structure of dictionary entries – results of empirical investigations. In Cornelia Müller and Roland Posner (ed.), *Semantics and pragmatics of everyday gestures,* 15–32. Berlin: Weidler.
Seyfeddinipur, Mandana. 2004. Meta-discursive gestures from Iran: some uses of the 'Pistol-Hand'. In Cornelia Müller and Roland Posner (eds.), *Semantics and pragmatics of everyday gestures,* 205–216. Berlin: Weidler.
Seyfeddinipur, Mandana and Marianne Gullberg (eds.). 2014. *From gesture in conversation to visible action as utterance: Essays in honor of Adam Kendon.* Amsterdam and Philadelphia: John Benjamins.
Shapero, Joshua. 2014. Gestures in Native South America: Ancash Quechua. In Cornelia Müller, Alan Cienki, Ellen Fricke, Silva H. Ladewig, David McNeill, and Jana Bressem (eds.), *Body – language – communication: An international handbook on multimodality in human interaction* (vol. 2), 1193–1206. Berlin: Mouton De Gruyter.
Sherzer, Joel. 1973. Verbal and nonverbal deixis: the pointed lip gesture among the San Blas Cuna. *Language in Society* 2. 117–131.
Sherzer, Joel. 1983. *Kuna ways of speaking. An ethnographic perspective.* Austin: University of Texas Press.
Sherzer, Joel. 1991. The Brazilian thumbs-up gesture. *Journal of Linguistic Anthropology* 1. 189–197.
Sherzer, Joel. 1993. Pointed lips, thumbs up, and cheek puffs: some emblematic gestures in social interactional and ethnographic context. *SALSA* I. 196–211.
Sittl, Carl. 1890. *Die Gebärden der Griechen und Römer.* Leipzig: Teubner.
Slama-Cazacu, Tatiana. 1976. Nonverbal components in message sequence: 'mixed syntax'. In William C. McCormack and Stephen A. Wurm (eds.), *Language and man: Anthropological issues,* 217–227. The Hague: Mouton.
Smith, J. David. 2014. Prototypes, exemplars and the natural history of categorization. *Psychonomic Bulletin & Review* 21. 312–331.
Smithson, Lisa, Elena Nicoladis and Paula Marentette. 2011. Bilingual children's gesture use. *Gesture* 11. 330–347.
Sparhawk, Carol M. 1978. Contrastive-identificational features of Persian gesture. *Semiotica* 24. 49–86.
Sperber, Dan and Deirdre Wilson. 1986 [1995]. *Relevance: Communication and cognition* (2nd edn., 1995). Oxford: Blackwell.

Stange, Ulrike and Damaris Nübling. 2014. Multimodal forms of expressing emotions: the case of interjections. In Cornelia Müller, Alan Cienki, Ellen Fricke, Silva H. Ladewig, David McNeill, and Jana Bressem (eds.), *Body – language – communication: An international handbook on multimodality in human interaction* (vol. 2), 1982–1989. Berlin: De Gruyter Mouton.
Streeck, Jürgen. 1995. On projection. In Esther N. Goody (ed.), *Interaction and social intelligence*, 84–110. Cambridge: Cambridge University Press.
Streeck, Jürgen. 2005. Pragmatic aspects of gesture. In Jacob Mey (ed.), *Encyclopedia of language and linguistics* (vol. 5): pragmatics, 71–76. Oxford: Elsevier.
Streeck, Jürgen [2009] 2011. *Gesturecraft. The manufacture of meaning.* Amsterdam and Philadelphia: John Benjamins.
Takagaki, Toshihiro, Hiroto Ueda, Emma Martinell, and Maria. J. Gelabert. 1998. *Pequeño diccionario de gestos españoles.* Tokio: Hakusuisha.
Taylor, Archer. 1956. The Shanghai gesture. *Folklore Fellowship Communications* 166. 1–76.
Taylor, John R. 2003. *Linguistic categorization. Prototypes in linguistic theory.* Oxford: Oxford University Press.
Tessendorf, Sedinha. 2005. Pragmatische Funktionen spanischer Gesten am Beispiel des 'gesto de barrer'. Free University Berlin, unpublished MA thesis.
Tessendorf, Sedinha. 2008. Pragmatic and metaphoric gestures – combining functional with cognitive approaches. European University Viadrina, Frankfurt (Oder), unpublished manuscript.
Tessendorf, Sedinha. 2013. Emblems, quotable gestures, or conventionalized body movements. In Cornelia Müller, Alan Cienki, Ellen Fricke, Alan Cienki, Silva H. Ladewig, David McNeill and Sedinha Tessendorf (eds.), *Body – language – communication: An international handbook on multimodality in human interaction* (vol. 1), 82–100. Berlin: De Gruyter Mouton.
Tessendorf, Sedinha. 2014. Pragmatic and metaphoric – combining functional with cognitive approaches in the analysis of the "brushing aside gesture". In Cornelia Müller, Alan Cienki, Ellen Fricke, Silva H. Ladewig, David McNeill, and Jana Bressem (eds.), *Body – language – communication: An international handbook on multimodality in human interaction* (vol. 2), 1540–1558. Berlin: De Gruyter Mouton.
Tohyama, Yasuko. 2003. Japanese and American body movements: towards a potential database of world gestures. In Monica Rector, Isabella Poggi, and Nadine Trigo (eds.), *Gestures: Meaning and use*, 83–87. Porto: Ediçoes Universidade Fernando Pessoa.
Tomasello, Michael. 2008. *Origins of human communication.* The Jean Nicod Lectures. Cambridge, MA: MIT Press.
Torrego, Ester. 1974. Aportación al estudio gestual del habla de Madrid. Universidad Complutense, Madrid, PhD dissertation.
Tumarkin, Petr S. 2003. On a dictionary of Japanese gesture. In Monica Rector, Isabella Poggi, and Nadine Trigo (eds.), *Gestures: Meaning and use*, 89–92. Porto: Ediçoes Universidade Fernando Pessoa.
Tylor, Edward B. 1865. *Researches on the Early History of Mankind and the Development of Civilization.* London: John Murray.
Umiker-Sebeok, Jean and Thomas A. Sebeok (eds.), 1987 *Monastic sign language.* Berlin: Mouton de Gruyter.
Urios-Aparisi, Eduardo. 2009. Interaction of multimodal metaphor and metonymy in TV commercials: four case studies. In Charles Forceville and Eduardo Urios-Aparisi (eds.), *Multimodal metaphor*, 95–117. Berlin – New York: Mouton de Gruyter.

Ussa, Maria del C. and Mauricio Ussa. 2001. Les U'wa bilingues: un cas de gestualité multiculturelle. In Christian Cavé, Isabelle Guaïtella, and Serge Santi (eds.), *Oralité et gestualité. Interactions et comportements multimodaux dans la communication*, 591–594. Paris: L'Harmattan.

Van Ginneken, Jacques. 1939. *La reconstruction typologique des langues archaiques de l'humanité*. Amsterdam: Noord-Hollandsche uitgevers-mij.

Vávra, Vlastimil. 1976. Is Jakobson right? *Semiotica* 17. 95–110.

Vrugt, Anneke. 1987. The meaning of nonverbal sex differences. *Semiotica* 64. 371–380.

Vrugt, Anneke and Ada Kerkstra. 1984. Sex differences in nonverbal communication. *Semiotica* 50. 1–41.

Washabaugh, William. 1986. The acquisition of communicative skills by the deaf of Providence Island. *Semiotica* 62. 179–190.

Weiss, Paul. 1943. The social character of gestures. *The Philosophical Review* LII. 182–86.

Wharton, Tim. 2009. *Pragmatics and non-verbal communication*. Cambridge: Cambridge University Press.

Wharton, Tim. 2011. Pragmatics and nonverbal communication. An exchange. Reply to the review of Kensy Cooperrider. *Gesture* 11. 383–393.

Wiener, Morton, Shannon Devoe, Stuart Rubinow, and Jesse Geller. 1972. Nonverbal behavior and nonverbal communication. *Psychological Review* 79. 185–214.

Wilcox, Sherman. 2004. Gesture and language: cross linguistic and historical data from signed languages. *Gesture* 4. 43–75.

Wilcox, Sherman. 2014. Gestures in sign language. In Cornelia Müller, Alan Cienki, Ellen Fricke, Silva H. Ladewig, David McNeill, and Jana Bressem (eds.), *Body – language – communication: An international handbook on multimodality in human interaction* (vol. 2), 2170–2176. Berlin: De Gruyter Mouton.

Wolff, Charlotte. 1945. *A psychology of gesture*. London: Methuen.

Wollock, Jeffrey. 2013. Renaissance philosophy: gesture as universal language. In Cornelia Müller, Alan Cienki, Ellen Fricke, Silva H. Ladewig, David McNeill, and Sedinha Tessendorf (eds.), *Body – language – communication: An international handbook on multimodality in human interaction*, 364–378. Berlin: De Gruyter Mouton.

Wundt, Wilhelm. 1900. *Völkerpsychologie. Die Sprache* (vol. 1–2). Leipzig: Engelmann. Chapter 2 translated to English in *The language of gestures* [1973]. The Hague: Mouton.

Wylie, Laurence and Rick Stafford. 1977. *Beaux gestes: A guide to French body talk*. Cambridge: The Undergraduate Press.

Yus, Francisco. 2009. Visual metaphor versus verbal metaphor: A unified account. In Charles Forceville and Eduardo Urios-Aparisi (eds.), *Multimodal metaphor*, 147–172. Berlin – New York: Mouton de Gruyter.

Zamora, Alonso. 1983. Corte de mangas. In *Homenaje a José Manuel Blecua ofrecido por sus discípulos, colegas y amigos*, 709–713. Madrid: Gredos.

Zlatev, Jordan. 2007. Embodiment, language, and mimesis. In Tom Ziemke, Jordan Zlatev, and Roslyn Frank (eds.), *Body, language and mind* (vol. I), 297–337. Berlin: De Gruyter Mouton.

Zlatev, Jordan. 2008. The co-evolution of intersubjectivity and bodily mimesis. In Jordan Zlatev, Timothy R. Racine, Chris Sinha, and Esa Itkonen (eds.), *The shared mind: Perspectives on intersubjectivity*, 215–244. Amsterdam and Philadelphia: John Benjamins.

Index

Acquisition 1, 3, 69, 141, 157
Adaptor 3, 23–25, 31, 57, 105–107
Affect display 2, 23–25, 79, 106
Africa 82, 83, 128
America 83, 84, 87, 89, 99, 104, 125, 173
Amerindian 83
Ancient Greece and Rome 108
Anthropology 14, 16, 28
Arab 57, 124
Armenian 83
Articulated gesture 39–49
Australia 74
Autonomous gesture 1, 5, 26, 40, 41, 91, 94, 98, 148, 176, 177

Banyes gesture 1, 62, 63
Bilingualism 110
Body
–Hand 3, 10–12, 15, 18–20, 31, 34, 37, 89, 115, 125, 137, 158, 159, 162, 164, 169, 178, 180
–Head movement 17, 20, 101, 107, 112, 115, 132, 182
–Mutual orientation 168
–Pointing 59–61, 122, 124, 125, 128, 164, 177, 183
–Shrugging 101, 177, 178
Borrowing 111, 170
Botifarra gesture 1, 62, 63, 100, 139, 164, 172–174, 199, 203
Brazil 83, 89

Catalan 2, 18, 27, 39, 51, 60–62, 70–72, 74–76, 83, 91–102, 104, 107–112, 117, 121, 124, 130, 132, 137, 142, 145, 162, 166–168, 170, 172–174, 176, 179, 180, 182
Catalonia 63, 83, 100, 110, 112, 130, 142, 171, 181
Categorization 11, 12, 17–19, 21, 26, 29–31, 35, 38, 41, 42, 49, 116, 139, 141, 142, 151, 189, 190
Cheek screw gesture 110, 119

Cheek stroke gesture 110, 119
Chinese 83
Chin flick gesture 119
Classical rhetoric 1, 5–15
Classification 10, 12, 16–25, 27, 34, 43, 44, 51–54, 59, 67, 68, 71, 88, 113, 128, 129, 136, 139, 176, 179, 189
Clever gesture 128
Codification 22, 87, 91–94, 97, 98, 121
Cognitive dimension 11, 110, 153, 185
Colloquial 50, 51, 74, 78, 92, 182
Colombian 85, 214
Compilation 2, 64, 73, 78–84, 87, 88, 91, 93, 94, 104
Composite utterance 59, 132, 145, 155
Conventional 14, 15, 32, 35, 47, 49, 50, 54, 68, 70, 71, 140, 142, 144, 148, 177
Conventionalization 40, 49, 51, 67, 69, 71, 79, 94, 105, 135, 140–142, 150, 152, 158
Corte de mangas gesture 1, 62, 63, 173, 213
Co-speech gesture 40, 47, 66, 67, 79, 104, 110, 111, 115, 128, 141, 152, 156, 174, 190, 193
Cuernos gesture 62, 63, 207, 212
Culture 1–4, 10, 13–15, 20, 21, 23, 25, 39, 43, 54, 56–58, 60, 62–65, 68, 70, 72, 73, 76, 78, 82, 85, 88, 90, 94, 99, 103, 104, 106, 108–113, 115, 117, 119, 121–125, 130, 134, 150, 168, 173, 174, 185, 187–189, 191–192
Cultural distribution and variation 108–111, 115

Deaf 10, 14, 15, 17, 18, 73–75, 86, 181, 184
Deixis 2, 9, 17, 18, 21, 23–26, 47, 50, 52, 53, 59–61, 92, 105, 110, 111, 116, 124, 126, 150, 164, 172, 182, 191, 193
Descriptive emblem 20, 27, 40, 77, 84, 128, 150, 151, 175
Dialectology 51, 81, 92, 99, 108, 109, 113, 116, 129, 192
Dictionary 30, 39, 56, 70, 79, 82, 87–89, 91, 92, 117, 188
Disability 181

https://doi.org/10.1515/9781501509957-017

Ear touch gesture 110, 119
Ecological perspective 103, 133
Elicitation 121
Emblematicity criteria 2, 48, 91
Emblematic web 141–147
Emblematization 41, 51, 70, 71, 94, 104, 105, 135, 140, 141, 150, 155, 157–174, 190
Emblem, definition
–as a category 42–49
–as a semiotic category 27, 42
Emblem ecology 2, 103–134
Emblem, type and function
–Borrowing 110, 111, 170
–current speech 51
–deictic 50, 59, 60, 105, 182, 191
–greeting 50, 54–59
–insult 50, 62, 63, 140
–Technical emblem or emblem for special purpose 2, 64, 65, 85–87, 174
Emotion 6, 14, 18, 20, 32, 38, 67, 106, 123, 176
English 16, 21, 27, 30, 39, 44, 62, 70, 83, 100, 110–112, 121, 162, 163, 168, 170, 173, 179
Ethnography 1, 3, 13, 18, 27, 59, 62, 64, 78, 84, 109, 119, 123, 126, 129, 130, 136, 145, 154, 174, 181, 185, 191, 192
Europe 11, 56, 84, 104, 114, 115, 117
Everyday 15, 22, 31, 34, 50, 51, 54, 56, 63–65, 74–76, 78, 81, 85–88, 91, 97, 104, 121, 128–130, 154, 160, 174–175, 180, 182, 187
Evolution 3, 12, 16, 20, 103–107, 117, 133, 168, 173
Exemplar model 143
Expressive gesture 8, 12, 67, 180
Eyelid pull gesture 101, 119

Face 14, 19, 25, 35, 67, 78, 102, 107, 149, 172, 178, 179, 182, 188
Family gesture 112
Family resemblance model 63, 141, 143–147, 190
Fig gesture 63
Fingers cross gesture 119

Fingertips kiss gesture 101, 119, 121
Flat-hand flick gesture 119
Forearm jerk gesture 1, 54, 62, 63, 100, 119, 139, 142, 145, 164, 172, 173
French 2, 5, 10, 21, 22, 27, 39, 62, 73, 75, 82, 83, 87, 110, 112, 120, 170, 173, 175, 188
Functional grammar 9, 155

Geographic distribution of emblems 113–123, 134
German 19, 69, 82, 83, 84
Gesticulation 11, 13, 19–21, 34, 40, 45, 46, 67, 72, 152, 175, 192
Gestural continua 2, 39, 42, 44
Gestural dictionary 87, 89, 117
Gestural lexicography
–interview 96–98
–item 96–98
–repertoire 98, 99
–questionnaire 96–98
Gestural neologism 3, 107, 124
Gesture
–Definition 30
–Gesture, co-speech 40, 47, 66, 67, 79, 104, 110, 111, 115, 128, 141, 152, 156, 174, 190, 193
–Gesture, pragmatic 2, 29, 40, 67, 68, 105, 154
–as universal language 9, 10
Gesture-speech relationship 27, 46, 59
Greek 15, 83, 87, 113–115, 145
Greeting 2, 15, 18, 31, 49, 50, 54–56, 58, 78, 89, 109, 127, 138, 140, 178, 193

Hand 3, 10–12, 15, 18–20, 31, 34, 37, 89, 115, 125, 137, 158, 159, 162, 164, 169, 178, 180
Hand purse gesture 119, 120, 121
Head 3, 17, 18, 20, 31, 34, 68, 72–74, 78, 89, 101, 105, 108, 112, 115, 119, 130, 132, 133, 138, 147, 156, 158, 163, 164, 178, 180, 182
Head toss gesture 112, 115, 119
Holophrastic gesture 39–40
Horn sign gesture, horizontal 63, 119
Horn sign gesture, vertical 100, 119

Iconicity 17, 27, 44, 47, 49, 68, 71, 109, 110, 117, 163
Illocution 1–4, 38, 41, 48–50, 54, 61, 64, 66, 68–70, 78, 91, 93, 99, 105, 140, 141, 148, 150, 153, 174, 176–181, 185
Illustrator 2, 22–24, 26, 31, 41, 67, 68–70, 79, 88, 104, 105, 141, 193
Image schema 3, 104–106, 121, 122, 163, 190
Impair 181–183
Impudicus finger emblem 54, 63, 100
Indexical 17, 43, 49, 59, 158, 186
Insult 1, 2, 49–51, 60, 62, 63, 66, 99, 100, 104, 111, 122, 124, 140, 142, 148, 151, 154, 159, 164, 172, 176, 179–181, 193
Interaction 3, 4, 20, 27, 32, 38, 51, 55, 56, 58, 59, 66, 68–70, 72, 74, 77–79, 81, 92, 108, 123, 129, 130, 134, 135–187, 192, 194
Interactive gesture 68, 74
Intergrammar 27, 132, 155
Interjection 2, 47, 70–72, 111, 141
Irony 150, 157, 170, 172, 191
Italian 2, 5, 19, 20, 27, 39, 56, 59, 62, 82, 83, 87, 110–112, 123, 161

Japanese 74, 83, 90, 188

Kinesis 25, 27, 72, 155

Language-gesture origin 107
Language-gesture relationship 14, 27, 30, 42, 157, 173
Lexical gesture 39–40
Lexicalization 71, 135
Linguistics 1, 8, 17, 20, 46, 50–52, 59, 65–67, 70–72, 78, 81, 87, 90, 95, 98, 99, 107–119, 134, 139, 186, 187, 190

Mano a borsa gesture 69, 109
Manual 15, 149, 186
Meaning 34, 38, 48–49, 135, 137–141, 147–151
Medieval studies (Middle Ages) 1, 5, 10, 77, 103

Metaphoric gesture 14, 67, 68
Metaphorization 1, 3, 157
Metaphor 1, 11, 79, 102, 103, 150, 153, 157–170, 191
Methodology 2, 27, 77–102, 113, 115, 117, 120, 123, 189, 192
Metonymy 1, 3, 74, 153, 157–170, 191
Mixed syntax 132, 155
Mockery 63, 99, 104, 158, 159, 181
Movement 16, 19, 20, 30, 31, 34, 38, 48, 63, 69, 72, 101, 105, 107, 115, 122, 125, 132, 140, 158, 160, 162, 169, 173, 182, 183
Multilingualism 110, 111
Multimodality 3, 18, 26, 28, 157, 186–188

Neurology 157
Non-verbal 2, 14, 15, 18, 20, 22, 26, 28, 30, 31, 38, 39, 42, 49, 54, 65–76, 78, 97, 101, 109, 124, 135, 151–160, 166, 168, 174, 175, 177, 179, 186, 187, 193, 194
Nose tap gesture 101, 109
Nose thumb gesture 1, 99, 109, 158
Notation 2, 13, 38, 77, 78

Okay gesture 132
Origin and historical evolution of emblem 112

Palm 54, 56, 69, 73, 98, 100–102, 107, 111, 116, 119, 124, 125, 137, 138, 155, 166, 168, 169, 178
Palm-back V-sign gesture 119
Pam-i-pipa gesture 1, 99, 111, 122, 158, 173, 174
Pantomime 19, 32, 45, 46, 106, 138, 141, 150, 158, 172
Paralinguistics 27, 70, 178
Performative gesture 177
Performativity 9, 40, 68, 133, 177, 179, 193
Persian 83
Phraseology 3, 112, 152, 157, 162, 166–168, 172, 191
Pictorial gesture 9, 10, 12
Pilota, fer el expression and gesture 112, 167, 168, 170, 173

Pito Catalán gesture 99, 111, 173
Pointing 59, 60, 61, 89, 122, 124, 125, 128, 164, 177, 179, 183
Pointing lip gesture 126–128
Portuguese 5, 83, 173
Posture 30, 31, 173, 179
Pragmastylistics 185, 187, 189, 193
Pragmatic gesture 2, 29, 40, 67, 68, 105, 154
Pragmatics 3, 8, 9, 28, 49, 59, 60, 64, 78, 81, 85, 153, 177, 185–187, 189, 193, 194
Prototypicality 15, 30, 34, 36–38, 41, 46, 48–50, 54, 56, 60, 65, 66, 70, 78, 79, 94, 97, 99, 105, 140–146, 151, 162, 163, 174, 190
Pseudoemblem 93, 97–99, 176, 180

Questionnaire 80–82, 85, 90, 91, 94–97
Quotable gesture 5, 40, 41, 53, 128, 129, 148

Recurrent gesture 68, 69, 76, 79, 94, 177
Regulator 3, 23–26, 31, 74, 106, 107
Relevance 1, 3, 4, 38, 43, 49, 59, 71, 98, 121, 133, 135, 136, 140, 141, 147–157, 172, 185, 191, 193
Repertoire 1–4, 10, 27, 29, 47, 53, 61–65, 68–72, 76–108, 111, 122, 129, 130, 133, 135–137, 139–146, 148, 151, 175, 176, 179, 180, 182, 183, 187–192
Ring gesture 69, 109
Ritual 56, 74, 160, 173
Russian 63, 83, 84, 87

Schema, image 105, 106, 163
Semiotics 8, 28, 82
Shanghai gesture 1, 99, 104, 111, 112, 122, 158, 173, 174
Sign 2, 8, 14, 15, 17, 18, 42–46, 63, 71–76, 86, 100, 115, 119, 122, 123, 140, 148, 150, 163, 179, 184
Sign language 2, 17, 18, 44–46, 72–76, 123, 182

Social distribution of emblem 3, 123–134
Social interaction (human interaction) 123, 152, 185–187, 194
South Africa 82, 83, 128
Spain 27, 56, 63, 84, 87, 89, 90, 104, 121, 122, 130, 156, 181
Spanish, American 117, 169, 188
Spanish, Iberian Peninsula 112
Speech 5, 8, 9, 19, 38, 41, 45–51, 54–56, 59–62, 68–72, 74, 78, 79, 81, 85, 91, 99, 105, 106, 108, 113, 115, 124, 129, 135, 140, 141, 150–157, 162, 173, 176–178, 181–184, 189, 191–194
Speech Act Theory 38
Speech-gesture relationship 27, 46, 59
Swedish 84
Symbolic gesture 1, 5, 14, 17, 20, 27, 39, 86, 111, 117

Taboo 62, 96, 124, 129
Taxonomy 141
Technical repertoire 64, 87, 183
Teeth flick gesture 119
Thumb gesture 1, 126, 128, 133
Transcription 70, 77, 78, 81
Trope 63, 135, 136, 157–174, 191
Turkish 74, 82, 84

Universal 9, 10, 84, 103, 106

Velas, estar a dos expression and gesture 166, 173
Venezuela 22, 84, 156

Web, emblematic 141–145
Whistle, Catalan 99, 111, 173

Yes/no emblem 46
Yiddish 84

www.ingramcontent.com/pod-product-compliance
Lightning Source LLC
Chambersburg PA
CBHW031806220426
43662CB00007B/549